THE
BRITISH
EXPERIENCE
1945-75

Nuremberg: The Facts, the Law and the Consequences
Survey of International Affairs 1947–48
Survey of International Affairs 1949–50
Survey of International Affairs 1951
Survey of International Affairs 1952
Survey of International Affairs 1953
Middle East Crisis (with Guy Wint)
South Africa and World Opinion
World Order and New States
World Politics Since 1945
Suez: Ten Years After
Total War: The Story of World War II (with Guy Wint)

The British Experience 1945–75

Peter Calvocoressi

Pantheon Books
New York

Library of Congress Cataloging in Publication Data

Calvocoressi, Peter.
  The British Experience, 1945–75.
  1. Great Britain—Social conditions—1945–
2. Great Britain—Politics and government—1945–
3. Great Britain—Economic conditions—1945–
I. Title
HN390.C34 1978   309.1'41'085   77-90401
ISBN 0-394-50067-9

Manufactured in the United States of America

First American Edition   Str. 8.95|4.50|8|15|78

CONTENTS

PART I
Hopes

1 Postwar tasks

In July 1945, a couple of months after the German capitulation and a couple of weeks before the Japanese, the first British general election for ten years was held. The Labour Party, which had never before won a majority of the seats in the House of Commons, scored a spectacular victory, winning 12 million votes against 8.5 million given to the Conservatives and ending up with 392 seats in a House of 620. Practically everybody was astounded. The causes related to both past and future. The Conservatives had ruled Britain for virtually the whole of the interbellum period and they were not judged to have ruled it well. These years had imprinted memories of slump and slum, of fearful unemployment and misfortunes, which the Conservatives had seemed to face with a too easy equanimity and with the fortitude reserved for those capable of keeping out of harm's way; memories too of Hitler's atrocities and preparations for war which the Conservatives (though not they alone) had seemed to observe with unbecoming insensitivity and perilous passivity. In short, the Conservatives had a bad name and not all the achievements of Winston Churchill, a rogue Conservative in the thirties and a sporadic one before that, could wipe them out.

But the Conservatives were defeated by more than the record of the past. There were also hopes for the future which, no less than the record, pointed to the Labour Party which was expected to change everything that anybody thought wrong about Britain. What was wrong was summed up in phrases like 'social justice' or 'the welfare state', by which two things in particular were indicated: that the poorer people were much too poor and that the distinctions between classes were too big and blatant. The electorate hoped and believed that the Labour Party would make great strides towards the elimination of absolute poverty and excessive inequality whereas the Conservatives could be expected only to meander towards these goals.

The problems of the Labour government were not the same as the motives or instincts of the electorate, although they overlapped. At the end of the war Britain had two main sets of problems—and seemed bent on tackling both simultaneously. These were the problems of getting

9

back and the problems of going forward: getting back to a leading industrial and commercial role in the world, above all by reconverting industry from war production to peace, modernising it and recapturing export markets; and going forward to a juster society by more generous social services, better education for more people, full employment and a redistribution of wealth. The first set of problems was economic, the second social, and the commonly used term 'socio-economic' blurred the fact that, unless the economy expanded or the social aims were muted, they were in conflict—for resources.

The wartime background to these problems was likewise twofold. It embraced on the one hand the economic damage and losses of the war and on the other schemes for social betterment, some already worked out under the wartime coalition government. There was in addition, if less generally remarked, the remoter background of Britain's economic decline over half a century and more. The end of a war seemed a splendid moment for a new start, and so it was psychologically, but in practical terms it was not. The programme was huge. It needed a lot of money and—depending on the money available—time, whereas the elation of victory and the pressures for derationing, demobilisation and reform demanded that much be done in no time at all. There was too little calculation of the gravity of the programme in relation to resources and so a danger of disenchantment if the going got too hard. This it did almost at once with the cutting short of the Lend-Lease programme on the morrow of final victory, and although the fifties seemed bright with performance and promise this brightness was used for self-deception rather than recalculation.

The war reckoning was as sombre in economic terms as the moments of victory were elating. War damage at home and to shipping amounted to some £3 billion. Overseas assets worth more than another £1 billion had been sold or lost and the income from foreign investments halved. The external debt had been increased by £3.3 billion. The export trade had been halved and exports were paying for less than a fifth of imports. The balance sheet position was cruelly disappointing, the on-going situation daunting. A nation which had for generations drawn its livelihood from trade had been forced by war to stop making the goods which foreigners would buy in exchange for their own products and had in addition forfeited foreign investments which had been producing £170 million a year towards the cost of these foreign products. Unable to live of its own, Britain was left without the manufactures and the foreign cash with which it had been used to pay for food and other imported raw materials. During the war Roosevelt's secretary of the treasury, Henry Morgenthau, had judged that Britain was 'busted' and yet Britain aimed to recover its prewar position by redirecting and renewing its industries, recovering foreign markets and replacing its lost foreign investments. Since these aims were not seriously questioned, the main question was where the money was to come from pending the day when the country could once more pay its way at the level it was setting itself.

The sudden end of the war against Japan brought with it in the same month of August 1945 the equally sudden and unexpected end of Lend-Lease. Lend-Lease was a device introduced in 1941 when Britain ran out of cash to pay for American arms and other supplies. In essence it was an agreement to allow Britain to go on ordering but pay later. How much later was not made clear and Churchill for one may have hoped that in the end Britain's exertions and sacrifices would be set against the debit balance and the slate be wiped clean. But when war ended Truman, without proper briefing and in the absence of his principal advisers, signed a piece of paper which discontinued Lend-Lease forthwith and with a heavy debit due from Britain. From that moment Britain had to pay on the nail for whatever it bought including food and raw materials and manufactures vital for the reconversion and re-equipment of industry. There would be no breathing space, no time in which to put industry back into a condition to pay its way. Paying now meant not buying, and not buying meant no recovery. If the credit given by Lend-Lease must cease, Britain had to get credit some other way or accept economic anaemia.

In 1945 Britain was spending abroad more than £2000 million (excluding munitions) and was earning abroad about £350 million. The balance, something like five-sixths of the total, had to be acquired on credit or not at all. On the most optimistic view—which included maximising exports, cutting imports to the bone and drastically reducing spending in military and other establishments overseas (including British forces in Germany)—the gap could not be closed before 1949 and during the intervening 3–4 years Britain would have to borrow at least £1700 million in order to ensure a basic food ration and essential restocking and retooling of industry. There was no possible source of money of this kind except the USA and although Keynes had for a while hopes of getting it as a gift or an interest free loan it soon became clear that neither would be considered by the US administration or Congress and furthermore that there would be strings to the loan.

Keynes, who led the British delegation which went to Washington to beg for a loan, began by asking for $6000 million (nearly £1500 million) which he thought would be enough. He was pushed down to $3750 million which clearly was not, at 2% and repayable over fifty years from December 1951, with provision for waiver of interest (but not capital repayments) in years in which British overseas earnings fell below certain levels. This offer was flanked by a generous settlement of the Lend-Lease account but also by onerous conditions—the latter a fore-taste of the lesson that borrowers cannot set the terms on which they borrow or find lenders willing to lend without strings (an irritant to pride as well as an economic burden which became acuter in the sixties and seventies).

Lend-Lease had worked both ways. Britain had contributed to the account as well as drawing on it, but very unequally, and at the end of the war Britain's debit balance was $20 billion. This was cancelled. Further, Britain acquired for $532 million American goods and property in Britain which were clearly worth at least ten times that sum. Finally, Lend-Lease goods in transit were written down to $118 million, so that the total debt was reduced to $650 million, a mere phantom of the true figure. This sum was allowed to remain outstanding at 2%, so that in effect the USA was lending Britain $4400 million, most of it new money and a smaller amount being the written down Lend-Lease balance carried forward. Canada added $1500 million, making a grand total not far short of £1500 million. The big question was how long these loans would last. The date 1949 was kept as a target and it became a main aim of the British government to get to 1949 without exhausting the loans and with a fair prospect of balancing overseas accounts in that year and beginning the repayment of the loans two years later. If the loans were to run out before a balance was achieved, then either Britain would have to raise fresh loans (which is what happened) or it would once more face cuts in food and industrial imports and so rationing and unemployment.

The conditions attached to the American loan made Britain's task impossible. There were two main ones, both derived from the American vision of an international economic system embodied in the Bretton Woods agreement of 1944. They were, in economic shorthand, non-discrimination and convertibility. Non-discrimination in this context meant that American goods must be allowed to enter Britain as freely as similar Commonwealth goods and without quotas; the Americans saw the Commonwealth as a restrictive, preferential system which placed obstacles in the way of general free trade and of American commerce in particular. Of more immediate importance was American insistence that sterling be made freely convertible into other currencies by July 1947, a condition which would lead to a run on the British reserves and the consequent evaporation of the loan if by that date the British economy were not strong enough to support the pound at the value of $4.03 fixed for it at Bretton Woods. This condition meant in fact that British exports must come near to balancing imports not in 1949 but in 1947.

The British cabinet seriously considered breaking off the negotiations for the loan on this point and in the House of Commons 23 Labour members and 71 Conservatives voted against the terms in spite of the urgency of the situation and the immense prestige of Keynes who, however dispirited, recommended acceptance. The alternative to a loan on the best terms available was considerable domestic austerity and industrial privation and the forgoing of the opportunity, which was believed to exist, of putting the British economy back on its feet in the brief space of four years. But having settled for the inevitable the government had to live for the rest of its term with the knowledge that everything depended on having money in the kitty, that the bulk of the money was borrowed American money and that, even if this money lasted until the light at the end of the tunnel was reached in 1949, enough had to be earned thereafter on overseas accounts to begin repayment at the end of 1951. It was a very tight squeeze and it coloured British attitudes to the USA.

It was easy to see the end of Lend-Lease and the conditions clamped on to the loan as an exercise in ungenerosity and arm-twisting, to believe that Roosevelt would have treated his main ally less scurvily than Truman and some of his advisers did, and to complain that the postwar USA forgot with unbecoming speed that Lend-Lease had been something more than a commercial deal since it enabled the British to go on fighting and being killed while the Americans girded themselves up to come and help. There was in Britain some bitterness over the apparent American failure to remember that part of the account had been paid in blood (Americans could justly claim that they had not forgotten, as the final reckoning showed) and this bitterness was refuelled when the

Quebec and Hyde Park agreements of 1943 and 1944 on the postwar sharing of atomic secrets were broken by the McMahon Act of 1946 (see Part Four, Chapter 2). The war, and particularly Churchill and Roosevelt in person, had fostered a belief that the two countries were normally on the best of terms and had little difficulty in understanding one another. Yet this was quite untrue. Between the wars there were at government level considerable hostility and distrust on both sides, beginning in Britain immediately after the first world war and in a most sensitive spot – naval superiority. At the turn of the century Britain, no longer able to maintain unaided its superiority in all oceans, had fallen back on the Anglo-Japanese alliance to counter Germany's naval challenge which, above all else, was pointing Britain towards war. But as soon as this challenge was defeated the USA set about destroying the Anglo-Japanese special relationship. Anglo-American hostility, thus engendered, persisted between the wars, no less pervasive for being suppressed, but during the second war it was overlaid and both countries emerged from the war with an easy assumption about the relationship having become different in kind from other international relationships and easier to maintain. On the British side its maintenance was also regarded as an essential element in British foreign policy. Clement Attlee and his foreign secretary and closest political friend, Ernest Bevin, followed Churchill's line in making the Anglo-American alliance a cornerstone of policy and Bevin's vigorous anti-communism, reinforced by frustrating experiences with Molotov and other Russians at postwar foreign ministers' conferences, worked to the same end of making the alliance something like a fact of nature. This attitude persisted throughout the first postwar generation since it affected the heirs of Attlee and Bevin as well as Churchill's; and in spite of the loan negotiations the alliance—both the need for it and its nature—continued to be uncritically appraised, a factor which differentiated Britain from France where a more detached view of the alliance prevailed (again arising largely from personal attitudes, the Roosevelt–de Gaulle relationship having been the reverse of the Roosevelt–Churchill one).

The American loan was not finally approved by Congress until July 1946 but it became immediately a necessary assumption of economic planning. Presenting his budget in April of that year, the Chancellor of the Exchequer, Hugh Dalton, predicted a deficit on external account of £750 million for the calendar year. This was the second of Dalton's four budgets, the first having been presented in October 1945. Dalton aimed to keep prices stable, the cost of living down and money cheap and he did so for psychological as well as stricter economic reasons. He used his budgets as social as well as economic regulators. Thus in 1945 he relieved two million people of income tax altogether and increased surtax; by taking from one group what he put into the pockets of another he was practising social levelling in a modest way as well as taking anti-inflationary precautions. In 1946 he again reduced direct and indirect taxes but in reducing estate duty at the slimmer end he increased it at the fatter end. He budgeted for a deficit in 1946–47 of only £694 million on a total expenditure of £3837 million and said that his next budget would balance. In the event the deficit in 1946–47 turned out to be even smaller (£569 million) in spite of what the Chancellor called his contributions to socialism and in April 1947 he was able to budget for a surplus of £270 million. In 1947–48 defence was to be cut by nearly half while civil spending would go up by only 3%. This time there were some shifts in taxation but no reductions. It all looked like a good housekeeping job but before the year was out the Chancellor had to introduce a new budget, raise taxes, stop all petrol for private purposes and ban the use of any money whatever for holidays abroad.

The economic substructure provided by the American loan was crumbling. Although in 1946 the government had hoped to make substantial savings in defence costs—the cabinet took the view that Britain was no longer an Asian power and could not in a future war defend its Mediterranean positions—the onset of the Cold War dashed these hopes even before the outbreak of war in Korea led to extravagantly costly rearmament. The value of the loan was sharply reduced by the American government's inflationary policies which increased the cost of the things that the money was meant to buy: prices in the USA rose by 40% between the fixing of the total of the loan and mid-1947. Germany was taking far more money than had been expected since it became necessary not merely to station an army there but also to buy food for the Germans to eat. The British share of the cost of feeding Germany rose from $5 million a month in 1946 to $20 million a month in 1947 and this item alone threatened to take a tenth of what was left by then of the American loan. If industrial recovery and social reform could with difficulty be paid for simultaneously, they certainly could not be paid for at all on top of worldwide defence commitments on a prewar scale.

The drawing of the loan accelerated in 1947. In the first three months of that year $700 million was drawn. This was more than double the rate in the second half of 1946 and at this new rate the entire loan would be gone before the end of February 1948. Then, in accordance with the loan agreement, sterling was made convertible on 15 July 1947. The result was catastrophe. Convertibility was brought to a stop on August 20th but in the last week alone of this short and frantic period the reserves sank by $237 million as people with money in the Bank of England rushed to take it away and put it into dollars. The Bank's reserves were down to £600 million but since the conventional wisdom decreed that the last £250 million was untouchable the Bank had no more than £350 million to spend. There was still £125 million of the Canadian loan left and the Chancellor could draw £320 million from the International Monetary Fund (IMF)—but over four years. The American loan, reduced to $400 million (less than £100 million), might be completely exhausted by October and could hardly be expected to last out the year. Exports had not responded as vigorously as had been hoped; the terms of trade had turned against Britain; political changes had produced unlooked for foreign expenditure; convertibility had finally punctured the whole fabric. The economic strategy, of which the American loan had been an essential guarantee, had collapsed. It had not bought enough time and exports were still far from paying for imports.

The solution, or more properly the expedient, chosen by the government was to borrow again—to buy more time on the assumption that, with time, the sums could be made to come out right. The basic policy of recovery was not abandoned, nor does it seem that the question of abandoning it was even discussed. What was discussed were means of achieving it and, as in 1945, the essential need was money. There was, however, some trimming domestically. Stafford Cripps, who became chancellor of the exchequer after a minor indiscretion by Dalton which the former Chancellor treated with pleasing rectitude as a resigning matter, reduced rations and imposed potato rationing for the first time. Dalton had already made cuts in capital investment. Belts were tightened for a second attempt, for which the means were already looming up.

Early in 1947 Britain's financial burden in supporting Greece and Turkey had been transferred to the USA. The American motive in accepting it was political, the containment of communism or Truman Doctrine, and the same motive played a major part in June in the much wider Marshall Plan for sustaining, with dollars, European countries in distress. Britain was not the only such country. Much of Europe was far worse off and the exceptionally harsh and long winter of 1946–47 had come near to breaking a lot of nerves as well as doing a vast amount of economic damage in countries which were just beginning to recover from war. Politically these disasters were seen as opportunities for communism. Western European governments, so General George C. Marshall, the US Secretary of State, was told, would keel over and red revolution would triumph if the USA did not come to the rescue. Hence the Marshall Plan, offered to all Europe including the USSR out of a mixture of calculation and compassion and accepted by the western half of the continent. This second helping of American aid—a second instalment of the Anglo-American debit-credit relationship—beginning with the Truman Doctrine and Marshall Plan and culminating two years later with the North Atlantic Treaty (April 1949) was more enduring and more complex than the first which, embodied in the loan agreement, was strictly bilateral and economic. The Marshall Plan and the North Atlantic Treaty were the centrepieces in a new continental, economic and military strategy which linked the fortunes of democratic and capitalist Europe with the emerging conflict between American and Russian power and ideologies, a conflict which would be enlarged to global dimensions and would dominate international affairs for at least a generation and would lead in the fifties and beyond to a British dependence on the USA for costly weaponry, prolonging and emphasising Britain's dependence on the USA for a financial lifeline in the forties.

By the Marshall Plan the USA took upon itself to finance for four years and as an emergency measure the dollar gap created by the incapacity of Europeans to grow or make exportable surpluses to pay for essential imports of food, timber (for housing), fertilisers and other raw materials. Most of the aid disbursed was a free gift, though part of it was on loan. Over the four years 1948–51 Britain received net £681 million and in 1950 the third Labour Chancellor, Hugh Gaitskell, was able to predict that Britain would break even on its external account in 1952 without American aid. But the panic caused by the convertibility crisis of 1947 had made a permanent mark. Recovery seemed not only hard but remote, even problematic. The introduction of bread rationing in July 1946 (it lasted two years) had been a jolt only partially offset by the thought that it was needed in order to help the war-shattered continent. The pains of the winter of 1946–47—the worst since 1880, producing shortages, power cuts, traffic chaos, industrial closures and unemployment—might be blamed on nature but there was no getting away from the fact that the cost was around £200 million and that Britain was in no state to take setbacks of that kind. There was no margin. The optimism of 1945 had been encouraged by the export figures for 1946 which were £150 million above the target of £750 million and twice the value of exports in 1938, but by 1947 and even before the convertibility crisis the public mood was turning sombre and those who found export statistics puzzling could see and feel for themselves the serious gap in coal supplies and in manpower in a number of industries. The government suffered severe losses in local elections in November 1947 and the Conservative opposition, which had by and large endorsed Labour's social policies, began to utter warnings about too much government spending. The Labour ranks too were uneasy. Doubts were replacing hopes.

Exports and the reserves were not the only worries. There was also the fear of inflation. It is a harsh truth that if war is inflationary, so too are postwar circumstances. The second world war, like the first and like the Napoleonic wars (to go back no further), was inescapably inflationary even though prices were prevented for the time being from rising by the wartime controls which are so much easier to impose on a democracy than controls in times of peace. Inflation was handled more expertly than in 1914–19; the increases in the national debt and in the rate of interest on the debt were kept under reasonable control; but wages rose both during the war and after and there was at first no hope of matching these increases by increased productivity from war-damaged plant. The ending of the war released psychological and economic demands: private people no longer felt the restraints of war and were eager to do things in the home which they had postponed and to indulge themselves a bit, while businesses big and small set about putting themselves straight and getting going again. The natural consequence of the end of a war is a boom and, given the difficulties of meeting demands and the reluctance of government to prolong austerity, inflation. Even countries which could hardly afford it and tried to damp it down were not immune: inflation spreads from one country to another if there is trade between them. The USA set the pace by removing price controls in 1946. Prices shot up, wage claims followed and were won, prices went up further. Apart from reducing the value in terms of goods of the American loan, these American price increases created an inflationary demand in Britain as people, ordering from America goods which they could not get at home, increased their own spending and the country's import bill.

The government tried to check inflationary demands by holding down domestic prices within their control through food and other subsidies and by appealing to the unions to mitigate their claims for the time being. Such appeals worked moderately well for a short time but were constantly threatened by rising costs (in markets in which shortages were not quickly relieved). The saga of prices, wages and inflation is more fully described in Part Two of this book. At this point we merely note that in 1948 the government's White Paper on Incomes, Costs and Prices put a toe into the waters of wages or incomes policy—a polite phrase for keeping wages down by hook (exhortation) or by crook (legislation)—and outlined positions and arguments which would become much more familiar when a second and more damaging bout of inflation hit the country twenty years later. The government was helped by a few promising signs in 1948 when the rise in the import bill slowed down and exports improved. In each of the last two quarters the overall deficit on the balance of payments fell below £100 million. But in 1949 it began to climb again and by the middle of the year it was apparent that the year's deficit would be double that for 1948. The gap was getting worse and in September the pound was devalued from $4.03 to $2.80 in order to make British goods more attractive in price to foreigners. This was the end of the attempt to see the postwar pound worth the same number of dollars as the prewar pound. It never was, for the war itself had seen to that. For a time the British economic performance, whether measured by industrial output or investment or foreign trade, had been very creditable, but the attempt simultaneously to maintain the external value of the pound at this level was a romantic extravaganza that failed. The failure damaged the government which had striven to avoid it and, a more serious matter, the misplaced attempt damaged the economic achievements of these years.

Devaluation was also a shock to confidence, largely for irrational reasons. A devaluation is an admission that the currency is not worth what it has been said to be worth and to that extent a devaluation is an admission of failure. On the other hand there is habitually a massive over-investment of nationalist emotion in the currency's external value, and devaluation is taken to be a humiliation akin to the defacing of statues of national heroes. Devaluation reflects too on the capacity of the government, all the more so since its spokesmen have to say until the very last moment that they are not going to do what they then do. In fact a government may be just as open to censure for not devaluing (in 1964 for example) as for doing so. What matters most is the timing—not leaving it until there is no choice—and the effects—ensuring an increase not only in the volume of exports but in their aggregate value. The immediate impact of the 1949 devaluation was to weaken a weakening government. Exports rose and Britain was able to forgo Marshall aid a year ahead of schedule, but within a year Cripps was having difficulty in obtaining a further instalment of wage restraint as the cost of living rose with the cost of imports (devaluation is not a certain cure unless imports can be controlled, which the devaluing country cannot achieve unless it devalues from strength) and the government was being pressed by the opposition to cut the food subsidies which were a large item in government expenditure but contrariwise were also a principal weapon in keeping the cost of living and so wage claims down. In his 1950 budget Cripps set a limit to the subsidies but did not reduce them. Wage claims accumulated and wage restraint could hardly be said to exist any longer. In February the government survived a general election by the skin of its teeth. The ups and downs of the economy, the continuance of rationing and other controls, the failure to build houses quickly enough were the main causes of a Conservative reflux. The Labour vote went up and Labour won more votes than it or any other party had ever got, but the Conservative vote went up more. Labour got 13.3 million votes and 315 seats, Conservatives 12.5 million votes and 298 seats, Liberals 2.6 million votes and 9 seats. The Communists, who put up 100 candidates, polled badly, very few of them winning more than 2% of the relevant constituency's vote. The poll was exceptionally high (84%) and the swing from Labour to Conservatives 3.3%. By common consent Labout lost about 30 seats as a result of its redistribution and redrawing of constituency boundaries under the Representation of the People Act 1948: the Home Secretary, Chuter Ede, was thought by neutral as well as Labour opinion to have displayed an excessive non-partisanship.

An intangible contributory cause of Labour's comparative decline was the fact that the government was running out of steam. Attlee's administration had been built round a nucleus of remarkable men: Bevin, Cripps, Morrison, Dalton. His cabinets came near the top in British history for intelligence and industry, but the senior members of them did not all love one another and by 1950 they were ailing. Bevin was a very sick man who was clinging to his office from which Attlee refused, until nearly the end, to remove him because of the rare trust and affection which existed between the two men. Cripps, the cabinet's outstanding intellect, was on the verge of resignation and death. Dalton had slipped out of the front rank after his resignation from the Treasury in 1947 while his propensity for intrigue marred the achievements of a sharp mind and robust personality. Morrison too was ill. The most experienced and professional politician of them all, not excluding the Prime Minister, he may have felt that he ought to have had and perhaps might still reach the top post, but his senior colleagues did not like him and he carried with him into national politics too much of the air of local politics (he had been a strikingly successful leader of the London County Council) to appeal to the bright new generation of Labour MPs. In 1945 Attlee himself had held a commanding position which he had abdicated by 1950. He owed his repute, and still does, to the fact that he had been the titular number two to Churchill during the war and he possessed certain traits, contradictory or complementary, which inspired confidence in his character and his efficiency: reserve with crispness, middle-class values with long service to a working-class constituency. Before the war Attlee's position in the party, which he had successfully contested against the pacifist Lansbury after the 'betrayal' of Macdonald and other big shots in 1931, was not assured; and after the war it declined again sooner than met the eye. A move to depose him in 1947 was foiled only by the loyalty of Bevin (who had refused to lend himself to a similar intrigue against Churchill during the war) and apart from Bevin no senior member of the cabinet remained completely loyal to the enigmatic Prime Minister whose placidity seemed to his close colleagues to derive no longer from skill but increasingly from feebleness. Moreover all these men had held high office continuously for a decade in the most testing circumstances of war and peace.

Among younger Labour leaders Aneurin Bevan was outstanding for his energy, his oratory, his intellect and his devotion to parliamentary democracy which was in no way lessened, as it was in some of his political progeny, by his being decisively on the left of the party. By 1950 Bevan was the one member of the cabinet clearly in the first class in status and mind, but he alienated colleagues and his unalloyed and undisguised hostility to his political and class enemies made some Labour politicians and voters uncomfortable. Probably he was not designed by nature for a subordinate position, even a high one, and before the end of the Attlee period he had become embroiled with another and very different rising star in Hugh Gaitskell. Attlee, characteristically but probably foolishly, was averse to any step which might look like conferring the succession on anybody, thereby observing the rule that it was not his to give but also generating or exacerbating harmful rivalries.

The election of 1950 was no more than a reprieve for Labour. The record of 1951 was similar to that of the previous year. There was a Festival of Britain and another summer crisis. The cost of living went on going up. Following the outbreak of war in Korea the government adopted a huge rearmament programme which it had no chance of achieving and which checked investment in civilian industries. In cabinet Bevan argued against the view that the Korean war had been instigated by Moscow. He was sceptical about the conventional view of Russian intentions and capacities, pointing out that the USSR lacked the steel and other essential requirements for war. He opposed not only the scale of British rearmament but also German rearmament for which the USA was pressing. In these matters, a generation later, Bevan would seem to have been substantially right but at the time he was a divisive element in a cabinet which was trundling along on established lines and had little verve for taking a hard new look at the way the world had changed since 1945. Disagreements were brought to a head by the budget. Gaitskell, who was probably better equipped to be chancellor of the exchequer than any of his predecessors or (to date) successors, proposed in a deflationary programme to impose charges for false teeth and spectacles supplied by the National Health Service. The amount to be recovered was small—about £13 million—and Bevan argued that it could either be knocked off the defence estimates or be dispensed with altogether in a year of budgetary surplus. As the creator of the Health Service and by now the protagonist of the social services and champion of the Labour conscience, he was moved to suspect that with Attlee away ill this item had been contrived by Gaitskell and Morrison to bait him and get him out of the government. He treated the matter as a question of principle and resigned. Two junior ministers, Harold Wilson and John Freeman, went with him. The commotion did the party no good and when Attlee unexpectedly decided to go to the country again in October Labour lost 20 seats and the Conservatives came back to power with a majority of 20. The other old guard took over.

2 The welfare state

The programme of social reforms of the Labour government elected in 1945 derived from the party's socialist premises and principles. Early in the war the TUC, backed by Labour ministers, pressed the coalition government to prepare, during the war and not after it, plans for an extension of the social services provided by the state, and in November 1942 there appeared Sir William Beveridge's Report on Social Insurance and Allied Services, the most famous document produced during the war, not excluding the Atlantic Charter, and one which made its author's name, as he himself remarked, better known than any save Churchill's. Two years later Beveridge published a second report, this time as a private individual and with private finance, entitled Full Employment in a Free Society, which, together with his first report and the Education Act 1944 sponsored by R. A. Butler, constituted the core of the specific wartime inheritance of the first postwar government.

The first Beveridge report was prepared by an interdepartmental committee of twelve representatives of the civilian departments of state. In origin this committee was intended to review existing social insurance schemes and make recommendations, but as soon as it became clear that the second part of this task would involve questions of high policy proper for ministers rather than civil servants, the form of the committee was altered, its members becoming advisers to the chairman and the chairman being charged with sole responsibility for the contents of the report. Thus the report when it appeared bore the sole signature of Beveridge.

The Beveridge committee did not start from nothing. The state, which had for centuries accepted a minimal obligation to the destitute who came within the ambit of the Poor Laws, had also accepted obligations to the needy and so had got into the business of defining need, and the model which Beveridge was to adopt and greatly expand was provided before the first world war by Lloyd George's National Insurance Act and Winston Churchill's Unemployment Insurance Act. Both these statutes rested upon the assumption that a given category of persons would in given circumstances need to be helped and should be. Beveridge universalised the principles underlying these measures which guaranteed those within their scope against future risks. Both schemes provided for weekly in-payments by certain classes of people and their employers, against which out-payments were made when the event insured against arose. The schemes were, within their limited spheres, contributory and compulsory. They were derived from nineteenth-century German models and were elaborated between the wars, particularly in relation to unemployment which was the subject of some two dozen Acts of Parliament and by the addition in 1926 of a contributory pensions scheme for certain classes of widows and orphans and the old. The state guarantees provided by these measures were an insurance in the popular sense that they gave individuals assurances against defined eventualities, but they were not insurances in the accepted commercial sense since the in-payments made by or on behalf of a particular contributor did not actuarially suffice to finance future out-payments to him; these were made possible only by the totality of the contributions by (or for) the whole class of possible beneficiaries supplemented by government contributions derived from general taxation. Nevertheless the word 'insurance' has stuck to schemes of this kind.

Beveridge proposed that the insurance model be extended to the entire population with the object of ensuring adequate subsistence for all in all circumstances: anything beyond a basic level of decent subsistence would not be the concern of the state but would be left to individuals to secure for themselves through private schemes as they saw fit. All social insurance benefits would be guaranteed to the individual through a single weekly contribution and there could be no opting out. The Beveridge report made three assumptions about the postwar world: the extension of national insurance and, in addition, universal family allowances and a high level of employment. Full employment was taken to mean no more than 3% unemployment. (For the greater part of the ensuing thirty years it was under 2%.)

Beveridge and his supporters were disappointed and indeed embittered by the reception given to his report by Conservative ministers, the Conservative press and Conservative strongholds generally. Their response seemed unimaginative and ungenerous and he particularly resented attempts to stifle discussion on the grounds that it would detract attention and effort away from the business of winning the war. He resolved therefore to devote as much of his time as he could to further study of how to prevent the kind of unemployment that had disfigured the thirties, to showing that this was practicable and getting the political parties to commit themselves to full employment. He was so successful as a gadfly that the coalition anticipated the appearance of his second report by itself publishing in 1944 a White Paper on employment. As a result all the political parties crossed the line from war to peace as proclaimed disciples of Keynes and with a commitment to 'a high and stable level of employment', a revolutionary innovation to be implemented, if need be, by maintaining expenditure on goods and services, i.e. by spending, probably government spending.

The Labour Party had a further commitment (which will be discussed in detail in the next chapter). It was pledged to bring into public ownership, to nationalise, certain sections of the economy. Partly this was a piece of Labour doctrine,* which saw a conflict of interest between public good and private profit. Partly it was a consequence of particular experiences, notably the conflict between the miners and the mine-owners in the twenties and the clash in 1931 over economic policy when the banking and financial establishment insisted that cuts in unemployment benefit were in the 'national' interest. Partly too it was a partisan attempt to reduce the political power of private capital and its Conservative owners and allies and to reduce also a major source of the private profits which went to the few rather than the many.

Overall the Labour view was that a great deal of government intervention was necessary for social planning and social justice; that without such intervention social justice would not arrive. Nationalisation was therefore a twin of social services. Nevertheless the party's commitment to nationalisation was in practice less firm than its programmes and manifestoes made it out to be (as we shall see). What was firm was the determination to secure two things: full employment for those of working age and capacity; and, for those who could not work because they were too young or too old or permanently or temporarily ill, safeguards and services in cash or in kind sufficient to abolish poverty and ensure a minimum standard of living. The social services born of this determination fall into three groups—social security, a national health service and

* 'Doctrinaire' is commonly used as a word of abuse. This is sloppy. Doctrinaire means having a view and sticking to it—two excellent characteristics, certainly preferable to not having a view or not sticking to it. Having a wrong view is of course deplorable, but attacking other people for having and holding views is more deplorable.

education. The rest of this chapter is concerned with the first and second of these enterprises, while education is considered in Part Three of this book.

The centrepiece of social security legislation was the National Insurance Act introduced and passed in 1946. It was flanked by the Family Allowance Act 1945 and the National Insurance (Industrial Injuries) Act 1946. Many statutes were enacted in the next thirty years to modify or extend these basic Acts, but only one significant innovation—the Redundancy Payments Act 1965—was added to them.

The National Insurance Act 1946 brought the whole population into a comprehensive scheme covering unemployment, sickness, maternity, guardianship, death and retirement. A new Ministry of National Insurance was established to administer the scheme with local offices scattered about the country. The Act created a National Insurance Fund to be fed by weekly contributions from insured persons and their employers and to disburse to individuals the sums to which they might become entitled upon the happening of the events insured against. Every insured person had a card to which a stamp had to be affixed every week, the cost of this stamp being shared with the employer; self-employed persons had to pay the full cost of a cheaper stamp. The assets of existing state insurance schemes were transferred to a National Insurance (Reserve) Fund which immediately made an initial grant of £100 million to the National Insurance Fund. In addition this Fund was to receive annually lump sums from the Exchequer rising from £36 million initially to £60 million in 1955, but these payments were interrupted for a short time from 1952 when the Fund was too healthy to need them and in the first twenty years employers' and employees' contributions met 73–93% of the annual outgoings. After the introduction of graduated contributions (see below) these became an increasingly important source of revenue to the Fund and from 1973 exceeded the total of flat-rate contributions, thus further reducing the burden on the Exchequer. In 1975 94% of all benefits paid out of the Fund was covered by the flat-rate and graduated contributions of employers, employees and the self-employed.

The most striking feature of the scheme was its universality. There were a few exceptions (e.g. full-time students); married women could choose not to be separately insured, in which case their benefits would be fewer; transitionally some people were bypassed because of their age or would fail to qualify for benefits until the Act, and their contributions, had run an initial course. But there was no contracting out and individuals who wanted to make separate arrangements might do so as an addition but not as an alternative to the national scheme. Beveridge had strongly insisted on universality. He was influenced by the camaraderie of war, by the desirability of emphasising common citizenship rather than separate classes and also by the fear that the scheme's finances would become unbalanced if, as a result of widespread contracting out, the state's supplementary and eleemosynary role outweighed the contributory element. It followed that if everybody had to pay, then everybody must be eligible for benefits. A contributor acquired rights, regardless of his means. Nevertheless universality had its opponents and they became more numerous in the sixties when the cost of social services came under worried scrutiny and it was argued that a selective scheme would be cheaper to administer than a universal one (which was probably not true) and, more pertinently, that large sums were in aggregate being paid to people who did not need them (to which one answer was that the better way to discriminate against the rich was graduated taxes rather than means-tested social services).

First among the hazards covered by the National Insurance Act was unemployment. The chief source of poverty was not having work. After the war aggregate unemployment did not become serious until the end of the sixties but it was always serious for each individual unemployed, however few his fellows might be. From the point of view of social security the cause of a man's unemployment was immaterial. He might be out of a job because of the state of the economy as a whole, or the decline of an industry or district, or the collapse of a particular employer. Some—a number difficult to assess but reckoned in the years of full employment at about two-thirds of the total of unemployed—might be unemployable through some physical or mental disability or for some other reason. But whatever the cause (other than a strike) an unemployed person became entitled, after the first three days of unemployment, to receive a weekly payment for 180 days, extended in 1966 to twelve months. A man or woman who then got a job and lost it again after not less than thirteen weeks qualified for a fresh stint of unemployment benefit. As with other benefits under the Act a claimant had to have paid a minimum number of weekly contributions and to have been virtually fully paid up in the year immediately preceding the claim.

So long as the labour market was healthy unions and their members concentrated on the size of the wage rather than the security of the job.

When most people could get jobs what mattered to them was the pay rather than the place. There were nevertheless two statutory innovations in the sixties which strengthened the worker's hold on his place. By the Contracts of Employment Act 1963 an employer was obliged to give each employee a written statement of the terms of his employment and minimum notice of dismissal—one to four weeks depending on length of service. By the Redundancy Payments Act 1965 the employee moved a sizeable step nearer to having his job recognised as a franchise or possession of which he might not be deprived without compensation. This compensation was based on wage, age and years of service. The Act was also meant to make labour more mobile but it is doubtful whether this aspect of the new Labour government's industrial strategy was much helped in this way. The Redundancy Fund created by the new Act was fed by employers but not by employees or the state.

Neither of these two Acts affected national insurance but a new National Insurance Act in 1966 did so by introducing—for unemployment and also for sickness, widowhood and industrial injuries—supplementary contributions and benefits over and above the first Act's flat-rate payments in and out. These were called earnings-related payments and they were invented for two main reasons. On the one hand rising costs were making benefits increasingly inadequate. All governments shrank from tying insurance benefits to the cost of living. They preferred to nudge benefits upwards from time to time and usually belatedly, but there came a time when the increases, however justifiable in terms of rising costs, were costing so much that governments were tempted to limit fresh increases to those who could also increase their contributions out of their relatively higher earnings. The second reason was a change in attitudes about the purpose of social security payments. Beveridge and the 1946 Act had both postulated minimum payments to stave off poverty which was regarded as something capable of absolute definition. A line would be drawn and everybody would be kept above it and the line was the same for everybody. But there was another view which held that need was not absolute but relative, and therefore not the same for everybody. According to this view a man or woman ought, within limits, to be sustained at a level not too far removed from what he was used to: he ought not through misfortune to suffer too great a fall. This view was a mixture of generosity flourishing in an expansive climate; of the self-interest of the better paid and their preoccupation with preserving their differential standards of living; and of experience of hard cases created by the difficulty anybody must have in cutting back fixed expenses (rent, for example) which cannot be suddenly reduced. The Act of 1966 therefore provided that, upon a prescribed median band of an employee's wages, employee and employer should pay an additional contribution and the employee become entitled to increased benefits. The state's contribution to this ancillary scheme was nil, an additional attraction from the government's point of view. In the case of unemployment these increments were payable for six months after twelve days out of work. A year after the introduction of the scheme some 110,000 unemployed persons were drawing these extra payments, as well as 250,000 sick and 70,000 widows.

Sickness benefit, the second category under the 1946 Act, was compensation for loss of earnings during enforced absence from work. It was distinct from the medical and other services provided free (or nearly free) by the health service. It could be drawn indefinitely up to retirement age when it was replaced by a pension. It was not paid to people in prison.

Maternity benefits were of various kinds: a maternity grant, a lump sum fixed initially at £4; a post-natal attendance allowance for four weeks after the child's birth to help the mother to get help at home; and a maternity allowance for 13 weeks to compensate for absence from work. The last two benefits were alternatives. In 1953 the grant and the attendance allowance were combined in a single lump sum and the maternity allowance was expanded to 18 weeks covering 11 weeks before and 6 weeks after the birth and the week of the birth. Grants were not given to student couples or, for some strange reason, to unmarried non-working mothers.

Grants occasioned by death were even more various. The death grant itself, a small contribution of £20 (raised in 1967 to £30) towards funeral expenses, was paid to the deceased's personal representatives without any inquiry into these expenses. An orphaned child's guardian could claim an allowance provided one of its parents had been insured under the 1946 Act. By a later Act of 1957 the divorced wife of a father who had been supporting his child received, on the father's death, a special child's allowance, provided she had not remarried. But the most substantial benefits arising on death were widows' benefits. For the first 16 weeks, extended in 1966 to 26 weeks, a widow under 60 (i.e. not qualifying for a retirement pension) was given a widow's benefit in what was thought of as a breathing-space for readjustment to life without a husband. She might also get: a continuing allowance between the ages of 50 and 60; an allowance for children below school-leaving age or in full-time education beyond that age and up to 16 (later upgraded to 18); an allowance if, having been drawing this last allowance, she had at the end of it reached the age of 40 (later upgraded to 50). The second of these allowances recognised the peculiar difficulties a woman might have in finding a new job after a certain age. Widows' benefits were payable only during widowhood and settled cohabitation counted in this respect as remarriage. Under the Act of 1946 a widow could not draw these benefits unless she had been married to her husband for ten years but this period was reduced in 1957 to three years. Also in 1957 various provisions for payments up to the age of 60 were amended to that age or later retirement.

Finally within the ambit of the National Insurance Act 1946 came the important category of retirement pensions. Before 1908 state pensions, which go back to the Superannuation Acts 1834 and 1859, had been restricted to those who had served the crown in military or civil capacities. From 1908 old age pensions were paid to certain classes of people over 70 provided they were deemed worthy, e.g. by being able to show that they had saved and put by. The contributory principle was introduced by the Women's, Orphans' and Old Age Contributory Pensions Act 1925 which provided for pensions to poorish people at the age of 65: this age applied to both sexes. The Act of 1946 chose 65 for a man's retiring age and 60 for a woman's but also provided that for a period of five years a man or woman might defer retirement in return for a higher pension later or might, within limits, go on earning subject to slight reductions in pension during these years. These provisions ceased to apply at the ages of 70 and 65 respectively. The main reason for this five-year grey area was the feeling that the limit at 65 or 60 was somewhat on the low side, coupled with the fear that on this definition of old age the old would become embarrassingly numerous. In fact about a quarter of the persons in the twilight zone deferred their retirement. From 1959 the flat-rate pension might be supplemented by a graduated pension obtainable in return for graduated contributions, and the Social Security Pensions Act 1975 applied to the retirement pensions, as from 1978, the earnings-related principle already operating for unemployment, sickness and widowhood. Insured persons and their employers would pay additional contributions at the rate of $1 \cdot 5 \%$ and $2 \cdot 5 \%$ respectively on earnings within a prescribed bracket in return for incremental pensions. The numbers of persons drawing retirement pensions in 1965 and 1975 were approximately 6·5 million and 8·25 million, with women twice as numerous as men.

A National Insurance (Industrial Injuries) Act was enacted alongside the National Insurance Act 1946 and in the same year. This Act's pedigree started with the first ventures into workmen's compensation in the nineteenth century. The Beveridge report recommended that the obligation to pay compensation of this kind should be assumed by the state instead of leaving the injured victim to take proceedings against his employer (who might not be worth powder and shot). The scheme propounded in 1946, which embraced some industrial diseases as well as injuries inflicted by accidents, was non-contributory. The claimant became entitled to injury benefit for six months, succeeded by disability benefit thereafter either as a lump sum in minor cases or as a continuing allowance in more serious ones. Supplementary allowances could be claimed to cover *ad hoc* needs or specialist injuries (a footballer's legs or a pianist's hands). The Act also provided death benefits which usually took the form of pensions to widows.

Children constitute a special category within social security legislation, the principal statutes being the Family Allowance Acts of 1945, 1956 and 1968. Legislation of this nature had been talked about, although not enacted, as long ago as the closing years of the eighteenth century. The nineteenth century was more concerned with the exploitation of child labour, but in the present century attention shifted to the child as a member of the family and the financial needs of poor families with children. The Act of 1945 gave mothers (not fathers) a weekly allowance for each child after the first who was below school-leaving age or in full-time education up to 16. The Act of 1956 increased the allowance for all children except the second. The Act of 1968 increased the allowance again, this time including the second child but still excluding the first. The age-limit was raised with the school-leaving age and, for children in full-time education after leaving school, to 19. Adopted children, stepchildren and illegitimate children were included and also unrelated children being brought up as part of the family. In 1970 the Family Income Supplements Act provided further but discretionary payments to parents in straits. In 1975 4.6 million families in Britain were drawing family allowances and 67,000 were drawing family income supplements.

Children's allowances, as distinct from family allowances, were also available. These were not payments to parents but deductions from taxable income and so available to taxpayers only. The first such allowance was accorded in 1909 to a parent earning less than £500 a year. The income qualification was removed in 1920, the amount of the allowance was progressively altered and children in full-time education were brought within the scheme if they were over 16.

Finally, the state, following wartime practice, provided certain benefits in kind, for children mostly in schools. These included routine medical and dental inspections; free milk in schools, although this was whittled away in stages—in 1968 when it was withdrawn from secondary schools, and in 1971 when it was limited to under-sevens or special medical cases; and school meals which at the end of our period were being given to nearly six million day pupils.

Such was the framework of this comprehensive and beneficent reform. Gradually two big questions presented themselves—the cost and the fulfilment of the aims. Changing standards of what was due to the individual or family occasioned throughout the century, but particularly after 1945, a massive growth in social services and security benefits and their cost. By 1975 the services and benefits reviewed in this chapter (excluding therefore education and housing services) were costing £15·6 billion and accounting for nearly a third of all public expenditure (excluding debt service).

By 1975 too the shape of the services had been altered in two material respects. The first of these was the increasing part played by supplements to the basic scheme. It was no doubt inevitable that some persons should fall through even the best constructed net but it was depressing to discover how many remained in poverty in spite of this postwar apparatus of benefits. There seemed still to be a need for something like the old Poor Law and in 1948 the National Assistance Act was passed to cater for those who remained penurious (full-time workers and strikers excepted). Its purpose was, by single sums or weekly payments, to succour those who were unable to secure the basic requirements of themselves and their dependents. Its operation required therefore case by case investigation of circumstances and means; there had to be rules or guidelines for deciding who qualified for national assistance and to what level this assistance was to hoist them. In principle there was nothing against a long-stop system of this kind, but almost at once those in receipt of national assistance became an uncomfortably large proportion of the total of recipients of national insurance benefits—

contrary to the expectation that national assistance was only for the anomalous few. There was therefore a drift towards means-testing and selectivity over a large area instead of merely at the fringe, a derogation of rather than a minor corrective to the Beveridge principle of flat-rate payments to all as of right. In 1966 the National Assistance Board, which operated the national assistance scheme alongside the Ministry of Pensions and National Insurance, was replaced by a Supplementary Benefits Commission within the renamed Ministry of Social Security, but the functions remained broadly the same and so did the need.* There was some evidence of, and disproportionate attention to, exploitation of the system by cheats in spite of safeguards and a rising number of prosecutions. The principal safeguard was that supplementary benefits to an unemployed person might not exceed the pay which he would have got from his job; that assistance would be stopped if a recipient refused the offer of a suitable job; that a suspected layabout might be sent to a re-establishment centre; and that in the last (and rare) resort a person might be prosecuted and sent to prison.

A second departure from the Beveridge plan and the statutes of the forties was the abandonment of flat-rate contributions for equal benefits. The introduction in 1959 of graduated contributions for graduated pensions and in 1966 of earnings-related supplements for unemployment and sickness benefits and widows' allowances led to a comprehensive recasting of the system in the seventies, initiated by the (Conservative) Social Security Act 1973 which was superseded before it came into effect by the (Labour) Social Security Act 1974 which, coming into effect the next year, turned the system into one which levied earnings-related contributions in return for flat-rate benefits plus earnings-related supplements. The Social Security Pensions Act 1975 likewise converted pensions to an earnings-related basis from 1978.

Distinct from but no less important than social security was the national health service created by the National Health Act 1946. Medical services were provided in 1945 by 3000 hospitals and tens of thousands of general practitioners, each active in a chosen locality either

* In the years 1965–75 the beneficiaries of the National Insurance Acts numbered 25 million. Supplementary benefits were given to help 4–4·5 million of them.

in competition with other doctors or, in country areas, as effectively the only doctor whom the patient might choose. GPs were available for fees which they themselves set. Persons within the National Health Insurance scheme inaugurated in 1911, i.e. persons at work earning no more than £8 a week but not their wives, were treated free in what was a sectional health service financed by the state. This service had been bitterly opposed by the medical profession but by 1945 two-thirds of the profession were working for it part-time and many derived a substantial part of their income from it. The hospital service was haphazard and in parts antiquated. Many hospitals were very small. Some provided little more than a bed; in some the surgery was positively dangerous. Others were excellent; the major teaching hospitals continued to enjoy worldwide fame. Rather more than half the hospitals belonged to local authorities.

Reorganisation under state control was recommended by a planning commission set up by the profession which envisaged a service covering 90% of the population. It would be manned by GPs working in groups and paid salaries by the state; the sale of practices would cease; hospitals would be reorganised in regions and their staff too would receive state salaries. Doctors would however be free to take private work for private fees, so that their salaries would not necessarily constitute the whole of their remuneration. These proposals, which emanated from the profession and seemed to have its general support, were endorsed by Beveridge but were almost immediately denounced by doctors who, violently if belatedly, decided that they wanted to be left alone and developed fantasies about state regulation on the scale recommended by their own commission. Opposition to the commission's scheme was led by the British Medical Association, the principal collective organ of the GPs.

When therefore Labour won the election of 1945 and Aneurin Bevan was appointed Minister of Health, the medical profession was speaking with two voices. Bevan began by defining the points on which he would not bargain: no more selling of practices, authority to prevent a GP from going to an over-doctored area (but no authority to direct him to an under-doctored one), and the acquisition (but not the running) by the state of all hospitals in municipal or private ownership, including mental hospitals but excluding the teaching hospitals. His main aim was to secure a more even distribution of services across the country. The doctors were to retain much of what they were asking for: private practice, paying beds in hospitals, the patient's right to choose his doctor, clinical freedom, and local as opposed to central administration of the hospitals. But many doctors wanted more and some wanted no national service at all. The former wanted guarantees against becoming in future full-time state employees wholly dependent on state salaries; some also wanted to retain the sale and purchase of practices. Doctors' leaders became frenetic in their opposition to the Minister and, as was later the case in the conflict over comprehensive secondary schools, the professionals became more enraged than the politicians on either side, although the three Royal Colleges and the *Lancet* supported Bevan on several occasions and tried to offset the extremists of the BMA who were attacking him in astonishing and shameful language.

The National Health Act became law before the end of 1946. It decreed free medical and dental services for all. It established local health centres and invited doctors, dentists and pharmacists to join them. The remuneration of GPs was to consist of a basic salary augmented by capitation fees inside the service and private practice outside. Hospitals, municipal and voluntary, passed into the hands of the Minister but were to be run by regional boards and committees. The sum of £66 million was provided for what was in effect the purchase by the state of all private practices.

The Conservatives supported the principle of a national service but entered protests against the payment of doctors by salary and, nostalgically, against the take-over of the voluntary hospitals. The BMA tried to wreck the Act by organising a boycott. Emotions ran high. Speakers at mass meetings foretold the end of medicine and likened the new service to nazi totalitarianism. Doctors were balloted and voted against joining the service in the first of a series of jousts between the BMA and the government. A second ballot showed that many GPs would join the service, even though a majority still voted against doing so. The BMA extremists overplayed their hand and damaged the cause of those doctors who were genuinely worried about a possibly serious loss of independence. Eventually nine-tenths of them joined. The outcome was a triumph for the Minister, who had mastered his subject, made up his mind what to take and what to give, played firm and fair and was neither intimidated nor deceived by the vociferations of a minority. Ten years later a reviewing committee, the Guillebaud Committee, reported that the service had been organised on eminently sensible and satisfactory lines. For its customers it was a godsend, perhaps the most beneficial reform ever enacted in England, given that it relieved so many not merely of pain but also of the awful plight of having to watch the suffering or death of spouse or child for lack of enough money to do anything about it. A country in which such a service exists is utterly different from a country without it.

Such a service cannot come into existence smoothly. The sudden provision on this scale of varied and expert services hitherto available much less than universally meant queues and delays and exceptionally strenuous workloads. People who had to wait complained without remembering that the alternative at this stage to a slow service for all was a prompter service for fewer. The pressures on doctors, nurses, administrators and other staff were severe and occasioned further acrimony between the professions and the authorities which now employed them. Costs rose alarmingly. The cost to the public purse in 1948–49 was £208 million; by 1965 it was £1275 million and by 1975 £5260 million, slightly more than defence. The largest element in this bill was the hospitals, which accounted for more than half of it, largely because of the teaching hospitals (twelve in and twelve outside London) which were internationally famous but commensurately expensive to equip and run. The arguments for maintaining these hospitals at a peak of excellence were compelling although financially the effect was to weight the health bill on the side of in-care and cure as against preventive medicine and out-care.

Thirty years after the inauguration of these services the number of doctors had doubled, the number of nurses had doubled and the money spent on the nation's health had doubled in real terms. The people, not just some people, were being cared for. But this vast expansion had its gaps and strains. Half the hospital beds were in buildings built before 1900 and much equipment was far less good than its users knew it could be. The human strains were attracting more attention than the benefits. These strains were of two kinds: on the one hand pay and remuneration at all levels and on the other the intertwined issues of the doctor's right to private practice and the provision of private paying accommodation in hospitals where part of this practice was carried on. There were some 4000 paying beds in these hospitals, contributing significantly to their finances but also causing resentment because they enabled the patient with money to jump the queue. (The resentment was not lessened when the patients were in addition foreigners.) In 1975 consultants and junior doctors in a number of hospitals refused to to do more than work to rule until their terms of service were reviewed; nurses, midwives and domestic staff claimed rises of 30%, and there was a boycott of services to paying patients, beginning at the new Charing Cross Hospital's 40 penthouse suites and spreading to 150 other hospitals. Disputes on wages and hours of work were compromised. Nurses and midwives got in some cases more than they had asked for, but considerable bad feeling persisted among doctors, exacerbated by the fact that much of what was conceded to junior doctors with one hand was denied with the other in order not to transgress the rules in force under the wages and incomes policy. The government proposed to eliminate 1000 of the paying beds in a matter of months and the rest in an unspecified period. At the same time and in order to prevent the private sector from leeching the national service it proposed that private nursing homes should be permitted to create no more than 4900 new beds to supplement their existing capacity of about 2500. The consultants, fiercely suspicious of the Secretary of State, Barbara Castle, regarded these measures as a betrayal of the promise not to impede private practice. The provision of a national health service imposed severe strains not only on the national budget but also on the loyalties and tempers of overworked and, in some areas, underpaid professional and ancillary staff.

This great programme of social reforms was of the essence of socialism and had considerable support beyond the ranks of the Labour Party since that party, although the focus and driving force of socialism in Britain, has no monopoly of it. On the right the epithet 'socialist' might be used as a term of abuse, increasingly so when the cost of socialist measures became alarmingly high, but there were many Conservative politicians and voters who endorsed socialist aims even when they jibbed at so describing them. Social policies helped to hold the Labour Party together in spite of divisions about timing and pace, whereas these same social issues tended to divide Conservatives who were, on the contrary, united when it came to economic and industrial questions, especially the nationalisation of industry—upon which Labour in its turn was less united than it wished to appear.

Social policies and the welfare commitment confuse politics by bringing moral criteria into a pragmatic sphere where such arguments are normally suspect. Social reforms are undertaken primarily, though by no means exclusively, because they ought to be. The imperative behind the relief of poverty is a moral imperative, but it is a moral imperative which used to operate upon individuals or churches or other charitable bodies rather than upon the state. One of the principal innovations of modern times has been the transfer of this imperative to the state and so the extension of the area of 'ought' in politics. From doing the least possible for the most abject the state has progressed to setting and securing minima which, under the pressure of conscience or of potent lobbies, constantly rise. Since the beneficiaries of this trend are the sick, the poor, the young and the old, the burden of giving them what they are held to be entitled to falls on the rest of society. If the economy of the society is growing, the sacrifices demanded of the healthy, the rich and the middle-aged may not be too heavy, but if the economy is shrinking these sacrifices induce a less generous view of what one lot owes to the other. It is easy to agree that certain props and aids ought to be provided for those who need them, but less easy to contribute without resentment to such schemes when one's own standard of living is thereby eroded. It is in short impossible to develop a welfare state without class conflict unless the national cake is getting bigger all the time. The one telling argument against the welfare state is that it generates class conflict.

The conservative classes in particular were in a dilemma between welcoming a welfare state and not wishing to pay for it. (The left was nimbler at sidestepping the economic implications.) Initially, Conservatives were not only enthusiastic about social reform but claimed as much of the credit for it as they could. A few voices on the party's right prophesied unbearable levels of public spending but in the forties the descriptions heard twenty years later of the welfare state as a scrounger's paradise would have been considered bad form. The Conservative Party produced its Industrial Charter which was socialist in content and applauded by nearly all the party's big names. In the forties and fifties the main thrust of Conservative criticism was not yet directed at levels of expenditure but at the maintenance of controls which, to Conservatives, were relics of wartime necessity and out of place in peacetime, offensive to the British way of life and obstacles to economic efflorescence. Conservatives rejected in these years the notion that problems of peace, no less than problems of war, might require government intervention, and public opinion was on their side when they said that Britain had not fought a war in order to be nannied at the end of it. The

Churchill government of 1951 therefore set about removing these controls but had no intention of demolishing the social services.

These attitudes left unspoken what to do if after all it transpired that the welfare state and the *laissez-faire* state were incompatible. Both parties shirked this question. Yet it could become acute, particularly in Britain with its powerful addiction to the freedom of the individual. It could even be argued that here is one of the great questions of the age: how far does the provision of social services require restrictions on personal freedom, and justify them? In a complex modern society meeting the needs of the disadvantaged on the scale now regarded as right and proper cannot be compassed merely out of the abundance of the private generosity and impulses of the hale and hearty. It is impossible to protect individuals against the ills of poverty, sickness and decrepitude without some recourse to the machinery of the state, and the incursion of the state entails limitations on the freedom of the individual to do as he likes with his own. Even if state interference amounts to no more than taxation, the individual is being forced to give up something that belongs to him.

Socialists accept the implications of this situation and bring the state into play, but they like to gloss over the unpalatable fact that another implication is the restriction of personal freedom—or at any rate the personal freedom of the more fortunate. Their opponents make the most of the threat to freedom but gloss over the fact that if they are to defend this to the limit of their protestations they must also stop welcoming the welfare state. Both sides try to find ways of getting the best of both worlds. Let there be, they say, a measure of redistribution of wealth through government action in order to maintain social services at decent levels. But this equation begs the question since either the redistributive mechanisms are too onerous for the one side or the welfare levels are too low for the other. The problem has not gone away. Consequently the tale of social reforms is a tale of ups and downs, unlike the tale of political reforms in which, for example, an extension of the franchise was never followed by a cut-back but only by a standstill or a further step forward.

A different criticism of the social services was that something basically simple became appallingly complicated. In 1946 it seemed that everybody would pay standard contributions and get in return standard benefits, but this pattern was quickly muddied and then submerged. The main reason was that the rates of benefit were soon too low but the cost of raising them to appropriate levels alarmingly high. So in adjusting the benefits governments abandoned the principle of universality in order to pay increments to a select number rather than to all. They grafted selectivity on to universality and produced a hotchpotch. Up to a point selective supplementary benefits—which were mainly discretionary rather than fixed rights and might be allowances or single payments (to pay an electricity bill or buy a child a pair of shoes)—were accretions which did no more than help the poor and ignore the rich; they complicated things but roused little resentment. Their main defects were those of all means-tested reliefs. Many of those entitled to them failed to apply for them because they did not know of their existence or shrank from the humiliation of asking for charity for themselves or their children. By the end of the period covered by this book at least a million people were failing to draw what parliament had decreed to be their due. Furthermore, by the time the various selective increments, whether payments or rebates (on rents for example), had grown to several dozen bewilderment was compounded by resentment. It became possible to find a family receiving in supplementary benefits plus further discretionary grants more than a similar family whose head was working. Such cases, though exceptional, focused attention on weaknesses in the social security fabric and provided grounds for political attacks on it: scroungers, it was said, were battening on a system which paid a man not to work. Fundamentally, however, what was needed was an overhaul of something that had proliferated in bits and pieces until its basic principle had become overgrown and it was no longer either intelligible or sensible. Above all, the fact that by 1975 supplementary allowances and pensions were being given to no fewer than 2·8 million people showed that a distressing multitude was keeping above the poverty line only through recourse to emergency alms, proof that standard benefits—and wages—were too low.

The sixties and seventies were a bad time for grasping such nettles. The British did not begrudge this beneficial system but they were scared by its cost and irritated by its bureaucratic apparatus; and as time went by they became more scared and irritated. In the mid-sixties social security, the most costly item among the social services, was costing more than defence—which might be gratifying to some but was a shock to others. The social services as a whole, including the health service and education, were taking over 40% of government expenditure —£5·5 billion as against, for example, £2·1 billion for defence: social security benefits were running at about £2·5 billion a year (8% of GNP). Ten years later, at the close of our period, the social services as a whole were taking £22·5 billion and had risen to 45% of government expenditure. Social security benefits had risen to £9 billion (9·5% of GNP). These benefits took the lion's share (40%) of the cost of the social services; within the benefit area the largest slice went to retirement pensions (65%). Besides the hugeness of the sums involved there was a seemingly inexorable escalation.

Fear of these costs sharpened attacks on the socialist commitment to the welfare state and the egalitarianism which inspired it. Egalitarianism is both a dogma and an ideal. As a dogma, derived from Christianity, it asserts that all are equal in the next world; as an ideal it argues that they should be less unequal in this—in their material circumstances and their opportunities. Socialists are not as such interested in the dogma but they are very much concerned with the ideal. Antisocialist polemicists, using arguments which go back to Alexis de Tocqueville's *Democracy in America*, charge socialists with believing that all human beings are equal in this world—or ought to be—and so endangering it by promoting an unnatural equality which stifles talent. This accusation is largely a cloak for the conservative reaction which has followed every substantial advance towards social justice in the last two hundred years, but it contains also a more constructive concern for elite values threatened by the indiscriminate application of the egalitarian ideal—as we shall see more particularly in connection with education.

3 Nationalisation

The public ownership of industrial, commercial and financial under-takings runs counter to the dominant presuppositions and patterns of modern capitalism and indeed of post-Renaissance individualism. The public ownership of cultural undertakings is less obnoxious to these conceptions. Private ownership has been the norm, but public ownership has been gaining ground for a century or more and has advanced so rapidly in living memory as to set up strong emotional resistances. Among democratic countries Britain has swung notably towards public ownership although it has gone less far than some (e.g. France), but public ownership, although no longer as abnormal as it used to be, re-mains unpalatable to the general public which requires governments to make a strong positive case for each fresh proposal for nationalisation. Since the first postwar Labour administration even governments of the left have fought shy of nationalisation and the topic has become divi-sive within the Labour Party itself.

State intervention in cultural activities is relatively non-contentious— so far as the ownership of museums and galleries is concerned, wholly so. Yet even in this sphere the British have preferred to make the inter-vention indirect or veiled. State patronage of the arts—essential since the disappearance of the opulent private patron like a Duke of Urbino or a Prince Esterhazy*—is mediated through an Arts Council whose functions are hazier than the French government's control of the Comé-die Française. The state's powers over the BBC, although they include the right to take over services in an emergency and the right to require certain matters to be broadcast or not broadcast, are not in practice obtrusive and are not opposed by any significant body of people, least of all on the right, where most of the opposition to state intervention is to be found: the introduction of commercial television under a Con-servative administration in 1955 owed less to doctrinal opposition to state control or monopoly than to successful lobbying by entrepreneurs

* The modern millionaire does more collecting than patronising. He has also become a hoarder and speculator in rising values.

who saw a way to make a lot of money and did. In these areas it is generally accepted that the state has a role to play because only the state can find the money needed to sustain the arts at a level which is generally regarded as desirable and proper. The argument therefore is reduced to two ancillary points: the mechanisms most appropriate for channelling and apportioning the money, and the degree of state supervision appropriate in view of the fact that this money has first been extracted from the taxpayer. These are matters which have on the whole been settled with a typically British political deftness.

State intervention elsewhere is another matter altogether. It extends now to public services from utilities such as electricity to railways but hardly at all to financial services, and also to industries as various as coal-mining and atomic energy. In most recent times particular companies rather than whole industries have passed into public ownership. The motives are various. The main impetus has been given by socialist thinking. Private ownership is opposed by socialists where the undertakings are so important nationally that their direction ought, in the socialist view, to be governed by considerations of public policy rather than private gain. Private ownership, it is contended, is incompatible with public purpose. Such considerations include levels of investment and research and the size of the industry. Closely allied is the argument that such industries ought to be planned as a whole, i.e. nationwide and not company by company, and ought not to be conducted on the basis of competition between component companies seeking to damage one another; and that such planning is impossible except by a public authority or by a cartel (which is undesirable because private monopolies prey on the consumer). A different socialist argument derives from social premises rather than consideration of the national interest. It objects to the profits of industry going into the pockets of the few (owners, shareholders and senior managers—classes which increasingly overlap but remain a very small proportion of the population*) rather than the many. This argument has gained strength since the private owner ceased to be an adventurer risking his own money in his own energies and ideas and has become instead a passive rentier or calculating

---

* Shareholders are not a large army but a relatively small one. In the last decade of our period families derived between 3 and 4% of their income from investments. For the vast majority of families this source did not exist.

investor, a financier rather than a maker or merchant, a man who commands much less admiration than the individualist whose fortune in the early days of capitalism was earned—or lost—in imaginative and venturesome effort. No less important than socialist doctrine has been example. The nationalisation of coal, which was approved by thousands of people ignorant of socialist doctrine and suspicious of all doctrine, owed more to the historical failures of coal-owners than to anything else. And finally there were financial arguments. Industries needed more capital for rehabilitation and modernisation than they could find for themselves from profits or borrowing. This was uncontested in the case of a new industry like atomic energy, and in the older industries nationalised in 1945–49 huge sums had to be invested by the state which could not have come from anywhere else. Finance of this order was needed if the mines and railways, gas and electricity were to survive and prosper in any sort of acceptable shape. The alternative to state finance was decay.

The forms of public ownership are as numerous as the motives for it. As long ago as the eighteenth century a government passed a Regulating Act which was in effect a measure to legalise government interference in the affairs of the East India Company on grounds of public policy. That company having acquired an empire for which it needed an administration, an army and a judiciary, there was a public interest in seeing that it conducted itself in certain ways; and succeeding measures increased the degree of government intervention. This example was followed in the nineteenth century by the creation of a number of supervisory commissions which enabled the government to interfere otherwise than through the established departments of state, new wheels on an old machine. The modern British usage has grown out of this innovation. As the scope of government broadened, so have its instruments been diversified. Another method, much debated in the nineteen-fifties and -sixties —namely, the purchase by the state of shares in private companies— was anticipated by Disraeli when he bought shares in the Suez Canal Company and by Asquith when he bought shares in the Anglo-Persian Oil Company (later British Petroleum). Between the two world wars a number of public corporations were created—the Central Electricity Generating Board, the London Passenger Transport Board, the Forestry Commission, the BBC, the Tote, the British Overseas Airways Corporation and (earlier) the Port of London Authority and the Metropolitan Water Board. Largely under the influence of Herbert Morrison this kind of instrument was favoured by the Attlee administration when it came to create the National Coal Board, the Transport Commission, the Electricity and Gas Councils, new airways corporations and the British Iron and Steel Corporation.

The public corporation is a hybrid with a special appeal to those who do not want things to be black or white (e.g. the British). It is not a private company but it is not part of the normal structure of government expressed in departments of state and local authorities. It manages its own day-to-day affairs but it is not free from ministerial control since a minister can issue general directions. It does not have to make profits in order to declare dividends (it has no shareholders) but it is expected to earn surpluses in some years to set against deficits in others. Its staff are not state employees but neither are they quite like the employees of private companies, and its senior managers neither go out like ministers on a change of government nor carry on indefinitely like most company chairmen subject only to an age-limit (they normally serve for fixed terms of five years). The public corporation, as a type, has had many admirers abroad as well as at home, although these are not always to be found within the corporations themselves where the functions of chairman and minister dovetail imprecisely and uneasily. The specific corporations created since 1945 have had to live in difficult and above all expensive times and, quite apart from the buffetings of doctrinal debate, have not managed to earn the goodwill of the public mainly because they most frequently catch the public ear when they put up their charges or borrow huge sums of public money.

The first and simplest act of postwar nationalisation was the nationalisation of the Bank of England which was then unique among national banks in being still the property of private stockholders as it had been since its foundation in the wake of the Glorious Revolution.* There were 17,000 of these stockholders. The more substantial of them, those owning £500 worth of stock or more, appointed the governor, deputy governor and other directors. All the stockholders were bought out in

* Britain is a country so eccentric that it left its central bank in private hands until the middle of the twentieth century and allowed it to be directed for 24 years in that century by Montagu Norman, an autocratic and inarticulate neurotic who regarded banking as having nothing to do with economics, let alone politics, national or international. This apotheosis of naked individualism derived from a characteristic confusion of individualism with excellence.

1946, receiving a new government stock in place of their Bank stock, and the Treasury was empowered to give certain general directions to the Bank. There was no serious opposition to this change although some Conservatives maintained that it was unnecessary. It was a solitary incursion by the state into the areas of finance and credit, for the principal institutions of the City of London—its exchanges, commodity markets, joint stock banks and merchant banks, and insurance companies—were held in great respect and even awe, so that although France, Italy and a number of Commonwealth and other countries nationalised commercial banking and insurance, in Britain these activities remained in private hands for fear of disturbing the arcane mechanisms whose services earned large surpluses for the balance of payments ('the City' was thought of and publicised more in external than domestic terms). The Attlee government confined itself therefore to taking regulatory powers over the capital market by an Investment (Control and Guarantees) Act which was inspired by memories of the undignified free-for-all that followed the first world war. With capital in short supply somebody had to fix priorities and the government took power to arrange the queue instead of leaving it to influence or the blind workings of first come first served. Additionally the Treasury was authorised to guarantee pump-priming loans designed to assist postwar reconstruction and expansion.

The public ownership and centralization of gas and electricity were in principle no more contentious than the nationalisation of the Bank. Transport, partly a service and partly a profit-making industry, was a more debatable area where the nationalisation effected by the Labour government was later partially undone by the Conservatives. Coal, an industry and a basic one, had been recommended for nationalisation at the end of the first world war and was generally recognised to have for historical reasons no escape from that fate: nobody was prepared to put up a fight for the owners in 1945. Iron and steel, another basic industry, was destined for an unsettling round of nationalisation, denationalisation and renationalisation.

Gas, the older of the two major suppliers of light and heat, was supplied to domestic and industrial users by hundreds of different undertakings, many of them small, many of them out of date, about a third of them municipally owned. The industry was ailing and in 1945 the Heyworth Report recommended that it be reorganised and entirely nationalised. Private and municipal owners were bought out by the

Gas Act 1948. The industry was organised in twelve regions under a Gas Council consisting of the twelve regional chairmen plus a national chairman and deputy chairman. These were experienced and expert men who found themselves charged, first, with the technological revolution involved in getting gas from oil instead of coal and then, secondly, with the unexpected expansion and brightening of the industry upon the discovery of large amounts of gas under the North Sea. By the Continental Shelf Act 1964 all minerals under the British half of the North Sea were vested in the crown. Licences were granted to prospectors and the first find of gas was made in 1965.

The public ownership of electricity services had been envisaged from the beginnings of electricity in the nineteenth century. The electricity industry was both like and unlike gas. It was unlike gas because in 1945 it was a flourishing industry, but it was like gas inasmuch as supply was in the hands of a patchwork of suppliers using different voltages and currents, some of them privately but most of them municipally owned. Supply therefore was decentralised and partially in public ownership. Generation on the other hand had been centralised and wholly nationalised by the Conservative government which created in 1926 the Central Electricity Generating Board, charged with the generation of electric power and also the construction of a national grid to feed the several suppliers. In 1945 some areas in England were still without electricity. The Electricity Act 1947 unified supply. It established fifteen regional boards (three of them in Scotland, later reduced to two) under central authority which was somewhat decentralised by an amending Act in 1957. This reorganisation, coupled with postwar recovery and re-equipment and rapidly increasing demands which had to be met in the face of a serious shortage of coal, were challenges which the newly nationalised industry and its boards met with success.

The modern history of coal in Britain has been unhappy. Nationalisation had been talked about in the nineteenth century and was recommended by the Sankey Committee in 1919. Between the wars productivity slumped and miners' wages slipped further and further behind wages in other major industries. Pay and conditions in the mines caused the strike of 1926 which turned briefly into a general strike in which the owners (or their protagonists—they were not all of one mind) prevailed not only over the workers but also over politicians like Baldwin and Churchill who deplored their harshness and had hoped for a compromise. The obduracy of the owners was due to their concern about their profits. The coal industry had been expanded during the war but had lost its export business and the return to the gold standard in 1925 at the prewar rate of $4·86 to the £ made the recovery of these markets extremely difficult. The owners sought to safeguard their finances by insisting on a longer (8-hour) working day, by cutting wages and by negotiating on pay and conditions locally and not nationally with the union. Having won this battle, the owners were not obliged by the economics of their situation to face the need for modernisation, although in shirking it they worsened their long-term problem and the plight of the industry. Productivity continued to lag. In the year of the strike it was nearly as high as in Poland, the European leader, and about the same as in the Ruhr and the Netherlands. Ten years later it was not much more than half what was being produced per man in Poland and had slipped significantly below German and Dutch levels. Labour relations were appallingly bad. During the second world war the Reid Report on the coal industry gave a devastating exposure of inadequacies and backwardness and when peace came an unregenerated and demoralised industry was facing the competition of nuclear power as well as gas while one third of the coal produced was no use to anybody except the Electricity Generating Board.

The Coal Industry Nationalisation Act 1946 transferred mines and minerals to the state in exchange for compensation which was subsequently assessed by a special tribunal at £164·6 million to be divided between 850 claimants. A National Coal Board of nine, appointed by the Minister of Fuel and Power and subject to his general direction, was charged with the arduous business of reviving and re-equipping the industry. It produced in 1950 a *Plan for Coal* which was revised in 1956 by *Investing in Coal* and again in 1959 by the *Revised Plan for Coal*. The aim in the early fifties was to increase production and productivity but by 1959 there was over-production in Europe and targets were brought down. At the date of nationalisation production was just over 200 million tons a year, which the 1950 plan proposed to raise to 240 million tons by 1965, but which was then cut in 1959 to 200–215 million. Manpower, which totalled 720,000 at nationalisation, was to be reduced by 1965 to 672,000 (the 1950 plan) and then (the 1959 plan) to somewhere between 587,000 and 626,000. The latter plan envisaged the closure of 200 out of 750 pits but also an increase in productivity from 280 tons per man per year to 375 tons (it topped 400 tons in 1967). These were big and hurtful changes and they involved a costly programme of mechanisation which soon outran first estimates. For a generation to come the industry was plagued by prospects of closures and unemployment on the one hand and abnormally heavy expenditure on the other against a background of falling demand, an ageing work force and a mood of pessimism.

The plans of the fifties were revised again in the sixties in an attempt to shrink the industry further without inflicting an unacceptable rate of dismissals on the men working in it. By the Coal Industry Act 1965 the state paid the electricity industry to take coal which it did not want in order to keep the pace of shrinkage within bounds; from 1969 onwards the electricity supply industry was taking more than half of all the coal mined in Britain. Prices were kept down by ministerial direction but with the inevitable corollary that the Coal Board's deficits rose. By 1965 they had reached £91 million (aggravated by overstocks of coal mined but not sold in the declining market) and parliament revamped the Board's finances by extinguishing a large part of its debt in return for an undertaking to pay into the Treasury surpluses earned in good years when these should occur. Mechanisation was paying in terms of productivity, which arose by over 20% in the last decade of our period. Many pits were profitable, but there were also many unprofitable pits which the Board could not close fast enough because of the unemployment which would result.

Between the wars little attention had been given to the finances of nationalised industries. There would be a price to pay to expropriated owners but after that the industries would finance themselves. They would no doubt need to borrow, as any great industry did, but they would do so on normal terms in the capital market. That they should become dependent on government funds was not part of anybody's plan, nor was the size of the sums needed or the fact that the shrinking capital market would throw the financial burden on to government and taxpayer. The Coal Industry Act 1965 in effect cancelled the interest service on £415 million of capital and subsidised the human cost of pit closures, but this was not enough and more money had to be found to cushion the human effects of closures or to subsidise pits kept working for non-economic reasons. Directly or indirectly the state provided funds to protect or compensate miners who would in an earlier age having been turned away with little or no unemployment or redundancy pay. On top of the costs of modernisation and mechanisation the state was paying for the reshaping of an industry that was no longer king in the realm of energy. At the end of 1972 two-thirds of the debt of the Coal Board (£475 million) was cancelled and £515 million was promised up to March 1976, with the prospect of £150 million more to come, to cover the economic cost of slowing down the contraction of an industry which had a powerful union and significant public sympathy: for the miners, in their own eyes but not theirs alone, were not just an industry but a community, the proletariat *par excellence*, a special case.*

The case of the railways was in some ways similar. The railways, like the mines, were in need of a technical face-lift. Gladstone had toyed with the idea of nationalising the railways while he was still a Conserva-̇tive but did nothing about it either then or after he became a Liberal. Governments limited their intervention to taking power to regulate fares and charges. The first world war provided an opportunity to rationalise the untidy patchwork bequeathed by Victorian competitive-ness and between the wars virtually all lines were concentrated in four, mostly unsuccessful, companies. These companies had to fight the road hauliers for an adequate share of the freight business but could not make up their minds whether to do so by keeping charges low (which was to some extent imposed on them by government) or by putting fares up and so earning enough money to improve their services and attract custom. To a considerable extent they abandoned the fight and either urged government to put shackles on road transport or bought their way into road transport themselves, thus implicitly accepting a decline in the future and fortunes of rail services and incidentally foreshadowing the Labour government's solution of combining all forms of transport in one organisation. The heyday of the railways had been when roads were appalling and there was no such thing as a lorry.

During the second world war the railways were under public control and the Attlee government could have taken the comparatively simple step of converting this control into ownership. It decided on something more radical by tackling all transport as a unitary problem† and brought

---

* This is not new. Mediaeval miners had laws and lawcourts of their own.

† Except air transport. Civil air services were organised in three public corporations, two of them new and a third—BOAC—which had been in existence since 1939. These were reduced to two in 1949 when British South American Airways became part of BOAC and to one in 1973 when British European Airways and BOAC were merged as British Airways.

in a Bill to nationalise and reorganise rail, road, inland waterway and dock services together with all other properties such as hotels owned by the undertakings thus acquired. Coastal and other shipping, except ferry services, were excluded from the Bill and so were some specialised road services such as tankers, which remained in private hands, and local bus services, which were retained by their municipal or private owners. Expropriated owners were compensated with British Transport Stock issued and guaranteed by the Treasury (parallel with the similar issues of Gas and Electricity Stock) on the basis of the stock exchange value of their shares or debentures. This assessment was regarded as unfair by the owners who maintained that the threat of nationalisation had depressed stock exchange quotations, but contrariwise it was argued that these quotations had exaggerated the true value of the undertakings by leaving their monopolistic character out of account. In the event the nationalised undertakings were saddled with very big annual interest payments which they were required to bring into account before striking a profit and loss balance, and the biggest of all the compensation bills was for transport—£1217 million, nearly twice as much as gas and electricity together.

The vast and varied new transport dominion, comprising 52,000 miles of track, over 2000 miles of canals and 450,000 road haulage vehicles, was committed to the direction of a British Transport Commission with a number of subordinate functional executives. A number of these contrived to make surpluses for several years but rail services had financial troubles from the start and even before embarking on the costly modernisation entailed by the end of steam and the advent of the diesel locomotive and electrification. The accounts of nationalised transport looked even sicker after 1953 when the Conservatives, by the Transport Act of that year, began to return profitable road services to private ownership. By this Act the Transport Commission was required to sell off the undertakings and assets of its Road Haulage Executive, but since buyers could not be found for all these properties another Act in 1956 consolidated what was left in public ownership as British Road Services. The railways were back to competing with road freight and passenger coaches at a time when the contraction of the coal industry was reducing earnings from the traditional bread-and-butter source of carrying coal. Once more the railways had a choice: to cut back or to modernise. Once more they tried to get the best of both worlds by cutting back economically marginal or unprofitable services and spending on main lines. But non-economic factors entered into the argument. The least profitable services were frequently those passenger rail services which, if excised, would leave people with no other way of getting around, and people did not take amiably to the idea of reverting to the comparative dearth of public transport which had satisfied their grand-parents. They felt that the state owed them something better and, by implication, should find a way of paying for it. This meant either subsi-dising the Transport Commission to go on running loss-making lines or allowing the Commission to raise charges on these lines to the point where they would pay for themselves—which charges would probably be more than the traffic would bear anyway. The Commission might be willing enough to operate such lines provided it were not charged with the losses, but governments shrank from subsidies for economic reasons, which, by this time, were paramount over social considerations. Under Lord Beeching's chairmanship (1961–66) the Commission set about retrenching, proposed substantial closures of passenger services and was authorised to effect much but not the whole of its programme. These cuts, designed to make the Commission's books balance, caused con-siderable resentment and failed to balance the books.

The fact was that the railways could not be made to pay in any accepted sense. The act of nationalisation had imposed on the Com-mission, not on the Treasury, the permanent burden of the interest on Transport Stock, while the advance of technology and the neglect of a previous generation combined to impose the heavier burden of building a new railway system while charging the users at rates related to past custom rather than current cost. The modernisation was tackled with considerable success but while it was being paid for solvency of the kind expected by company auditors and devoutly desired by commuters and taxpayers was impossible. For a period the railways could not 'invest in the future' and 'pay their way'. In the fifties this dilemma was faced but underestimated. Inter-city electrification and a revolution in freight services were undertaken at a calculated cost of £250 million which would be provided partly by the Treasury and partly out of higher charges with the expectation that by 1962 the railway system, refurbished and also slimmed, would be one of the best and fastest in the world and would pay its way. The £250 million was quickly con-sumed. So was the £400 million to which it was increased. Hopes of attracting traffic back to the railways were disappointed. Despite modernisation railways were still stigmatised, especially by the road lobby, as old-fashioned affairs with more than the sniff of the museum about them; road–rail competition was still being won by the roads; and the profits of road hauliers were no longer available to the Transport Commission, which had become something less than a transport commission and in fact a rail commission. In addition wages shot up, especially after the Guillebaud Report of 1955 which ruled against the Commission's view that it was prevented by statute from raising wages so long as surpluses were not available from which to pay them.

One result was the Transport Act 1962 designed to give interim financial relief so that the railways might become self-financing by 1968 instead of 1962. Interest on half the accumulated deficits was reduced to nil while the remainder was to be repaid by instalments beginning in 1965: in other words the Commission would apply to capital repayment sums previously earmarked for interest payments. But this arrangement was almost immediately suspended and when 1968 arrived yet another Act gave yet more financial relief by slashing the burden of indebtedness and authorising subsidies for unrewarding services. These successive adjustments, painful to orthodoxy and to the economy as a whole, were a way of expressing the cost of maintaining a certain kind of service when the alternative was not to maintain it but, applying commercial norms, to let it collapse or wither. That the cost was paid signified a political acceptance of something over and above commercial justification—that transport was a social service and not merely a commercial enterprise. But social services have to be paid for by somebody, the more so when their social justification is unmatched by commercial justification. In 1961 a White Paper on the nationalised industries (Cmd. 1337) had insisted that sound economic management take precedence over social service considerations and that each nationalised industry should earn both a return on capital employed and, over the years, surpluses to constitute a fund for development and investment. The trouble with these impeccable sentiments was that it was possible to practise sound economic management and still not earn the anticipated return and surpluses. A later White Paper (Cmd. 3437) on forward planning and investment in the nationalised industries tried to be more precise by setting a target of 8% as an acceptable average return using discounted cash flow (i.e. assessing future costs and future returns at values ruling at the date of assessment and adding 8%).

Transport has a very obvious social as well as commercial function, but there is no accepted way of measuring the social benefits. On the assumption, generally accepted, that there was a social benefit, it was logical to take this benefit into account when assessing the industry's performance. By so much should the required economic return be reduced; or, to put it another way round, the whole performance should be judged acceptable if the economic return and the social benefit together balanced the cost side of the account. But these are acceptable generalisations which cannot be reduced to figures. Since social benefits cannot be quantified it is impossible to strike such an account with the result that the accounts go on being presented in the old way without any allowance on the plus side for the social benefits provided. There are only two logical ways of dealing with this dilemma. The first is to forget the social element when presenting and measuring the performance of the undertaking. The social element then becomes an element in the background which is held to excuse to some vague degree the economic shortcomings disclosed by the accounts, or, alternatively, the social service element and the social purposes become gradually eroded or altogether eliminated. The second way is to make an arbitrary assessment of the social benefit, separate it from the economic performance and pay for it out of general taxation. Attempts to reconcile the economic and social obligations of such an undertaking in a single document are futile.

There remains the final act of Labour's nationalisation programme in these first postwar years: the Iron and Steel Act 1949.

The ironmaster has had a different place from the coal-owner in British history and mythology. The stereotype of the ironmaster derives from the prosperous Victorian middle-class entrepreneur, a hard man perhaps but a self-made man who owed his fortunes to his exertions. The coal-owner on the other hand was more often than not a land-owner and an aristocrat who owed his minerals to the happy accident of where his land lay. There was much more class feeling in the coal industry than in iron and steel. There was too a wide difference in political attitudes between 1945 and 1948 when the Iron and Steel Bill was brought in. By the latter date the Conservatives had recovered from their unexpected and humiliating shock at the polls in 1945; much of wartime solidarity between parties and classes had already drained away; and the ending of a parliamentary term (a general election could not be delayed beyond July 1950) was a better time than a beginning for a fight. The Conservative Party, which had no heart to fight the nationalisation of coal, was determined and eager to fight the nationalisation of steel and suffered none of the embarrassment about doing so which the record and social image of the coal-owners had imposed in the earlier case.

The owners too were well equipped for the fight. The steel industry was more highly centralised than coal, more confident and more intelligently led. The owners' association, the British Iron and Steel Federation, exercised significant authority over its constituent companies and provided leadership which was united and politically weighty; the companies themselves were not unmanageably numerous. The industry as a whole was neither markedly inefficient nor short of cash (two of the criteria for nationalisation) and its labour relations were incomparably better than those in the pits. There were nevertheless arguments on the other side. Steel, like coal, had been in embarrassingly short supply during the war and most of the blame for underproduction rested on the owners. Unemployment in the twenties and thirties had been extreme, reaching in some areas and in the worst year 50%; for long stretches the industry had been working at half capacity. Its organisation was haphazard, based on separate companies with distinct functions where perhaps a regional organisation would work better. Parts of the industry were completely outmoded and technically unfit to compete with foreign plants. The costs of modernisation might well prove beyond the borrowing powers of the companies. The importance of the industry to the national economy was beyond question. It was vital for other industries, e.g. the motor-car manufacturers, and no less for armaments. It was tending towards monopoly under the increasing authority of the Federation, a process facilitated by the legacy of wartime concentration. Some measure of public direction or intervention seemed therefore justifiable on any view, while a socialist case for public ownership of the commanding heights of the economy could not possibly bypass steel. The nationalisation of steel had been part of Labour's policy since the thirties.

The subsequent fate of the industry owed much to the fact that the Labour Party did not wholly subscribe to this socialist view. It fumbled nationalisation and so invited denationalisation. The steel industry became involved in internal labour dissensions as well as in the politics of Labour *versus* Conservatives. It is at least possible that if Labour had been as clearly resolved on the nationalisation of steel as it was on the nationalisation of coal, the act would have been done more quickly and would have been accepted as irreversible—by 1951 an accomplished fact best left alone, however much deplored by many. In the event, however, the Labour Party and cabinet were divided on the nature of the measure to be introduced and the Bill was delayed until it could be rendered ineffective by the election due in 1950.

The gerarchs of the Attlee cabinet were, with one exception, in favour of what was called full nationalisation, i.e. a statute vesting all relevant raw materials and undertakings in the state. This was the view of Bevin, Cripps and Dalton, and it was also the view of Bevan who was the outstanding figure in the next generation. But it was not the view of Morrison who did not want to nationalise steel—or did not want to do so yet —and, with Attlee's blessing, entered into discussions with the Federation with the aim of getting agreement on a half-way measure. The cabinet, however, rejected Morrison's proposals partly because it thought a half-way measure was the worst of all possible courses and partly because it was affronted by Morrison's tactics of concerting a scheme with interested parties before the cabinet had discussed it. Attlee, by failing at this point to back Morrison, added to the confusion and bad feeling. The TUC also was divided. The principal union leaders, supported by a majority of the Congress, sided with Morrison but a surprisingly large minority voted for full nationalisation.

These divisions and delays introduced a fresh complication. Consertive opposition to an Iron and Steel Bill made it likely that the Parliament Act 1911 would have to be invoked to circumvent the Conservative dominance of the House of Lords, but delays had spun out the timetable to the point where the Parliament Act would fail to ensure the passage of a Bill before the natural expiry of the parliament elected in 1945 and in that case the Bill would be wholly lost even if Labour won the ensuing election. In 1947 the government introduced a new Parliament Bill which became law in 1949 and abbreviated to one year the delaying competence of the House of Lords. Even those who approved the substance of this measure could hardly escape uneasiness about its immediate motive and the opposition did not fail to denounce it as opportunist gerrymandering with the constitution—and, incidentally, an evasion of the more serious issue of the reform of the House of Lords.

During the controversies over the Parliament Bill the government introduced, in November 1948, its Iron and Steel Bill which had the formal endorsement of the entire cabinet. It proposed the purchase of specified companies chosen mainly for their size (107 were named in the Bill but the number was later reduced to 96) and the creation of a British Iron and Steel Corporation empowered to reorganise these companies by merger, liquidation or otherwise and to provide central services and research. The debates on the Bill in the House of Commons threatened to become more protracted than the government was willing to tolerate. It was by now in a hurry and it had been irritated by opposition tactics on previous Bills which seemed to be directed at least as much to delaying as to amending them. Consequently the Labour majority cut the debate short by the guillotine over predictable accusations of gagging. The House of Lords then made a number of changes in the Bill and inserted a provision postponing the vesting of the specified companies in the Corporation until after the next general election. The government, no longer able to get its Bill even by recourse to the new Parliament Act, accepted the Lords' amendments and the Bill became law in November 1949, a year after its introduction. The contest over steel had been bitterer than other nationalisation issues and in spite of the passing of the Bill Labour seemed to have lost.

But in the following February Labour won the election. With 46·8% of the votes cast and 315 seats the Labour Party was still the largest in the House of Commons: the Conservatives had 298 seats and the Liberals 9. The Conservatives, resorting to the mandate theory of politics dear to a losing party, claimed that the country had rejected the nationalisation of steel and that the vesting date should be again postponed until after another election. The Iron and Steel Federation did its best to obstruct the law by refusing to suggest candidates for posts with the Corporation. The government proceeded to implement the Act but in October 1951 time came down on the Conservative side when another election gave them 321 seats to Labour's 295 (Liberals 6).

The Conservatives had undertaken to reverse the Act of 1949 and did so by the Iron and Steel Act 1953 which created the more passive Iron and Steel Board with supervisory powers only and directed the Corporation to sell off the companies vested in it by the Act of 1949. This proved to be an unexpectedly lengthy and ultimately incomplete process. The previous owners did not rush to buy and when the process was brought to a halt in 1967 one major company, Richard Thomas and Baldwins, remained in national ownership. In 1967 Labour fulfilled its counter-pledge to renationalise by taking back into public ownership thirteen of the largest companies which between them accounted for nine-tenths of the industry's production and employed nearly three-quarters of its workers. The principal argument advanced for renationalisation—like denationalisation in the case of the Conservatives—was also a more or less blind process of the party's soul. The Acts of 1953 and 1967 were, more than a little, political reflex actions. But the financial argument was not a hollow one. In 1972 another Labour government put up £36 million for reorganisation, including closures calculated to eliminate 50,000 jobs. In the last ten years of our period the iron and steel industry's production and the number of its active furnaces shrank by 30%. Home consumption of iron and steel products sank by the same margin.

The Conservatives, denationalising steel and road haulage, were not plagued by doubts. The Labour Party, on the opposite course, was. Among the leaders of the new generation Hugh Gaitskell and Anthony Crosland saw nationalisation as a means to socialist ends but not the only one or a necessary one. Although they were talking about means they gave the impression of wanting a close season, probably a long one, for new ventures into public ownership. Yet the Labour cupboard was far from bare of further proposals. The party's 1953 programme included, besides the renationalisation of steel and road transport, a variety of new candidates: water supply to join gas and electricity; parts of the aircraft industry if, like coal, it was not doing a good job; parts of insurance; chemicals on the grounds that the industry was becoming a monopoly; machine tools, mining machinery, cement. There were also ideas for acquiring majority shareholdings in desirable companies, for advancing capital for approved schemes, for supplying expensive equipment on loan, for establishing and endowing research organisations. The net was wide and the public, no longer much interested, took the diversity to betoken confusion.

Four years later, with an election in the offing, Labour produced *Industry and Society* which advocated the purchase by the state of shares in 500 companies accounting between them for half the profits of private industry and half the direct investment in the private sector. This plan shifted the emphasis from the ownership of industry to its fruits and in fact adumbrated a new way of financing the activities of the state alongside the traditional methods of taxation and public borrowing. By holding shares the state, and so the nation, would garner a share of profits and capital gains, but this symptom of Labour's new pragmatism wore an air of incongruity, joining the capitalist system instead of deploring its weaknesses and iniquities: nationalisation, from being a means to secure the national interest and public purpose, was being put forward as a way of deflecting the profits of capitalism directly into the Exchequer. This might be a sensible idea but it was more obviously a new one and it did the party no good in 1959 when it lost its third election in a row. Gaitskell ascribed this unique rebuff to the electorate's distaste for indiscriminate nationalisation and, while maintaining that there were still things that ought to be under public control, again argued that ownership was not the only method, thereby provoking a commotion within the party and leaving it with a vague policy of creeping communal ownership to be achieved as and when necessary and by whatever means.

Whatever may be thought about the wisdom of Gaitskell's tactics after the 1959 election he was right about one thing. The electorate was not behind Labour's policy of nationalisation. This word was changing its connotations. It had stood for public ownership, and public ownership of coal or transport or gas had seemed at least proper and even thoroughly desirable. But by the fifties and thereafter nationalisation meant not so much the creation of public ownership as the destruction of private property. It had become enmeshed in a very ancient and deep debate, and the Labour Party was to be subliminally but fatefully tinged with the odious notion that it threatened a basic right of man. Probably this notion was already gaining ground when Labour left office in 1951. Certainly it was fostered in the years that followed.

Europe has known two distinct and incompatible traditions about private property. The one holds that private property is natural, the other that it is unnatural. The first tradition is rooted in Aristotle, the second is Christian. The Christian tradition dominated European thought in the Middle Ages until near their end. Christian thinkers varied in their denunciation of private property. Some regarded it as utterly wrong, while others accepted it as a necessary evil brought into the world by the fall and corruption of man. This Christian tradition began to go into decline around the thirteenth century, by which time the church had become the owner of private property on a huge scale and two exceptionally powerful minds—Alexander of Hales and Thomas Aquinas—found in the newly discovered writings of Aristotle grounds for taking a more benign view of private property. With the help of Aristotle they managed to controvert one of the most eminent of the Christian Fathers, St Ambrose, and one of the cleverest, St Isidore.

Private property has seemed natural ever since, both in the philosophical sense of being derived from natural law and in the popular sense of being a normally accepted institution. But it has never ceased to agitate a number of minds.

Property until close to our own day has meant land, and landed property was the source not only of wealth but also of status and authority. It also defined and underwrote the possessor's style of living. Attacks on property have therefore stung with double venom. The earliest attack of this kind in European history of which we know much took place in the last age of the Roman republic and the first decades of the principate.* It was clearly seen as an attack on power and privilege as well as an undermining of what we now call living standards and on all these counts as revolutionary. All attacks on property down to our own day have contained this revolutionary element and have raised the fears and bitterness associated with revolution.

One of the more revolutionary events in European history was the transfer of land from ecclesiastical bodies to secular lords and the middling classes, because this was a transfer of the political authority which went with land. The acquisition of land by the merchant class endowed it with political aspirations which it turned into political power, but enough was left of the Christian tradition to circumscribe this power. Before losing out to the layman the ecclesiastic, largely in order to salve his own conscience, invented the idea that although private ownership was (*pace* St Francis and others) proper, the enjoyment of privately owned property was not to be regarded as unshackled. The owner owed a duty to the propertyless and poor. This view reconciled property with conscience. It became standard and debate moved to the question how much care and subsistence the poor were entitled to look for. By analogy there have been throughout the modern centuries those who said that if the poor might have too little, some of the rich might have unconscionably too much, more than was good for them; but this did not become a popular view until the big prizes of modern capitalism gave a new twist to consciences and to envy, by which time property itself had changed its nature by becoming

---

* The social stirrings of the Gracchi and their successors may have been accompanied too by an early women's lib. movement if, as has been mooted, Clodia Metelli was something more significant than an upper-class whore.

typified by shares in industrial and commercial companies rather than by landowning.

Today property has less to do with status which derives more from office, for which social position and an adequate private income are no longer prerequisites—e.g. the office of general secretary of the National Union of Mineworkers, or for that matter chairman of the National Coal Board. But property still has a lot to do with living styles; there is still a substantial propertied class which lives differently and leads a more ample life than the unpropertied, even though some among the latter may attain from salaries plus 'perks' or from speculation a similar level of affluence. Private property is no longer necessary for political advancement*—there are other channels, better ones and worse—but it retains too many other attractions to be abandoned without a struggle, and those who struggle and protest easily persuade themselves that they are defending more than selfish interests and are saving the fabric of society from a baleful rift. Something that has been sanctified for so long by its mere existence does seem to belong to the natural order of things.

The most influential theorist on this topic after Thomas Aquinas was John Locke, a thinker with immense practical effect because his theory was a time-bomb. Locke agreed that private property was natural and went on to say why: it was natural for a man to own the fruits of his labour. But on that basis, as became apparent to the troubled mind of J. S. Mill (a secular troubled mind in the sea of Victorians troubled by religious doubt), the landowner had no right to his landed property unless he worked it himself and by the end of the century the Lockean theory was manifestly useless as a defence of the private property of the rentier and financier. A new theory was needed and in due course emerged. Property was not to be justified on the labour theory nor was it a natural right at all; it was however a good thing because it was essential to liberty. The first or historical half of this theory was valid within its own terms but the second was exceedingly vague. The proposition that property and freedom are indivisible had preoccupied Thomas Jefferson, who was inconsistent about it, and was boosted by Hegel and his descendants, who ended up by using libertarian arguments to attack both capitalism and socialism. It continues, however, to flourish without

* In the so-called developed countries. Over the greater part of the world land is still the main source of status and livelihood.

becoming any less vague and it is a measure of the confusion in which the twentieth century finds itself that, on the one hand, the century's archetypal liberal constitution, the Weimar constitution, approved the confiscation of private property by the state without compensation while, on the other hand, the 1936 constitution of the USSR, promulgated when the communist regime in that country had reached the limits of unfreedom, assured to the individual the ownership of what his labour earned. Democratic socialist theory holds that a man is entitled to own what he has worked for but no more, but democratic socialist practice shrinks from taking away from a man what he has already acquired in a theoretically unacceptable way and does little to prevent him from acquiring more in the same way. St Thomas and Locke both tried in different ways to find a compromise between Europe's two incompatible traditions about private property. So do we, accepting capitalism in practice because it is there and socialism in theory because it is nicer, and ending up with a compromise which consists of a practice and a theory that fit uneasily together.

PART II
Failures

1 Growth and industry

This book is about the thirty years that followed the second world war. The first of these years were years of endeavour and hope in which many difficulties were expected and some hardship accepted because the climate was optimistic and generous. The concluding years provided a harsh, sad—though perhaps not final—comment on these hopes. The early seventies were years of gloom, and this gloom was cast by economic problems and failures. By 1975 it seemed that too much had been attempted and too much hoped for; at the least it had to be said that too small a margin had been allowed for errors and misfortunes on the way.

The strategy of the first years aimed to recover for Britain, as a manufacturing and trading country, a position among the foremost in spite of the injury inflicted by war and by longer-term misdirection and changing world circumstances; and to enable Britain to live as well as it had been used to live, or better. Rising standards of comfort would be secured by industry which would produce both the goods for the home market in abundance and at stable prices and also surpluses wherewith to pay for necessary or merely desirable imports. These aims, which can be summed up as the growth of industry and the growth of exports, were not achieved. Industry lost ground to its competitors; exports, though by and large they paid for imports, did not also cover capital outflow; prices did not remain stable and in the seventies rose fearfully fast. It was Britain's turn to be the sick man of Europe, or one of the sick men, and alarm at this turn of fortune led even to speculation about the stability of the democratic political system itself.

Economics is a term derived from Greek words which mean home regulation or housekeeping. In public affairs it has a series of widening meanings. Basically it means balancing the books, the traditional business of the Treasury, for long its only avowed business and still the core of its activities. But balancing the books entails more than just bookkeeping; it involves choosing measures that are likely to make the books balance, i.e. policy decisions which may be regulatory like putting taxes up or down or expanding or constricting the money supply, or innovatory like introducing new taxes and so shifting the fiscal burden; and these measures may be either compulsory or persuasive, in the one case obliging people to pay or in the other inducing them, for example, to save or enticing them to invest. All these are delicate matters whose effects can never be forecast precisely. In addition economic policy requires decisions on whether to try to balance the books at a higher or a lower level: to go for more expenditure matched by bigger receipts or to cut both back. Parenthetically it may be remarked that in ordinary parlance the word 'economy' implies cutting back; the verb 'to economise' is not used in its basic sense of balancing accounts at whatever level but denotes a positive attempt to retrench. Professional economists are less inclined to assume that in bad times the right course is to constrict rather than expand but politicians, who are not normally versed in economics even when at the Treasury, have the ordinary person's propensity to favour retrenchment and fear expansion. Finally and most important, during the last half century or so economics as a national concern has ceased to be confined to balancing the government's books or choosing policies to make them balance or deciding at what levels to try to balance them; it has become concerned with the economics of individuals as well as those of government, and also with the entire economic activity of the nation as distinct from the economic activity of government.

Economics is inherently no more difficult than other subjects. Its central problems and theories are not intellectually more demanding than those of chemistry or sociology. Nevertheless economics often seems baffling and this is because it does have a peculiar feature: circularity. Arguments about economics have a maddening propensity to lead back to their starting point without solving anything; or to reach the conclusion that a given course will help to cure a present ill but will also and simultaneously produce or aggravate a different one. This makes the practical business of applying economic measures exceptionally tricky and induces in the general public a state of confusion and an unfair impatience with the politicians charged with getting economic policy right. So economic issues are more unsettling than others in the body politic. Take, for example, the question of money. Is cheap money a good thing or not? The individual with an overdraft has no doubt that interest charged at 3% is better than 8%. The businessman who wants to invest in his business and make it grow will borrow money to do so if he can get it cheap but not if he cannot. In the national accounts there is a hefty debit item for interest on the national debt (which stood at £24 billion at the end of the war) and it is in an obvious sense better if interest on so stupendous a sum can be kept down to 3% or less as Dalton wanted rather than rise to treble that rate. Local authorities have to borrow to do their many jobs and if borrowing is expensive either the rates go up or the jobs are not done. And so on. All spenders of money like to be able to get it cheap and so far as their spending is useful and well judged it is in the general interest that they should be able to get it cheap, since that way the economy grows and people prosper. But on the other hand cheap money usually means much money. The cheapness of money creates a demand for more of it and those who get it are very likely to spend it because that is what they want it for. They may save some of it, and in wartime they can be induced by patriotic appeals to save much of it, but most of it will be spent and the demand and the spending are inflationary. People out and about spending their money push prices up, and when they have done this—without in general realising that that is what they have done—they will not only complain about high prices but ask for higher wages and for subsidies on food and rents. (We will come to wages and prices later. Suffice it to say here that inflation of this kind could be contained if wages were held down by law or in some other way, but this is exceedingly difficult to do, particularly if free collective wage bargaining is regarded as an essential element in a democracy.) Consumer spending also draws more imports into the country and so tilts the balance of payments the wrong way. Moreover bankers have reason to like dear money rather than cheap money because depositors—the people who provide the money—do. A banker, whether a joint stock bank or the Bank of England, wants to attract money into his bank and the way to do this is to pay well for it. So is cheap money a good thing or a bad thing? It is not very satisfying to be told that it is both. This is only one example of the peculiarities of economic policy. The practical consequence is that economic decisions are largely a matter of balancing and timing, of combining opposites in fine adjustment and not of choosing between them as is commonly the case with other political questions which invite a decision yes or no. The answer to an economic problem is more often yes and no, or yes to some extent and at the right moment.

Economics provides a number of statistical indicators by which the signs may be read and the performance of the economy judged—and by which observers may become mesmerised. In terms of the growth of industry and exports the most popular among these indicators are the rate of growth of the gross national product (GNP) or gross domestic product (GDP) and the balance of payments, which are the subjects of this and the next chapter. No less hypnotic is a third indicator, the cost of living index which measures the movement of prices of selected commodities and services and so figures largely in wage rates, which are the subject of a later chapter.

Growth became something of a fetish in the postwar years. This was not unnatural although sometimes it verged on the obsessive, becoming a sort of economic virility test. In the nineteenth century growth had run at an average of about 2% a year and was largely unremarked. Between 1949 and 1967—the years of the two devaluations in our period—it did rather better than that and was improving and received constant, disparaging notice. This was because the growth rate, starting at 1·5% and rising to 2·5%, was lower than planners and prophets had said it would be and lower than other advanced industrial countries (except the USA) were achieving. It was a failure in terms of targets and current comparisons.

The intense preoccupation with growth had two main sources. Growth was a precondition of social justice without tears. If the national wealth did not grow, then it was impossible to provide a better living for the poor without cutting into the standards and expectations of the less poor. Only if the national cake got bigger could the poor have bigger slices and the not so poor go on having as much as before. Carving up a cake of the same size to the advantage of the poor must make the not so poor poorer. Secondly, growth was watched as an index of economic competitiveness in an age when the competition for markets was becoming fiercer because those supplying world markets were becoming more numerous while the markets themselves were no larger or, in some areas, smaller.

It became habitual to publish comparative tables giving an order of merit established by the growth of GNP in different countries. These tables were even front-page news and led to much depression as Britain slithered down from rubbing shoulders with Sweden to keeping company with Italy. The blame for this hurt to wealth and pride could be laid, according to prejudice backed where possible by evidence, on workers for not working hard or on management for not managing competently or on government for throttling instead of helping industry or on unions for exploiting their bargaining power in the context of full employment—or on all these groups. But it is easier to define the sources of growth than apportion blame for their failure to operate. These sources are: more men and women at work: freer movement of workers from less productive to more productive work including, in the case of manufacturing industry, movement out of agriculture into manufacturing (which had already gone very far in Britain before the war and was no longer a significant source); better tools and equipment; capital for investment and expansion; reorganisation, i.e. a more efficient disposition or grouping of resources; and more demand, domestic or foreign. The stimulation of demand requires particularly deft handling since increasing home demand entails a degree of inflation of the money in circulation, while export-led demand is intrinsically not inflationary.

The failure of industry and the concomitant failure even to maintain Britain's share of world trade became the centrepieces of politics and so an invitation to governments to take remedial action. The Attlee government, apart from nationalising half a dozen industries, had limited its intervention in industrial affairs to what seemed necessary to help industry in an immediate and critical postwar phase; and succeeding Conservative administrations were doctrinally non-interventionist. But this recipe had failed and by the sixties both parties had become converted to more active policies, and so had industrialists who wanted to be able to plan ahead and to touch more money. In strict logic neither planning nor finance necessitated intervention by government but in practice both did. As the prewar generation of politicians drifted off the scene a new generation appeared talking in new tones and no politician was more typical of this breed or more rhetorically expansive on industrial policies than Harold Wilson who became leader of the Labour Party on Gaitskell's death in 1963 and prime minister in 1964. Wilson had a vision of a new industrial efficiency to be attained through technical advance and political and economic planning. He was enchanted by new technology. The sixties would supplement the forties. Socialists of the older generation had laid the foundations of the welfare state. Socialists of the next generation, better at economics and more alive to business needs, would make it work. The state would provide direction and money: the modern state must be harnessed to modern invention and modern management techniques: so would industrial output grow.

Wilson's principal instruments were the National Economic Development-ment Organisation (Neddy), established in 1962 by his Conservative predecessors; little Neddies for particular industries: a new Department of Economic Affairs with regional economic planning committees; and an Industrial Reconstruction Corporation. These bodies were to improve central planning and the reorganisation, equipment and financing of industry. Further, Wilson made an approach to the thorny problem of the role and powers of trade unions by appointing a Royal Commission under Lord Donovan, a Lord of Appeal in Ordinary, which reported in 1968.

Economic planning is no more than thinking ahead about economic problems and how to meet them, but it has had an unpopular ring with devotees of laissez-faire liberalism, with old-fashioned sections of the right and with the public who think of planners as invaders of their freedom and privacy; and it has also had its ups and downs in the official world where politicians and civil servants debate whether medium-term planning should be part of the Chancellor's and Treasury's tasks or is something different. Cripps after 1947 was both an economics minister and a chancellor of the exchequer. In 1964 the new government contained an economics minister (Brown) as well as a chancellor (Callaghan) and a prime minister who himself took an active part in economic discussions. But Wilson refused to define the boundary between the new department and the Treasury and to make matters more difficult all these three senior ministers had very recently been opponents for the leadership of the party, Wilson and Brown had no love for one another, and Brown had only moderate respect for Callaghan. This experiment therefore came to grief for a complexity of reasons which make it difficult to pinpoint what went wrong. Brown, after some initial success on the wages front, departed from the Department of Economic Affairs to the Foreign Office towards the end of 1966 (he resigned from the government in 1968 and lost his seat in the House of Commons in 1970 and proceeded to the House of Lords) and after his departure the DEA withered and was ultimately engulfed in the Treasury. A plausible conclusion is that it is unwise to have two separate economics departments of equal status since each is bound to regard the other as a rival and a poacher.

This very mistake had been made in France before the war and avoided after it. In the thirties Léon Blum, like Wilson a generation later, institutionalised in two separate departments the inescapable conflict between the finances of short-term housekeeping and the economics of longer-term planning. De Gaulle's first postwar government made the same mistake and produced a conflict between René Pleven and Pierre Mendès-France which was resolved only by the latter's resignation, but then Jean Monnet's Commissariat du Plan sidestepped the conflict and achieved an alliance with the Ministry of Finance (and with the *patronat*, although less so with the unions). Monnet did this by having a department which was so small—only about thirty planners— that it did not look like a normal department of state and was not regarded as a threat to any other department or to anybody's career. It trod on very few toes. From this position the Commissariat embarked on its successful career, contributing massively to the regeneration of France from the status of sick man of Europe which, like Britain only sooner, it had earned from war injuries plus a century of economic decline and misdirection. The essence of the success of the Commissariat was threefold: first, it produced compelling facts and figures about the French economy and its prospects which everybody felt obliged to absorb; next, it used strong incentives or penalties to persuade industries into desirable courses without recourse to statutory compulsion; and thirdly, it worked its way through the economy sector by sector, choosing to tackle four or five areas at a time and not moving on to others until its studies and reports on these had been completed.

Wilson's DEA had no comparable successes. It produced in 1965 a national plan for 1965–70 based upon an estimated growth rate of 3·8% a year for six years. This was optimistic, although not at the time wildly so. An earlier Neddy plan had used 4% growth as a basis for its calculations, although it was never clear whether this figure was chosen as the likeliest forecast of what would in fact happen or because the plan's aims could not be achieved without it. With similar ambivalence the DEA's plan chose a growth rate of 3·8%, i.e. an increase of 25% over the planned period 1964–70. The national plan was swept away by the fierce deflation imposed by Wilson and Callaghan in 1966 in order to try to maintain the external value of the pound (see the next chapter) and so it is impossible to say whether the plan was well conceived or not. What can be said is that it had no chance if growth was not the government's first priority. It required political fortitude and political will, and these were lavished not enough on growth and too much on the external value of the pound. In the event growth over the period selected for the plan was not 25% but 14% and the plan itself became a melancholy museum piece. Growth was fatally arrested in 1964–66 and proceeded thereafter at an annual average of 2%.

The Industrial Reconstruction Corporation was equally unfortunate to be born in the stormy weather created by Wilson's and Callaghan's obstinate refusal to devalue. Its function was to assist the growth that was not to be. It was to inject money and ideas into the more promising and more crucial industrial areas and, if need be, reorganise them. Some reorganisation was undoubtedly needed (it always is) but it is less certain that mergers, which were too often regarded as the equivalent of reconstruction, were always the right way to go about it. Mergers are beloved of financiers (people who use money to make money) but not necessarily of industrialists (people who use money to make things). There was in the sixties a vogue for mergers. Many were successful in the limited sense that they put a lot of money into some pockets, but this was largely a consequence of the property boom and not of increased industrial efficiency or output. A would take over B because B owned property which A did not need and could sell. The result was a profit for A but no benefit to national growth or exports. A merger moreover could and frequently did create a conglomerate of incompatibles which might be more powerful than its parts but was also less efficient. Putting two motor-car manufacturers together might make sense (although size creates its problems as well as its economies of scale), since the outcome is still a motor-car company and is probably still run by people who understand the making and selling of motor-cars; but amalgamating companies of different kinds helps nobody except the financier who hopes thereby to increase his dividends (and who, when times get bad, does not even have the capital needed by the companies and becomes an extractor of cash instead of a provider, although his argument on buying the companies was that he would be able to provide them with cash which they could neither generate nor borrow for themselves). Mergers therefore looked good but did not so obviously do good. In so far as the IRC promoted mergers and added to their promiscuous popularity it was of dubious benefit, although in so far as it provided money for re-equipping or modernising enterprises capable of using the money profitably it was a salutary and even necessary device at a time when the traditional money markets of the capitalist system were finding it hard to supply all the money needed for these purposes. But in a stagnant economy it had no place.*

The government's foray into the minefields of industrial relations brought it no credit. The Donovan Commission presented in 1968 a searching and suggestive report (Cmd. 3623). Its terms of reference had been wide. Its report focussed on incongruities and particularly on the changed nature of collective bargaining. It pointed out that agreements were in practice negotiated and concluded at factory level rather than industry-wide. (This shift of emphasis from the union to the shop was partly a consequence of the war when the smaller local group had been encouraged as the dynamo of patriotic exertion: the shop steward was a stakhanovite before he became a bogeyman.) The results of bargaining in this way were untidy; they led also to leap-frogging; but the Commission accepted that this was the way things were. It recommended therefore the creation within the Department of Employment of an Industrial Relations Commission which would maintain a register of all collective agreements and would also seek to stimulate agreements where the parties had difficulty in reaching them—a helping hand but no statutory, mandatory authority. In the vexing field of unofficial strikes (95% of all strikes) the Commission found that the main cause was the breakdown of procedural agreements made at factory level. It concluded that making unions legally responsible for the acts of their members would be largely irrelevant and it rejected the view of the Confederation of British Industries that collective agreements should be made legally enforceable: this could not be done without giving unions wide powers over their members and so destroying the voluntary character of the union. The Commission stressed the importance of workers' participation in order to improve industrial harmony and industrial growth but did not prescribe how this should be achieved.

It fell to the Secretary of State for Employment, Barbara Castle, to make proposals for the statutory implementation of parts of the Donovan report. These were published early in 1969 in a White Paper

* Mergers and the vogue for bigness had a subsidiary drawback in the form of planning developed in unwieldy conglomerates and known as corporate planning. This over-valued way of looking at the future, based on statistical presentations, substituted extrapolation for purpose. It proliferated committees and debate to the detriment of constructive thinking and deciding by individuals.

entitled *In Place of Strife* (Cmd. 3888) which was ill received within the Labour Party and by the unions. The national executive of the party voted against it by 16 to 5 and in a debate in the House of Commons 53 Labour members voted against the government. The White Paper followed the Commission in proposing a register of collective agreements (which would not be legally enforceable) and a standing Commission on Industrial Relations. It proposed also that in the case of an unofficial strike the government might interpose a 28-day cooling-off period during which strike action would be illegal and that in the case of official strikes the government might insist on a preliminary secret ballot of the union's members. Fines might be imposed on individuals or unions if government action was in either case ignored, but penalties would not extend to imprisonment. Nevertheless the penalties were so vehemently opposed that the government had to abandon its proposals.

Wilson's technocratic socialism, designed (if that is not too strong a word) to supplement an ailing capitalism, did not deliver goods but it is impossible to judge how far this failure was inherent in his policies or occasioned by other aspects of economic policy, notably the failure to devalue, or how far it suffered the fate common to imperfectly thought out first shots. It was followed by a Conservative interlude (1970–74) in which industrial shortcomings were tackled from a different angle.

Edward Health, the modern Conservative where Wilson was the modern Labour man, also taking office as prime minister for the first time, determined to concentrate on industrial relations rather than industrial equipment and organisation. He brought in and passed the Industrial Relations Act 1971.

This Act was one of the most significant measures of the century. It had a number of admirable qualities which will be described below but it seriously misread the signs of the times and did more to undermine the rule of law than any Act of Parliament of modern times. The rule of law in a democracy rests ultimately on consent. A government must on occasion legislate against the sectional interests of a part of the nation but it may not, without imperilling the political order, make laws which a minority is likely to defy with the sympathetic assent of a significant part of the rest of the community. The Heath government challenged the unions in such a manner that the unions not only accepted the challenge to the point of breaking the law, but did so with a good measure of public support (notwithstanding that these were unpopular days for unions). Moreover, the resistance of the unions was successful and so undermined the authority of the judiciary which had been charged by statute to execute laws which proved unworkable. This was a portentous episode in British history and might have had most serious consequences if it had not been as short as it turned out to be.

The Act attempted to combine a number of different aims. Inspired by a liberal creed it laid down that no person might be compelled to join a union and that in certain circumstances a strike must be preceded by a secret ballot. It introduced salutary protections for workers against unfair dismissal and a cooling-off period in industrial disputes to be used to delay (but not outlaw) a threatened strike. It permitted the union shop, i.e. the right of a union to represent all workers in a given undertaking or plant, but banned the closed shop, i.e. the right of a union to brigade all the workers into membership of that union on pain of losing their jobs. It made agreements between unions and employers legally enforceable unless the agreement expressly provided the contrary. It tried to define unfair industrial practices and made them subject to legal action and damages. It created a National Industrial Relations Court to adjudicate causes arising under the Act, and this court was empowered to inflict heavy fines on peccant unions.

Soon after the passing of this Act its dangers became evident. The government, with a good deal of public support at this stage, was proposing to put unions in their place, to show them that they were not above the law and had no right to obstruct the elected representatives of the people in making and executing laws. The wider implications of this clash will be reserved to a later chapter on British politics which will consider the powers of the unions in the twentieth century and their place in a democratic polity. What matters here is the sequence of events. The first important case to reach the NIRC concerned a dock strike occasioned by the handling of containers by non-dockers. The dockers were threatened by a technical revolution, i.e. the packing of goods in large containers which needed less handling than hundreds of packages and could be carried to the point of loading by lorries. The dockers sought to safeguard their trade by reserving to themselves all handling of containers within a given radius of the port. Faced with the decline of their trade, they wanted to redefine it by area instead of by task. They refused therefore to handle the containers brought by lorries beyond the limits of this area. The lorry-owners complained that the dockers were engaging in an unfair industrial practice. The Transport and General Workers Union, to which the dockers belonged, was fined

£5000. The dockers took no notice of the court's ruling, whereupon the fine was increased to £50,000 on a motion for contempt. Summoned to appear before the court, the union refused and it looked as though eminent leaders would soon be in prison and a very big strike in progress, until the Court of Appeal found a way to quash the decision of the NIRC. However ingenious the arguments in the Court of Appeal, the superior court had evidently been placed in the position of having to find or invent grounds for overruling the court below in order to avoid serious economic and political trouble.

Meanwhile a work-to-rule on the railways, begun when unions stood out for a 16% rise in place of 12·5% offered, was met by a cooling-off order made by the NIRC upon the application of the Secretary of State, but the delay produced no settlement, the work-to-rule was resumed and the government successfully moved the court to order a secret ballot. This step too failed. The ballot produced a 6 to 1 majority in favour of industrial action and a startled and disillusioned government allowed a settlement to be negotiated between the two starting points of 16% and 12·5%. In this case the Act exacerbated relations without doing anything to restrain inflation.

The situation in the docks became acute once more when five dockers were sent to prison for contempt of the NIRC in a dispute over the blacking of a container depot. A general stoppage at the docks followed and once more a way had to be found, this time through the Official Solicitor (a bizarre *deus ex machina* of whom most people had never heard), to reverse the unhappy court's decision and get the men out of prison. Another union to get into trouble with the court was the Amalgamated Union of Engineering Workers which refused, wrongly in the court's judgment, to recognise a particular individual as a member and kept him out of branch meetings. The AUEW was mulcted of £61,000 and its assets were ordered to be sequestrated. A year later it was fined £75,000 for contempt and in May 1974 the court seized assets to the value of £280,000. In the ensuing frenzy some anonymous industrialists paid the fine and soon afterwards the Labour government which had been formed in February repealed the Industrial Relations Act and abolished the NIRC.

The short and unhappy history of this court focussed attention on the inepter side of Heath's legislation which had been partly prompted by hostility to the unions and their growing economic and therefore political power. But there was another side to it. The creation of the NIRC, which stemmed more than a little from the report of the Donovan Com- mission, reflected the view that wage-fixing had become too important to be left to crude bilateral encounters between organised labour and organised capital: there should be a third party involved but preferably not the executive arm of the state. The unions, however, continued to regard bilateral bargaining as a hardly won natural right which they were not prepared to abandon—quite apart from other features of the 1971 Act which they found obnoxious. Consequently the NIRC was a failure, although there was in the background a sound idea. The incoming Labour government put nothing in the place of the court. Instead it sought a loose agreement with the unions over the nature and limits of the bargaining that the unions would then bilaterally conduct with the employers: the social contract to which we will come in a later chapter.

Wilson's riposte to the Industrial Relations Act 1971, beyond re- pealing it, was the Industry Act 1975. This Act, as its name implied, was not directed to industrial relations but to industrial performance. Undaunted, so it seemed, by the failures of his first administration, Wilson was still eager to improve industrial efficiency and output through state intervention including, where necessary, public funds. At the same time some of his colleagues favoured intervention of this kind on theoretical rather than pragmatic grounds. They saw in it a way to acquire for public ownership a share in the profits and direction of industry, i.e. nationalisation to continue the programme that had been halted in 1951. For these divergent but not necessarily incompatible purposes the Industry Act 1975 created the National Enterprise Board which, with an initial £700 million and a promise of more to come (the IRC had started with £150 million), was empowered to acquire for the nation shares in healthy or ailing enterprises without limit (the Conser- vative Act of 1971 had provided money only to help sick companies and then to acquire no more than half the equity).

By this date the nationalisation of industry had become a complex issue. There were still those in the Labour Party but not dominant in it who wanted more nationalisation for the reasons which had produced the Attlee legislation. There were others who wanted to put up public money—which they could hardly do without attaching strings—in order to salvage enterprises in trouble, either because they were nation- ally vital or to save jobs. And there were the Wilsonites who wanted to concentrate on the efficient sectors and make them even more efficient by giving them money. Thus nationalisation in the seventies was much more of a jumble than it had been in the forties and financially riskier. The enterprises in its sights were a motley collection of occupants of commanding heights, lame ducks and front runners.

The Industry Act and National Enterprise Board represented Wilson's way forward. They superseded a resolution of the Labour Party's national executive in 1974 to nationalise 25 leading companies, a plan which offended the Prime Minister's tactical sense and seemed to him altogether too stark. He preferred to acquire particular enterprises by negotiation rather than by statute. Yet the Industry Act set no limit to what the Board might acquire in this way. It could acquire any part or the whole of the equity in an unlimited number of companies. The only significant limitation was the amount of funds available to the NEB at a given moment. But at the same time the party, as distinct from the government, was specifically committed to nationalising shipbuilding and repairing, aircraft manufacture and off-shore oil as well as renationalising road transport. In developing these policies Labour enthusiasts were helped by what the much less enthusiastic Conservatives had done when faced in office with the problem of lame ducks. Besides permitting by the 1971 Act the acquisition of minority holdings the Heath government had nationalised the major part of Rolls-Royce. This famous company, having subscribed in 1968 a foolishly drafted agreement for the supply of RB 211 engines for the American Lockheed Tristar, found itself in 1970, to the astonishment of a downcast public, on the verge of collapse; and the government, abandoning in these unexpected circumstances its policy of letting failures fail, lent it £42 million which however turned out to be too little for salvation, so that a few months later the whole company was taken into public ownership (except the motor-car section which became a separate non-nationalised concern). When therefore in 1974 the almost equally famous Harland and Wolff shipyards, employing 12,000 people in Belfast, were also discovered to be a member of the lame duck brigade, Anthony Benn, the minister involved and leader in cabinet of the left wing of the party, applied the same logic and this company too passed into public ownership. Not long afterwards Ferranti suffered, or enjoyed, a like fate. In the following year British Leyland got £100 million from the NEB because it was in danger of foundering and so leaving England without an indigenous motor-car maker; and Burmah Oil, caught short of cash, was rescued in the same way. Benn reaffirmed the policy of nationalising shipyards and aircraft manufacture and just after the end of our period a Bill was introduced for these purposes and led to conflict between the two Houses of Parliament. The Labour Party had a policy for industrial organisation and ownership but this policy did not command the party's wholehearted support and was not evidently a recipe for industrial growth. Governments, whether Labour or Conservative, reacted to particular emergencies, and each of them frequently did so by measures which the puzzled or cynical observer might have expected from the other.

2 Exports and the pound

The prime aim of industrial production was to maximise exports in order that they might balance imports and the outflow of capital. A trading nation must trade. Its goods must therefore be wanted in foreign markets, competitive in quality and attractively priced in the relevant local currency. This last condition depended not only upon costs of production in Britain but also upon the rate at which the pound was traded for local currency.

The balance of payments received, month by month, as much publicity and agonised attention as any set of economic statistics. The basic element in this balance is the balance of trade, i.e. the difference between the money value of imported goods and the money value of exported goods. This balance, taken by itself, has habitually and probably for centuries been adverse. It can be alleviated or aggravated by other money transactions across the national frontiers. One of these, normally favourable, is the so-called invisible exports which consist of money received in return for services rendered to foreigners: bank charges, insurance premiums, commissions of one kind or another, and anything else which requires foreigners to send money to Britain to pay for services of this nature. Invisibles also include dividends on foreign investments and the money that tourists bring here and leave behind them. Historically these earnings have more often than not more than covered the trade deficit, but in aggregate their contribution to the balance is less than half the contribution of visible exports: the British economy is by a wide margin an industrial and not a service economy. Then again there are movements of capital into or out of the country, as for example when overseas assets are sold and the proceeds of sale repatriated or, in reverse, when domestic capital is invested abroad. Finally, there is the money that the government has to send out of the country for the upkeep of military establishments, embassies and other offices.

All these movements in and out affect the reserves, the total of foreign currencies and gold held by the Bank of England which, if it falls too low, calls in question the external value of the currency which they back.

These reserves are built up from payments surpluses and also by attracting foreign money to London not on commercial transactions but on financial ones, i.e. when foreigners who have money and are in search of somewhere to deposit it on favourable terms choose to deposit it in London. When these sources fail the reserves have to be topped up by borrowing from other foreign central banks or international organisations such as the International Monetary Fund (IMF)—as happened increasingly in the sixties and seventies. Thus the state of the reserves may be affected at least as much by the actions, sometimes sudden, of depositors as by the balance of payments.

These depositors or creditors have been various. They included people who placed money in London and people who refrained from calling for payment of debts incurred by the British government. To a considerable extent these moneys were deposited in London for historical reasons, because in the past it had been the habit of foreign depositors to place their money in London in preference to elsewhere— a legacy of England's function as the centre of world trade and finance and, since the thirties, as the centre of the smaller but still very extensive sterling area. The sterling area, of which London remained for a while the financial capital, consisted of the empire minus Canada but, fatefully, plus Middle Eastern states which were to grow rich on the oil discoveries of the forties and the boom in oil prices in the seventies and so would find it natural to place their surplus cash in London. In the early seventies these oil exporters were earning surpluses of $3–4 billion a year, and much of this money flooded into London. This new money, the outcome of trade deficits, took the place of earlier balances which had been the outcome of war debts—debts incurred by Britain during the war on account of goods and services supplied by India and other countries and not funded until 1968 when Roy Jenkins negotiated the Basle agreement of that year.

These balances formed part of the reserves in the Bank of England and, subject to accepted banking practices and caution, were available to the Bank for use in its daily activities. From time to time, from a mixture of economic, psychological or purely gambling reasons the owners of this money take it away—and the reserves fall. When in this way the monetary backing of the pound falls, its fixed value in terms of other currencies is impugned. In the market—a free market if it exists or the black market if it does not—a fall tends to generate uneasiness and further falls, until people begin to think that the fall has been overdone and all the processes are gone through in reverse, but with less publicity.

The trouble about that part of the reserves which consists of deposits is the unpredictability of their behaviour in so far as the holders are entitled to remove their money at short notice. The money itself is not unwelcome—far from it—but its volatility can be very embarrassing: *qua* money it strengthens the reserves and the pound but *qua* hot money it makes them vulnerable. Even hot money is welcome so long as it stays put, although there comes a moment when it is so hot and volatile that the accounts showing it still there become misleading; for practical purposes it is more prudent to regard it as gone or at least going. The banker's interest is to have the best of two worlds by attracting the money in the first place (if necessary by offering high rates of interest) but receiving it on terms which prescribe repayment on fixed and preferably distant dates. This funding of the balances takes the heat out of them, stabilises the movements of funds and eliminates a prime factor in the destabilisation of the pound. During the negotiations for the American loan at the end of the war the US Treasury pressed the British government to default on its obligations to the holders of sterling balances, and while the war was still on Churchill wanted to cancel the big debt to India by charging the Indians an identical sum for having defended them against Japan. These scurvy measures were not adopted but some attempt should have been made to fund the balances at that time instead of delaying the problem for twenty years. After the devaluation of 1967 Roy Jenkins made them convertible with the aid of a loan of $2 billion from the Bank for International Settlements in Basle and a number of central banks; but by this date the size of the balances in relation to total reserves, coupled with an economic decline which forced any British government to act from weakness, made it impossible to effect this operation without substantial and costly outside help. In the late forties and fifties the sterling balances were a potential worry but not much more. In this respect the fifties were a neglected opportunity.

The same can be said of the balance of payments. In the first postwar years the balance was inescapably very adverse but, allowing for ups and downs, in the fifties the external accounts balanced. The main reasons were the quick collapse of the Korean war boom (which had made imported raw materials very expensive) and the good sense of the Conservatives in abandoning the exaggerated rearmament programme adopted by Labour when that war began. But two sinister trends could be noted: the hard-core deficit in the trading balance was growing substantially and, unless reduced, would require a commensurately strong increase in the credit balance on invisibles; and the pattern of imports was changing. In the past Britain had used the proceeds from exports to buy food and raw materials. Now, the proceeds were going more and more into purchases of manufactured and semi-manufactured goods, the very things which Britain traditionally had made for itself and others. Thus the very basis of the nineteenth-century industrial economy was undermined and the British were buying abroad what they were supposed to be selling. On this new basis the imbalance was permanent, since no new element had appeared on the credit side to enable Britain to buy foreign manufactured goods as well as food and raw materials. The fifties turned a hard row into a dead end.

A permanent deficit in the balance of payments is sooner or later intolerable since there comes a point when it can be covered only by burrowing sums which nobody is willing to lend, or which can be borrowed only at crippling rates of interest which themselves aggravate the imbalance. The problem of the sixties therefore was to find a way out of this impasse. The aim was to induce foreigners to buy more British goods and—since Britain had many competitors offering excellent wares—the only way to do this was to make British goods cheaper in foreign money. This could be done by reducing the cost of making them or by reducing the value of the pound: deflation or devaluation. Reducing costs meant keeping wages down either by removing the principal source of wage claims (rising prices) or by attacking wages head on by an incomes policy, voluntary or statutory. (An incomes policy is a euphemism for limiting wage rises by one method or another.) All these nettles were stingers and none was firmly grasped until both incomes policy and devaluation were forced on governments by the crisis of the mid-sixties.

We shall come to wages and incomes in the next chapter. Devaluation, instead of being regarded as a possible remedy, was treated as an enemy or even a sin. The even tenor of the fifties had been broken by a record deficit on the balance of payments in 1960, but this pointer towards devaluation was ignored by the Conservative government (which also turned its back for a while on deflation). The Conservative response to the deficit of 1960 was the stock one of raising the bank rate, so causing hot money which had evaporated to flow back and the reserves to look cheerier. The hot money soon dashed off again in pursuit of the West

German mark which was clearly undervalued, but whatever was happening in this (overdramatised) sector of the reserves, the balance of payments recovered until in 1963 a new chancellor, Reginald Maudling, decided to make a dash for economic growth by inflating. For the first time since the war unemployment was ringing alarm bells and the case for reflation*, always appealing to a new chancellor, seemed strong. In retrospect and probably rightly Maudling has been criticised not for choosing the wrong goal but for taking the wrong road. He used his budget in 1963 to give money and incentives to domestic consumers when, with a strong balance of payments, he could have reflated by stimulating export demand by devaluation instead of stimulating domestic demand by inflationary budgetary concessions. His dash for growth proved disastrous since it stimulated imports but not exports and so turned a favourable balance of payments into the staggering deficit of 1964 (£695 million: £382 million on current account and £313 million on capital account). This made inevitable the devaluation which he had either set aside or not thought of in 1963 and it fell to Labour to compound the disaster by resisting devaluation for another three years and then accepting it in far worse straits than obtained in 1964.

From 1964 to 1967 Labour behaved in its turn as though the apparent overvaluation of the pound was temporary when in fact it had become fundamental. Wilson believed that to devalue on taking office would fatally tarnish Labour's image. His senior colleagues, Brown and Callaghan, and also his professional (but not his academic) advisers were of the same mind, although Brown soon changed his. Many ministers could not help looking over their shoulders to 1949 when Labour had devalued and earned what was popularly regarded as a stigma. Labour's narrow majority until after the election of 1966 was another impediment, while Wilson himself seems also to have given even more weight than the Conservatives to American objections to a devaluation. (The dollar too was weak as a result of a long run of excessive spending overseas, culminating in the frenzy of the Vietnam war. The American administration feared that a devalued pound might further weaken the dollar.) So Wilson embarked on a fight to preserve the pound at its current dollar value and by the time he finally lost the fight in November 1967 a vast external debt had been uselessly incurred and harsh deflationary measures imposed. The new government began by imposing a

---

* Reflation is another word for inflation but sounds less alarming.

surcharge of 15% on imports—the nearest any government got in this period to tackling the imbalance by controlling the debit or import side of the account—but this surcharge caused a serious commotion since it infringed the rules both of the GATT and EFTA* and the rate had to be cut to 10% in April 1965: it was removed altogether in November 1966. The surcharge was followed by a November budget which was curiously vague and neutral: income and fuel taxes were raised but so too were pensions and other benefits and prescription charges were abolished, while the Chancellor's speech foreshadowed without specifying a Corporation Tax and a Capital Gains Tax. Neither this budget nor an increase in the bank rate by two points restored foreign confidence and the run on the reserves was resumed. But such was still the importance of sterling that the Bank for International Settlements and a number of central banks could be persuaded to lend huge sums to keep the Bank of England from running out of foreign cash, supplemented by standby credits from the IMF.

But the balance of payments remained sick and the run on the pound revived in the summer. By 1966 devaluation was regarded as certain by all except the Prime Minister and some of his colleagues, but Wilson tried once more to fend it off and after increasing his parliamentary majority from 1 to 97 in an election in March (the electorate approved what he was trying to do) he and Callaghan introduced a fierce deflationary package designed to reduce domestic demand by £500 million. It contributed to strikes—notably to a seamen's strike in May 1966 which the Prime Minister blamed on communists and a dock strike in 1967—which in turn aggravated the deficit on external account until even Wilson had to accept defeat. The final stages could not all be laid at his door, since war in the Middle East in 1967 further damaged the balance of payments. But he had fought the wrong fight. The pound was devalued from $2·80 to $2·40. This was done with prior international consultation and consent and was buttressed by a standby credit of $1·4 billion from the IMF and loans of $1·6 billion from central banks.

After devaluation big surpluses were earned on external account and at the end of 1971 £4 billion borrowed in 1964–69 was comfortably paid back, but the inflation of the ensuing years caused a relapse into

* The European Free Trade Association formed in opposition to the EEC. See Part Four, Chapter 2.

deficit and in 1972 the $2·40 value was abandoned and the pound was allowed to float for the first time since the thirties. Belatedly and in stages an overvalued sacred cow was sacrificed. After 1972 the pound declined, sometimes with dignity and sometimes without, to within sight of the unnaturally low value of $1·50. This decline was very demoralising to those who thought it unnatural that a pound might become no more valuable than a dollar.

Sterling had probably been somewhat overvalued for half a century. Its decline began in 1914. Until that date everything was measured in pounds, but the first world war began the shift to measuring everything, including pounds, in dollars. It also initiated the tradition of excessive sacrifices to keep the pound at its current dollar value which before the war was $4·87. The governments of 1914–19 used tariffs to restrain imports and keep the pound up. Nevertheless the pound went down to $3·66 when the war ended and the postwar government set out to put it back at whatever cost. Hence the return to the gold standard in 1925 at the anachronistic and ruinous rate of $4·87. With the pound still looking the dollar in the face in this way sterling remained a major international currency with all the ensuing benefits (considerable but very unevenly distributed) but also with inevitable costs in unemployment and the under-use of industrial resources as the exchange rate stifled foreign trade. After the debacle of 1931 the pound was given no new dollar value but was allowed to float and found its level around $3·28, ceasing to be the world currency it once was but becoming a part-world currency, the currency of the sterling area (which, during a second world war, a number of Americans were at pains to demolish). In 1949 the pound stood at $4·03 and was pegged at this rate until it was devalued in 1949—probably too much—to $2·80 where it remained—certainly too long—until 1967.

The overall reason for this decline in the value of the pound, beginning in 1914 and accelerating after 1945, was that foreigners preferred other currencies to sterling and so became sellers of sterling with the same effect on sterling as would be the effect on Queen Anne chairs if all the owners of Queen Anne chairs decided that they would rather sit in Louis XIV chairs. The reason why holders of sterling became dubious of it was the British industrial performance plus the belief—for there is a streak of mad psychology in economics—that other holders of sterling were about to sell, thus creating the need to sell as a self-fulfilling prophecy and the hectic air which sometimes overtakes money markets. Suddenly all the Queen Anne chairs were for sale at prices which made them a good buy. But behind the vagaries of dealers and their clients there is the hard core of fact, and the fact was that Britain had ceased to dominate the industrial world. Adjustment to this change was made needlessly tumultuous because governments of both colours added enormously to the country's debit balance by spending abroad not only the surpluses earned on trade and invisibles but very much more. For all the appreciation of loss of empire that undoubtedly existed governments adopted a pattern of overseas spending justifiable only upon the assumption that Britain's position in the world had not much changed.

Apart from the immediate postwar years Britain's balance of payments, excluding capital transactions, was unfavourable in three years only (1951, 1954, 1960) before the disaster of 1964. It was then adverse in 1965, 1967 and 1968, was healthy in 1969–72 inclusive and then went back into the red in 1973. The balance on invisibles alone was favourable in every postwar year after 1947. Visibles were in credit only rarely— 1956, 1958, 1970–71. The debilitating element was on capital more than current account. Deficits on capital account more than eliminated the favourable surpluses on trade and invisibles and became a crippling drain on the reserves in the latter part of our period. Much the greater part of this unrequited outflow was on government account and was part of the bill for maintaining Britain as a world power and a nuclear power—the costs of overseas bases and forces and of the terrifyingly expensive aircraft and missiles which this stance necessitated and which had to be bought from the USA. Britain was paying to maintain a role which was not merely out of date but was also made insupportable by the cost of trying to support it. (The argument that such an effort is necessary for salvation is senseless if the very effort is destructive. Defence questions and costs are further considered in Part Four of this book.) The net total of overseas government expenditure averaged nearly £700 million a year in the sixties, climbing every year until it was not far short of £1 billion a year at the end of the decade. Yet—to relate this outflow to the country's total external economic activity—even this massive expenditure by government overseas was less than 5% of the total value of all overseas current and capital transactions. In all financial calculations it is the margin one way or the other that tells. The final balance on external account was adverse, but the debit figure was, in relation to the total activity, small enough to be tractable. In the first twenty postwar years it averaged 1·25% of GDP, in the next ten years less than 2·0%.

In conclusion: in the context of this chapter, what mattered was the size of the reserves; these consisted of deposits from foreign sources and accumulated surpluses on foreign transactions; the deposits were always welcome, although their volatility became an embarrassment and the high cost of attracting them became burdensome; the surpluses were a compound consisting of balances (if any) on trade, on invisibles and on capital flows; the deficits which transformed an historically satisfactory situation were the deficits on capital account which consisted overwhelmingly of government spending on military establishments and weapons and debt charges; the deficits, however large in absolute figures, were not more than a manageable percentage of the whole account.

3 Inflation and wages

Inflation is one of those weasel words which sum up and oversimplify a compound of causes and effects and present it as though it were a single process with a cause capable of being isolated and reversed. Inflation means increase. Beyond that it is ambiguous. It is used to mean increase in wages, in prices or in the money supply, or the increase of all these things. It is frequently used to convey that the increase of one of them causes the increase of the others. It is easy to see that higher wages are likely to be inflationary since they increase the cost of the goods made by those who are being paid more to make them and because paying higher wages entails putting more money into circulation without any assurance that the higher wages will be matched by higher output: more money but no more goods shifts the equation between money and goods—the value of the one in terms of the other—to the disadvantage of money and this process, by making money less scarce, finds expression in higher prices. But in so far as wage demands originate in higher prices, which they partly do, it does not make sense to say that higher wages cause higher prices when it is evident that the higher wages are themselves caused by higher prices. There is a clear interaction between wages and prices but, it is necessary to add, the statement that either causes the other is too simple to be valid. This is a further example of the maddening circularity of economic argument already noted.

Prices certainly rise (in the absence of statutory controls) if wages rise and production does not, but they also rise for other reasons such as wage increases in foreign countries, the economic and political bargaining powers of foreign governments or corporations or even their irrationality, changes in rates of exchange for the pound, and the pressures of demand which derive not merely from economic causes such as the supply of money asking to be spent but also from psychological causes such as the postwar determination to have done with sacrifice, austerity and controls. Similarly wages rise for reasons which are not economic. The increased bargaining power of organised workers, coupled with a sense of inequity or with mere cupidity, is a political factor and one too well known to be laboured. Another is democracy itself.

Democracy implies political equality and it nurtures aspirations for other kinds of equality or, more properly, for the diminution of in-equalities. One consequence of one man, one vote is to give underdogs first a sense of rights and then the power to grasp them. In economic terms this means a levelling of living standards and, human nature being what it is, levelling means levelling up rather than levelling down. (There is something ugly about pulling people down except in the con-text of helping other people up.) Democracy coupled with industrialisa-tion entails better wages for the bottom half and the question is where they are to come from and how they are to be met without causing in-flation or aggravating it. The top half says, in effect, let the bottom half work harder and they will get more; but this does not work in practice, partly because output does not depend on labour alone, partly because the top half appropriates a share of the excess in the form of higher profits, and partly because the discontent of the bottom half is not to be satisfied by higher pay so long as inequality too blatantly persists. Theo-retically higher wages for some could be paid by a realignment of wage levels, i.e. by lower wages for others. (Such realignment is not the same as redistribution of wealth which operates on capital assets and only in-directly on personal incomes and not at all on earned incomes.) But satisfying the lower paid by reducing or holding back superior wages is virtually impossible outside an authoritarian state. It leads to an outcry about differentials—an extremely hazy subject since there is no rational way of deciding how one kind of job should be rated in terms of another —and can in practice only be applied in favour of those whose pay is all but universally regarded as scandalously low. Consequently democracy is inherently inflationary and the problem is how to confine the rate of inflation and how to get greater output from a man in return for his increased pay. This is not easy since there is no reason to expect a man to produce more simply because he is paid more (especially if he thinks the increase is due to him anyway, and least of all if he is lazy since money is no antidote to indolence). The usual answers to this conun-drum are two: investment in better equipment, i.e. shifting the problem from labour costs to capital improvements, and the psychological push to be provided by a worker's sense of participation in and so responsi-bility for the corporate activity. Hence the connection between industrial output and industrial democracy to which we will revert although nothing of any consequence was done about it in Britain in the period covered by this book.

If democracy produces higher wages and higher wages are conducive to inflation, then the exceptionally difficult problem arises of finding a democratic way to restrain or phase the inevitable rise in wages. Democratic means acceptable to a majority, and *prima facie* the majority is not disposed to accept such restraint either at the hands of the state or on the urging of the class of capitalist employers. Any attempt to limit wages looks like class jealousy, an inescapable outcome of the history of conflict between classes which has been central to the development of industry by private capital. The regulation of wages by whatever means is the most intractable political problem of modern industrial society, its nemesis.

The case for restraint and, if necessary, state intervention in potentially inflationary circumstances has been strengthened by the fact that wages have become a preponderant element in the economy, constituting in aggregate the biggest single item in the total of personal incomes; wages therefore have become an increasingly large factor in the costs of production of goods and services and affect prices more than salaries or rents. The level of wages has traditionally been a matter to be settled between those who get them and those who pay them, without government interference. Until recently the advantage in this contest lay with the employers (the coal strike of 1926 was a memorable illustration of employers' power), but this advantage shifted, first slowly and then more markedly, to the other side as a result of a number of things: the organisation of workers in unions with economic leverage and political articulateness; public sympathy with the poor partly on account of their poverty and partly because of a new inclination to regard dangerous or dirty work as socially meritorious instead of unspeakable or simply a sad necessity; and, as a consequence of both these developments, the increased political punch of organised labour, delivered if need be by strikes so long as these were not made illegal. But at this point of greater equivalence between the powers of employers and employed two considerable obstacles were conjured up in the way of the advance of the workers to standards of living nearer those of the middle classes. The first was the recourse once more to statute law by the middle-class parliament, the limitation by the Trades Disputes Act 1927 of the right to strike—a move which was nullified by the repeal of the Act in 1946 but which left a sour taste in the mouths of union leaders and others who had grown up in the twenties and thirties. The second was the argument that the state must, in the stringent economic situation of the postwar years, intervene in the wage-fixing process, at least by exhortation and possibly by statute. This argument was well grounded in left-wing doctrine regarding the role of the state in the nation's affairs, but this particular application of the doctrine was offensive to the unions (whose leadership in the first postwar generation was anything but left-wing) on two major grounds: it seemed to be changing the rules about wage-fixing at the very moment when the balance of bargaining power was shifting from the employers to the workers, and it raised the abominable spectre of unions becoming an executive arm of government as in communist countries instead of retaining their traditional stance of independence. Even in wartime free collective bargaining had not been abrogated, and after the war a Labour government found it almost as difficult as a Conservative one to persuade union leaders, let alone their followers, to accept an official wages policy inhibiting in any way the exercise of collective bargaining muscle.

Governments were saying that wage levels were of prime national concern and could not be left to private negotiation (the more so, it could be added, since many employers were ready enough to pay higher wages, avoid disputes, keep machinery turning and charge the extra costs to the consumer at home or abroad). Union leaders were suspicious of the argument but willing on the whole to see some force in it. They saw too that the government's commitment to full employment had further strengthened their bargaining position and had sealed the transfer to them of the determining voice in the fixing of money wages, but that at the same time their influence on the level of real wages had been reduced since, in times of inflation, the value of the money wage depended not merely on the bargain struck with the employer but also upon the economic policies pursued by government: these policies could affect for better or worse the purchasing power of the wage. Union leaders were therefore impelled, often unwillingly, towards demanding a voice in the elaboration of economic policy and so found themselves intervening in an area traditionally reserved to government while objecting to government intervention in an area traditionally reserved to unions. Nevertheless such intervention was, both ways, logical. The government's case for some regulation of wage levels in some way was incontestable, and in return the unions were entitled to point out that if economic policy had to include an incomes policy (a polite term for holding wages back), then those who were required to accept the incomes policy should have a say in the broader economic policies which were necessitating or dependent upon it.

Although rising wages were not a serious problem until the late sixties, the first attempt at a wages policy came very soon after the end of the war. In the first postwar years prices were kept remarkably stable and wage claims followed suit, but Dalton's cheap money policy faced two ways: while it kept the cost of some things down, it also encouraged demand and consumption and so pushed up the prices of others. In 1948 a White Paper on Incomes, Costs and Prices expressed views which were to reappear over and over again in the next thirty years. It said that personal incomes must rise no faster than productivity; that government did not wish to interfere in the fixing of the wages of the individual; that there would be no overall freeze but some flexible management of the economy to help move labour to those places where, in the national interest, it was more needed. The White Paper showed a marked inclination to keep off dangerous ground and avoid disturbing sacrosanct procedures. Nevertheless the TUC, also sounding notes that were frequently to reappear, was irritated, asking why it had not been consulted in advance and why there was nothing in the White Paper about controlling profits. But union leaders were well aware of the nation's plight and most of them were ready to support the government; they realised that there were still a number of grounds—increased productivity, anomalies and hardship—on which wage claims might be advanced without infringing the tentative generalities of the White Paper. Although a substantial minority at the TUC's autumn conference that year voted against wage restraint, the unions on the whole endorsed and observed it. But the hefty devaluation of 1949 increased the prices of imported goods and the outbreak of war in Korea in the next year created a worldwide boom in commodity prices which, besides shifting the balance of payments into the red, further raised the cost of living. Two years after the White Paper restraint had been washed away, the 1950 conference of the TUC voted against it, and as the government's life ebbed to its close unions and employers alike were ignoring it.

The 13-year Conservative rule which followed witnessed ultimately a considerable shift in Conservative policy. In 1951 the Conservatives were opposed to anything in the nature of a wages policy partly because it smacked of controls and they were out to abolish controls and constraints (except conscription) and partly because they were a bit afraid of the unions and very much at arm's length from them. Having abolished price controls they could not introduce wage controls and in any case they had a doctrinaire preference for monetary controls and fiscal manipulation. They abandoned cheap money but did not get rid of its chief drawback, for they kept public spending and borrowing high. They were helped by the quick termination of the Korean war boom and they reduced food subsidies. This led them into conflict with the TUC which was in expansionist mood and wanted higher subsidies and lower taxes (except on distributed profits) but could give no assurance that expansionist measures of this kind could be prevented, by increased productivity or saving, from unleashing uncontrollable inflation. The government, which seemed unsure whether it was expansionist or not, turned a politely deaf ear while on the industrial front a number of large wage increases were won by unions (normally through the medium of courts of inquiry which served as figleaves for inflationary increases) and tolerated by government which was anxious to avoid serious stoppages, had no guidelines for determining whether a particular claim was nationally injurious or not, and was captivated by its own rhetoric about unprecedented prosperity. In 1957 government made a first tentative move towards bringing order into the free-for-all of wage bargaining by creating a Council on Prices, Productivity and Incomes, an embryo doomed to inanition because the unions spurned it, half the Conservatives did not believe in it and, like Labour's initiative in 1948 but even more promptly, it was swamped by other forces. These were both of the government's own making and external.

In the mid-fifties the Conservatives were misled by their monetary doctrine and their urge to decontrol. The economy was booming and in 1955 Eden's chancellor of the exchequer, R. A. Butler, cut taxes by £135 million in the mistaken belief that this inflationary gesture could be contained by monetary controls. Later in the same year, and after an intervening general election, he had to introduce a second budget to undo much of what he had done in the first, but by this time weighty wage claims had been put on the table and by the end of the year Butler was put out of the Treasury. His errors were those of mismanagement, essentially mistiming. He not merely set the signals at go at the wrong moment but positively promoted top speed and then had to switch to stop. His successor, Peter Thorneycroft, was given the task of finding the right moment for the right measure of go (he and the Prime Minister, Harold Macmillan, were both moderate expansionists and interventionists): the Council on Prices, Productivity and Incomes was part of the regulatory mechanism designed to achieve this but its creation coincided with a summer crisis of foreign confidence in the pound as hot money was withdrawn from London in disturbing quantities, the government took fright and reached for all the traditional levers (bank rate, cuts in government spending, restrictions on credit and cuts in investment) to halt the exodus and save the external value of the pound. These deflationary measures, adopted by a puzzled and half convinced cabinet, did the trick although it was not by any means certain that they were necessary since the balance of payments was at this time healthy. More certainly they had a second consequence which was to intensify incipient signs of recession and unemployment. When in the next year Thorneycroft and other Treasury ministers insisted on continued restraint in government spending, the more expansive Macmillan abandoned them and they resigned.* The next chancellor, Derek Heathcote-Amory, reduced taxes but not until 1959, which was too late to avert or alleviate the recession of 1958 and gave a spur to the economy at what was once more the wrong moment.

These vagaries of the fifties, coupled with assertions that the material condition of Britain had never been so good, were disconcerting and paved the way for the more serious dilemmas of the sixties. They also prompted further excursions into planning and at least indirect controls, to which many employers and Conservative politicians became converted by the stop-go of the fifties and also by the new vogue for planning *à la francaise* already referred to. (The notion that France could become more efficient and prosperous than Britain was a stunning one which caused a lot of head-scratching in London.) So the Conservatives created the National Economic Development Council (Neddy), a forum for longer-term planning than the conventional one year dictated by annual budgets: ministers, union chiefs and employers were to meet regularly to discuss each other's views and attitudes. Unhappily these years were overshadowed by the deterioration in the balance of payments described in the last chapter and by the measures taken to redress it, so that wages and prices policies were barely tackled except within the narrow confines of budgetary deflation or expansion. Two more Conservative chancellors presided at the Exchequer, Selwyn

---

* Thorneycroft returned to the government in 1963 as minister of aviation and, as champion of Concorde, became a mammoth spender.

Lloyd and Reginald Maudling, and were succeeded before the decade was out by two Labour chancellors, James Callaghan and Roy Jenkins as well as, contemporaneously, by an economics minister in George Brown and a prime minister, Wilson, who made economic policy his own affair to a greater extent than any of his predecessors since Gladstone. The net result of the efforts of these public-spirited, intelligent (though for the most part economically untutored) men was the onset in the early seventies of a second bout of inflation far worse than the short inflation provoked by the Korean war.

It is not easy to give a succinct picture of the sixties. They were years of disturbing but manageable inflation producing by the end of the decade inflation of a different order which threatened to become unmanageable—but, within our period, did not. The centrepiece in this context was a forced and nervous approach to a wages policy. Wage increases were fuelling inflation, by 1970 very strongly. Although union pressures did not start the cycle (a cycle, being circular, has no starting point and it is futile to look for one), in a glowering economic climate unions and their members pressed for better wages and were often abetted by employers who either bid wages up in competition with one another or handed out ancillary benefits, financial or other, which were no less inflationary. Moreover wage-push inflation was promoted as much by economic exuberance as by economic gloom. Large profits were being made and brandished in some sectors and workers were determined that a share of these should come their way: in the absence of co-partnership higher wages were the only way to secure such a share. These were the years of the property boom and other speculators' paradises. The sight of easy profits, or the anticipation of them, can be as inflationary as anything.

The ebb of the reserves in 1960–61 had started another chain of misapprehensions. A battery of deflationary remedial measures was brought into play, including this time a pay-pause to last from September 1961 to April 1962. It was all the more unpopular for being combined with reliefs for surtax-payers who commanded nobody's sympathy but their own, and when it appeared that Selwyn Lloyd had erred in assuming that consumption and employment were rising and had by his deflationary budget contributed to the opposite trend he was abruptly dismissed and a successor was found to go into reverse (July 1962). The winter of 1962–63 was a harsh one and the next chancellor, Maudling, decided on a therapeutic reflation in 1963; but he not only left it too late but chose the wrong method and landed the country with an un-precedented deficit in the balance of payments. A year later the Labour Party took office under a new prime minister whose superior acquaintance with academic and practical economics entitled him to ideas of his own and who gave first priority to the defence (as it was called) of the pound at $2·80.

This policy required, as we have seen, severe domestic deflation. The home front had to suffer in a battle on the external front which should never have been fought. The inconclusive budget of November 1964 was followed by a squeeze in 1965 and a very fierce squeeze indeed after the general election of March 1966. This squeeze included a six-month freeze on wages, salaries and dividends, followed by a further six months of 'severe restraint'. A wages policy had arrived as a consequence of trying to maintain against all the world a fictitious value for the pound.

A wages policy means not leaving wages to be fixed by bargaining between those who pay them and those who get them, or their representatives. We have seen how Cripps in 1948 initiated a short-lived semi-pact between government and unions which kept claims down for a couple of years. This arrangement worked as long as it did because it was imprecise and non-binding and because prices were still fairly stable. During the fifties such ventures had been taboo both to governments and unions, but in the sixties Conservatives began to have second thoughts and after the change of government in 1964 George Brown, in the new office of secretary of state for economic affairs and the panoply of second-in-command of the government, secured in remarkably short time (December 1964) a statement of intent subscribed by employers and union leaders. This document, which was less remarkable for what it contained than for the fact that it came into existence at all, was a tripartite acknowledgement of the need for joint planning and regulation. It was one of those documents which are easy to deride for its content but should rather be applauded in its context. It made a point and won a short breathing space. It was followed gingerly by two White Papers (Cmd. 2577 and 2639) and the Prices and Incomes Act 1966 which were successive stages in the imposition of government control over wage increases. The first White Paper designed a new piece of machinery, a National Prices and Incomes Board, to act as a referee and the second prescribed a norm for wage increases of 3–3·5% (except in return for greater productivity). The Board had minuscule authority but its existence had some effect by slowing down rises which were referred to it and by accustoming people to the idea that some wage and price increases were destructive and that it was possible to adjudicate roughly what was permissible and what not.

Later in the year the government took a further step, announcing its intention to introduce legislation requiring advance notification of wage and price increases and authorising government to interpose a four months' stay. The policy was still consultative and, with the sole exception of the four months' stay, voluntary, but during the debates on the Prices and Incomes Bill 1966 the government inserted new provisions enabling it to disallow or reverse increases. It also proclaimed the six months' freeze to be followed by six months of severe restraint. The Prices and Incomes Act, passed in August, gave the government the power, which it exercised in October, to give this freeze full statutory backing. This was too much for some union leaders and Frank Cousins, who had been brought into the government on its formation (he was general secretary of the Transport and General Workers Union but not an effective MP or successful minister), resigned. The leading figures in the TUC were in these years more left-wing than the markedly conservative leadership of the early postwar years, but the Wilson government established in partnership with them a tentative control over wage increases which gradually became a familiar, if not an accepted, part of the political scene.

The devaluation of 1967 gave government and country some respite but it was short and the government was weakened by its handling of the Donovan Report and the revolt of the parliamentary party against the proposals contained in *In Place of Strife*. Impatience with wage restraint was fuelled by rising prices and there were some peculiarly exasperating strikes in 1969: a strike at Fords, beginning unofficially but rendered official, kept 42,000 men out of work for more than three weeks; a strike at Port Talbot steel works which lasted from the end of June into August, again begun unofficially but adopted by the union, was brought to an end only by recourse to a court of inquiry which, after severe criticism of both sides, approved the claim for £1 a week made for lower-paid workers and so showed that the refusal of this comparatively small sum had caused disproportionate commotion and loss in an unsuccessful attempt to stand by a principle or guideline. Throughout this year wages policy came under sporadic attack and at its annual conference the TUC voted massively against any prolongation of the Prices and Incomes Act 1966. But with attention still riveted on the improving balance of payments and the calendar year ending with a surplus on current account of £460 million there was a feeling that the worst of the country's economic troubles might be over. The financial year 1969–70 ended with a record budgetary surplus of £2·4 billion and when the Prime Minister decided to go to the country in June he was expected to win. But he did not. Labour lost 59 seats and the Conservatives came back with an overall majority of 30 and a new prime minister, Edward Heath, who had defeated Maudling for the succession to Douglas-Home in 1965. (This was the first election in which the qualifying age was 18 in place of 21. The total vote was higher than in 1966 although the proportion of eligible voters who voted fell.)

Heath's initial policy on wages was to keep the government out of the fray and put employers in the firing line, backed where necessary by courts of inquiry which would reject excessive claims. Trouble began in July with a strike by dockers refusing to accept a 7% pay rise. After the declaration of a state of emergency this claim was referred to a court of inquiry which mediated a settlement favourable to the strikers—rises averaging £2·50 a week and costing £20 million a year, and a basic working week of 40 hours. Later in the year dustmen who went on strike also got much of what they were asking for, again through a court of inquiry which was then attacked by the Prime Minister for its findings; and still in the same year electric power workers initiated a work to rule leading to another state of emergency and another inquiry which, in February of the next year, produced a report which was as confusing as it was unsatisfactory to the government but was adopted by unions and employers because each could interpret it in their own way. By this time the merry-go-round of strikes, inquiries and settlements was becoming something of a farce as well as failing to check wage rises and making government look weak and peripheral. Employers did not relish their exposed role and the tribunals could not be got to say that the claims should be rejected. Through its policy of non-intervention, or indirect intervention, the government was losing control and finding itself restricted to *post hoc* expressions of anger.

In 1971 a post office strike lasting six weeks ended with an award of 9% to workers who had been offered 8% but had stood out for 15–20%. The government was encouraged by this verdict but dismayed when the Ford Motor Company gave rises of 33% spread over two years in order to put an end to a two months' strike. It was not long before other major motor manufacturers, British Leyland and Vauxhall, had to give similar increases. A go-slow on the railways, however, ended after ten days with an award of 9·5% to men who were asking for 15–25% and had been offered 9%, an indication that a nationalised industry might be tougher than the big companies in the private sector. A more serious confrontation took place early in 1972 when an offer by the National Coal Board of £2 a week plus other benefits was rejected and the miners were out for most of January and the whole of February. A picket was killed and there were other cases of violence. Civil strife seemed to be in the offing. The strikers refused to allow coal from stocks to be delivered to power stations, a state of emergency was declared and the government contemplated ordering industry on to half time in order to save fuel. For the government this was an ill judged trial of strength. The evidence of polls showed that the public was on the miners' side by something like 3 to 1. The usual inquiry was instituted to get the miners back to the pits, the rest of the country back to a normal working week and the government off the hook. The inquiry recommended rises of £6 a week and in subsequent negotiations the miners got in fact slightly more. They felt that their rejection of the Board's offer had been endorsed by popular support and the findings of the court of inquiry and they thereby finally torpedoed Heath's policy of putting employers in the front line. The miners' victory encouraged other wage-seekers and demonstrated that if wage increases were to be held back the regulation would have to be done by government and not by employers.

Reversing his stance of aloofness Heath took the initiative and proposed to the TUC and CBI a voluntary policy based on the assumption that the economy would grow by 5% over the next two years: retail prices to rise by no more than 5% and pay increases to be limited to £2 a week for everyone unless retail prices did rise beyond that limit. Prolonged discussions of this plan broke down in November when the government finally took the plunge and imposed a statutory 90-day freeze on pay, prices, rents and dividends. The 90 days were later extended by a further 60. This was Phase One of the policy and it was followed by Phases Two and Three in April and November 1973. Phase Two limited pay rises to £1 a week plus 4% with a ceiling of £250 a year and prescribed that price increases had to be justified by increases in costs. Phase Three authorised pay rises of £2·25 a week or 7% and, in addition, so-called threshold increments at the rate of 40p a week for every 1% increase in the cost of living index above 7% (from a fixed initial date). Within these straitjackets unions and employers had to manoeuvre as best they could, unions using to the full the argument that the permissible limits were also the appropriate rises; employers too tended, for the sake of convenience and a quiet life, to give without much question the whole of what they were permitted to give. Protests from the workers' side were at first muted: a general stoppage on May Day was not strongly supported. But by the autumn prices, including food prices, were rising sharply and another war in the Middle East threatened to put inflation into top gear. Employers were seeking freedom not only to increase dividends but also to pay higher wages. Heath was pressed by his own party to make big cuts in government spending which, since defence was a sacred cow, evidently meant cutting social services or benefits. He resisted, arguing that the measures so far adopted sufficed and blaming the Arabs for the bad turn of events, but a few weeks before the end of the year an emergency budget cut government spending by £1·2 million, made hire purchase more expensive and introduced other deflationary measures.

Like Callaghan's 1964 budget this package satisfied nobody. The cuts were either resented or derided as inadequate. Already in November a state of emergency had been declared after threats of electricity and gas strikes and in the same month the miners challenged the government and Phase Three by rejecting a pay offer which went to the statutory limit. Heath said there could be no giving in. The miners banned overtime. Petrol coupons were issued. The union refused to conduct a ballot of its members on the rejected pay offer. Railmen added to the tension by rejecting a 12% offer and banning overtime. Sunday trains ceased to run. As a result of the oil crisis a 50-m.p.h. speed-limit was introduced on the roads (it incidentally saved a number of lives) and heating levels were prescribed. From the last day of the year industry was obliged to go on to a three-day week except in so far as it was able and willing to work without consuming power. Heath decided to seek popular support on a government versus miners issue. He did not get it. In an election at the end of February 1974 the Conservatives lost 26 seats. Heath tried to retain office by offering to form a coalition with the tiny Liberal Party but the Liberals refused, influenced partly by their distinctly anti-Conservative wing and also by the impropriety of denying office to the party which had just won the largest number of seats in the House of Commons. Labour, with 301 seats in a House of 635, took office, relying on the benevolence of the Liberals and the Scottish and Welsh nationalists. Michael Foot was given the Department of Employment and the task of getting the miners back to work, which he swiftly accomplished with the help of the Prices and Incomes Board whose ruling on what the miners ought to have was not far from what they were claiming. Rents were frozen for the rest of the year and the government got down to discussing what form wage restraint should now take. What emerged was a 'social contract'.

This concordat—certainly not a contract in any legal sense—was at first sight astonishingly vague. It had, however, some virtue. It bought time when there was little else that could be bought. It not only established a better relationship between government and unions (a Labour government could usually do that) but also outlined common ground where specific agreements could be sought and unwelcome policies could be made acceptable. Wage restraint was the basic aim but if wage restraint was to be made effective either voluntarily (by persuading union leaders who would in turn persuade their unions that the argument was no longer about whether but about how much) or by statute, then some assurances had to be given even if they were no more than expressions of intention. What was offered in return for wage restraint was commitment to social reform and, on the economic side, the maintenance at least of real incomes. Restraint was defined as limiting claims to one per year and limiting rises to whatever might be needed to keep pace with the cost of living or whatever might be earned by increased productivity (with something more for the lowest paid). The major weakness of the deal was that its endorsement by TUC leaders did not of itself carry with it a pledge by any particular union. It was a fragile document which, dubiously and temporarily, kept government and unions in partnership and so saved the government for the time being from having to resort to statutory controls.

Besides its declared intent to protect real wages the government proposed to proceed with social reforms. This would be compassed through the budget. Another new chancellor, Denis Healey, presented no fewer than three budgets in 1974 (March, July and November). In the first, besides increasing the overall tax burden, he raised retirement pensions and subsidised food to the tune of £500 million. In the second, besides reducing the basic rate of VAT (first levied in 1973) from 10% to 8%, he provided another £50 million for food and gave reliefs to rate-payers. Keeping the ostensible cost of living down was now both a social aim and, in view of the social contract, a necessary way of avoiding wage increases. The November budget increased pensions again and promised higher children's benefits; it also gave tax remissions to industry—in the hope of maintaining employment—and began to make significant inroads into government spending. Alongside these fiscal adjustments the government appointed a Royal Commission on the Distribution of Incomes and Wealth (the Diamond Commission) and proposed in a White Paper to tax gifts *inter vivos* at rates varying between 10% and (after £15,000) 75% and from 1977 to tax personal capital assets or wealth at rates of 1% on £100,000 to 5% on £5 million or more. Healey's fourth budget, in 1975, contained classic mopping-up increases and again cut government spending: food subsidies down by £150 million, housing subsidies by £65 million and subsidies to nationalised industries down by no less than £480 million out of £550 million. Even defence was cut by £110 million as part of an attempt to reduce government spending by £1·1 billion. These severe measures did not endear the Chancellor to the unions or fortify the social contract. It was a question how long the social contract could survive deflation of this order. Some unions continued to support the government on restraint but others were harassing it and calling in question the sincerity of its commitment to existing living standards and the social services. The miners won a rise which seemed to most people, including their own leaders, to breach the contract and the government came under fire from its opponents and its own right wing for not standing firm, but more claims were put in to offset the rise in the cost of living and when in June 1975 the railmen held out for 30% the social contract was in tatters. In July the TUC, by a decent but not overwhelming majority, proposed a new limitation—£6 a week for those earning less than £7000 a year and nothing for anybody else—to which the CBI riposted by proposing £5 a week or 10% (whichever was the lower) as a limit for everybody. The government opted for a maximum of £6 a week for one year from August 1st for everybody earning £8500 or less and nothing for those above this mark. Theoretically this was still a voluntary arrangement, or at any rate not compulsory in the sense that it was not made unlawful to make claims above these limits. Sanctions were directed not against unions but against employers and even these were contained in a White Paper and not in an Act of Parliament; the government declared that employers acceding to higher claims might neither receive government contracts nor get assistance under the Industry Act nor take their increased wage bill into account when seeking permission to raise their prices. The £6 limit, presented as a maximum, rapidly became a norm. In effect, however, and by these devious paths, wage limitation had come about, even though its terms would have to be argued annually and for some time ahead it would continue to be regarded as a temporary abnormality.

Government control of wages and prices in peacetime had been brought about by fear. It was still a very tenuous control. It lacked the broad and unifying force provided in wartime by fear or hate of a common external enemy: appeals to the spirit of war and the forms of wartime government were irrelevant or worse. Britain's industrial and financial crisis brought fears without unity, because the fears were of the kind that coerce but do not make men kin. This was particularly true of wages. Price rises were condemned by all wholeheartedly, but wage rises were not condemned by those who got or sought them. Restraint was accepted grudgingly, temporarily and in the expectation of a later reward in the shape of more pay some day or more political power or just an undefined something. Above all incomes policy remained a dangerously ambiguous concept. To some it meant measures to hold wages down, to others a process or mechanism to regulate their increase. In so far as it attempted to hold wages down it operated as a dam which was bound to break one day with destructive force. In so far as it sought an acceptable regulator it failed to find one. What was needed was not a way of preventing wage increases (except in the very short term) but a way to equate rises with one another and with the growth of or non-growth of the economy; but the longer government maintained an incomes policy of the first kind the more unacceptable did incomes policy of any kind become.

4 The crunch

Two parties shared between them the government of Britain in the thirty years that followed the second world war. Both had as a prime aim the restoration and expansion of the British economy by restoring and expanding industry and exports. Both failed. The economic decline of Britain which they inherited accelerated.

In Britain the conduct of public affairs is accompanied by intelligent and sophisticated comment and debate. In this debate the focus throughout these years was on what the government of the day was doing, on whether it was doing the right things or the wrong. The formulation is significant. It shows how government action and government policy had become central. The role of government in the direction and management of the economy had become paramount, even though many—including above all ministers themselves—deplored or sought to evade this development.

Every government acted within the established system. None tried radically to change it. This system was and remained a capitalist system. Labour governments made significant changes of emphasis within the system by acts of nationalisation which diminished the area of private capitalism and extended the public sector, but there had long been these two sectors and both were and remained capitalist in structure and operation. The mixed economy—not a very happy phrase if and so far as it conveyed a fundamental distinction in economic terms between the two sectors—was mixed in different proportions. Government intervention in economic affairs was not a consequence of nationalisation but an assumption of responsibility for the functioning of the entire economy in the trebly difficult times of economic stringency, social exuberance and demographic change: one of the most telling facts was the steady reduction, at a rate of 2% per decade, in the proportion of the population of working age and the growth therefore in the proportion of those who looked to the rest of the society to pay for services from education to old age pensions—the major element in government spending. (The scale of government intervention may have been, and certainly appeared to be, affected by nationalisation and the unexpectedly large calls of nationalised industries on government for finance, but it is far from clear that government could have avoided providing sums of similar magnitude if these industries, particularly coal and the railways, had not been nationalised.)

What then were governments trying to do? There was not so very much difference between them, extremists on either side excepted—and these were ineffective. All governments accepted an obligation to contribute positively to the prosperity of both sectors. This contribution was in the nature of things essentially financial; governments provided money or facilitated credit, and with this money private and nationalised businesses would invest, modernise and grow. At the same time, and from the very earliest postwar years, governments of both colours also saw it as part of their job to intervene in economic affairs to keep wages in check, whether by bargaining with the unions or by subsidising the cost of living or by law. Broadly speaking therefore governments were actively involved in priming industry and restraining wages. This was their economic strategy. It did not distinguish fundamentally between the private and the public sector, which were treated as parts of a single whole. There was no fixed dividing line between them.

Government intervention of this nature was inflationary. The inflation was modified so far as wage rises were restrained (or matched by higher output) but some inflation was inseparable from a policy which set out to make things happen by supplying money and credit to make them happen—the more so of course if governments were simultaneously supplying money for social services and social security benefits, the former as of right and the latter in return for contributions which did not cover the whole cost. For about twenty years inflation proceeded at around 3% a year. Then, in the early seventies, it averaged nearly 10% and was soon to shoot up much higher.

A modern democratic capitalist economy is based on inflation, and in these years the wherewithal for recovery and expansion was provided to a significant degree by government, either through fiscal policy or by direct central or local government expenditure. (Complaints that governments were impeding industry and commerce, e.g. by excessive taxation, were at bottom pleas for further inflation.) At the same time governments hoped that the private sector in particular would quickly get on its own feet, attaining a degree of profitability which would make it sturdily independent of governments; wages policies were designed to this end and when the end was not attained government, in the later years of our period, remitted taxes on business, thereby shifting the fiscal burden from companies to individuals.

These policies did not work. Unions were powerful enough to insist, if sometimes tardily, on wage rises to match or more than match the rise in the cost of living. Wage claims were increasingly geared not to price rises but to these plus anticipated further rises. Profitability remained therefore elusive, or was achieved only on paper by presenting accounts in new ways: on the hard test of how much cash there was in the bank profits were meagre. Real wage increases were also elusive. By the late sixties not only rates of profit were falling but so too was the share of wages as a proportion of the national product.

Governments were committed to inflation because they were themselves part of the system which required it. Modern capitalism thrives on expansion and credit, and without them it shrivels. Equally however it requires the right context, which is an expanding world economy: a national economy is distinct and severable from other national economies in some senses but not all. If the total economy of which it is part does not expand, then the inflation in the particular economy ceases to be fruitful and becomes malignant. Furthermore, the more the particular economy flourishes, the more dependent is it upon the total economy to which it is directing a part of its product, and the more dangerous is any pause in its alimentation—the easier is it to turn from boom to bust. Finally, any government operating within such a system becomes overwhelmingly committed to maintaining it, more especially when symptons of collapse appear—as they did in the last decade of our period when governments felt compelled to help not only lame ducks but lame eagles too. All this was inflationary. No government could simply deflate: every government did both, aiming to deflate on balance but constantly inflating to such an extent that the compensating deflation became increasingly harsh and politically dangerous. Simply to turn off the tap would have been a double disaster, not only putting millions out of work but also ringing down the curtain once and for all on Britain's career as an industrial and trading nation. If industries were allowed to shrivel and fail they would cease producing the goods which the country exchanged for food (which it had ceased to produce for itself when it took the industrial option) and for the industrial raw materials which it did not possess within its own borders (now much reduced by loss of empire).

This fearful dilemma was not, strictly speaking, a consequence of inflation. It was a consequence of too much inflation. Inflation is one of those things which are healthy in small doses but lethal in large ones and the difference between the first twenty postwar years and the next ten was that inflation became too great round about the mid-sixties. The main reason was external. Government policies were themselves inflationary and therefore risky since they created a situation in which an extra dose of inflation would be dangerous, but it was the extra dose that actually did the damage. In order to understand this it is necessary to look at the wider economy of which Britain was inexorably a part and over which Britain had ceased to exercise the kind of control it had once wielded. That position had passed to the USA with the uncomfortable result of leaving Britain as part of something which it was increasingly powerless to direct. It was the behaviour of the international economy under American direction, or non-direction, which from the sixties onwards most severely boosted inflation in Britain. The correct criticism to make of postwar British governments is that they conducted the British economy as though this risk did not exist, forgetting or ignoring that the decline of British industrial and economic power required them to retain a much larger margin of safety in their own planning than their predecessors had been compelled to allow.

The international economic system was designed by and for the benefit of the advanced industrial countries. Consequently, like the economies of these countries, it needed to be expansible and to be based on credit and paper with only a sufficient hard core of bullion. The Bretton Woods system created in 1944 was not based on gold but on gold plus US dollars. This was possible because the dollars had two vital characteristics: they had a fixed value in relation to gold and were convertible into gold, and (like gold) they were in short supply. Since everybody wanted them and everybody knew their precise value in gold, they were the equivalent of and supplemented gold (on which the defunct gold standard system had been based). Further, the system could be expanded as soon as other major desirable currencies could be harnessed to it. This would be done in two stages—first, by fixing the value of each currency in terms of dollars just as the value of the dollar was pegged to gold, thus making each currency a further supplement to gold at second remove; and secondly, by making these currencies freely convertible into dollars. The first or fixed-parity requirement was a basic element in the Bretton Woods system from the start and the second was achieved by the beginning of the fifties (albeit with a disastrous false start by the pound in 1947). The pivot of the whole system was the dollar, tied on the one hand to gold and on the other to other currencies, and itself the currency of the most powerful national economy in the world. The dollar was in these early years continuously in strong demand.*

But before the end of the fifties dollars ceased to be so much in demand. There were too many around and their value sank. The principal reasons for this unexpected change were the outpouring of dollars on overseas military establishments (ultimately hugely increased by the war in Vietnam) and the hardly less lavish outpouring by Americans buying up or setting up businesses overseas. This second expenditure was nurtured and made possible by successive American administrations which inflated the domestic money supply and credit in order to boost the American economy and so placed in the hands of American corporations large quantities of dollars which they were able to invest or spend abroad. Western Europe in particular became flooded with dollars, at which point logic prescribed that the USA should stop pumping dollars into the international economy. But the American national interest was not identical with the needs of the international economy and American administrations were slow to take steps which would check the domestic boom and reverse extravagant foreign policies (including wars) which were regarded as necessary and even virtuous. So the Bretton Woods system was punctured. The scarce dollar had become a superabundant dollar, the values fixed for other currencies no longer fitted the facts; at the beginning of the seventies the dollar was devalued and the fixed-parity system abandoned. Meanwhile American inflation, reflected in the prices of American products, was exported to wherever these products were bought, especially to those countries whose armed forces were buying American aircraft, missiles and other equipment which they could not get elsewhere.

The increase in the price of oil and other imported commodities in the seventies exacerbated these developments. The increase in oil prices was large and sudden and made a particularly disagreeable

---

* The earliest example of a particular currency serving an international economy in this way was the silver-backed Athenian drachma in the fifth century BC.

impact, but it was a contributory and secondary source of inflation. It pushed up domestic and industrial bills but in Britain the total cost of imported fuels remained nevertheless at about 1 per cent of GNP. The main trouble with this increase was that those who made the money did not know what to do with it. Some, like the Shah of Iran, had ways of spending it at home, but others had no way of spending such large revenues in tiny states with small populations (Kuwait, Abu Dhabi) or even large states with small populations (Saudi Arabia) and, once personal exuberance had been quenched, could only invest their surpluses abroad, largely in the countries which bought the oil and to which they returned the cash.

A functioning, expansive international economic system, such as the Bretton Woods conference had tried to devise, would have enabled the leading industrial economies to continue to expand within it, reaping the benefits of inflation and avoiding its traps. The breakdown of the system made expansion impossible and projected constraint and stagnation into national economies already suffering domestic and imported inflation. Inflation, which was necessary for the system for the reasons given, became also lethal; in which case deflation too was necessary. Deflation unquestionably reverses inflation and, given enough of it, eliminates inflation. But deflation does other things too, including shutting industry and destroying the economy as surely as inflation. If inflation were the ultimate evil, deflation was the cure. If not inflation but its consequences were the evil, then too much deflation could be as harmful as too much inflation.*

Inflation had domestic as well as international sources. The latter tended to be played down by political critics of whatever government was failing to cope, so that debate centred on the main domestic sources. There were two principal lines of attack. One was that inflation was due primarily to the wage explosion, from which all else flowed. The other was that it derived primarily from the expansion of the money supply, from which all else flowed. In this extreme form each argument was fatal to the other: both could not be true, although both could be partly

---

* One of the worst economic crises in the history of western Europe, that of the early fourteenth century, was caused by a shortage of money, not a superabundance. It was followed by wage restraint by statute, the Statutes of Labourers in England, which were in turn followed by the Peasants' Revolt.

true. The first required an incomes policy, the second a reduction in government spending.

The second was the more fashionable in the early seventies although also the more obviously dubious, if only because British government expenditure was a smaller proportion of GDP than that of other advanced European industrial countries (where also taxes and social security contributions were a higher proportion of GDP than they were in Britain). The argument was fundamentally whether inflation was caused mainly by government action or by private action. In the crisis of the seventies governments brushed the argument aside and acted on the assumption that both causes were operating. Government spending was sharply cut and an incomes policy was imposed. Government retrenchment caused unemployment and stopped growth but enabled the government to borrow abroad, in the hope once more—as in 1945 —that the economy could be stimulated, men and women put to work, and non-growth become growth: the loans would be paid back and the country would pay its way internationally. Incomes policy strained relations between government and unions and reduced the standard of living of millions of people but helped the government to get its loans and arrest lethal inflation.

Incomes policy had haunted all postwar governments. It was rigorously opposed by the Conservatives in the fifties but then adopted by the Macmillan government; eschewed by the first Wilson government but then nibbled at; rejected by Heath but then applied with a vengeance; and finally decried by the second Wilson government but then firmly applied. This chopping and changing was not simply the reflection of government's impoverished intellect or impoverished power. It reflected real and justified doubts. The situation required some regulation of wages in relation to industrial output and economic performance, but it did not follow that governmental regulation would work or that organised labour would willingly accept, or could be forced to accept, the abrogation of free collective bargaining for more than two or three years at a stretch.

If the international economy had behaved differently, and if—a separate question—Britain had at least maintained its prewar share of international trade, then Britain might have been able to stage an industrial recovery and at the same time finance the social improvements necessary to create the welfare state and assuage the national conscience. But in retrospect the combination of these two large and complex aims seems not merely crippling, as it proved in fact to be, but foolhardy too: France, it has to be observed, which went from weakness to strength, relaid its economic base before proceeding to social reform. Exercising the historian's privilege to be wise after the event one may wonder why, in the daunting economic stringency of the postwar decade, priority was not given to less costly but hardly less urgent reforms such as overhauling the tax system, which was not only a tangle but also a paradise for moneyed wide boys, and converting the industrial scene from one of crude conflict to more fruitful partnership between employers and employed.

Yet it is over-simple to explain all that followed as a direct consequence of miscalculating the equation between what was attempted and the resources available to back the attempt. This equation was not obviously wrong. It was, however, too narrow to allow for mistakes or misfortune, and mistakes and misfortune came—unsure management of the economy and misuse of resources from the mid-fifties, accompanied by an increasingly obstinate and myopic insistence on maintaining that the pound was worth more than in fact it was worth, and—misfortune compounding mistakes—the straitening of the world economy in our last decade and the shift in the terms of trade away from the manufacturing nations and in favour of the possessors of raw materials.

Whatever their causes, failures led to political division and criticism not only of the policies of government but also of its role. Governments had disagreed over the right means to stimulate the mixed capitalist economy, but they had not denied that this was something that governments ought to be doing. Still less had they questioned the existence of a mixed economy. But the failures of this economy in this period led to questions about the viability of such an economy. On the political periphery there was a whiff of real reaction or revolution, although both the one and the other seemed quite unreal to 90% of the people.

Two broad conclusions emerged. Governments had been in charge and had failed. Whether failure came from ineptitude or bad luck or a mixture of both, the verdict remained adverse and it was easy, if not entirely logical, to go on to judge that governments had taken on what they did not know how to discharge and had better get out of the business again. They had bitten off more than they could chew. There was, besides, a second reason for re-examining the role of government. In taking a hand in industrial affairs government had got into industrial

relations. It seemed proper that it should. But if priming industry entailed holding back wages in order to ensure profits at what had been
traditional levels, then government risked getting into the class war as
tertius non gaudens. The record, although admittedly very short, was
not encouraging. Either wages were restrained little and briefly, or,
when governments got tough (Heath's Industrial Relations Act and
Wilson's *In Place of Strife*), they failed to carry public opinion sufficiently and jeopardised their power to govern. Government intervention in wage-fixing had been economically trivial and politically disastrous: it had perhaps on occasions bought time but without discovering
what to do next. In times of failure governments are not given time to
develop new ideas and instruments. Instead the public, its impatience
increased by alarm, begins to listen to those on the one side or the other
who say that the whole strategy is wrong. Perhaps there should be much
less government intervention; or much more. Hence agreement between
the main parties not, as before, on the broad strategy but on the fact
that this strategy was wrong—and widening disagreement on everything else, as the one side was drawn towards more state intervention
and financing through a National Enterprise Board and the other looked
for ways of retreating to a pristine capitalist system in which the private
sector dominated, capital and labour fought for the spoils in that sector,
and the government was confined to keeping the books and watching
out for infringements of the rules.

The lugubrious failures we have been considering in this Part were
economic failures, essentially industrial failures and still more particularly the failure of a handful of industries which could make all the
difference to the volume of exports. Such failures have a number of
contributory causes but the prime responsibility must rest on those who
ran these industries with results that could only be described as poor.
Management, with the inevitable exceptions, was stamped as mediocre.
The assumption that those in charge and the proprietors at their backs
knew best was replaced, sometimes with justification, by the assumption
that the owners knew little about the business or how to run it. (Imagine,
for example, a publishing company managed by people who know next
to nothing about publishing and do not read books.) The finger could be
pointed at other groups too—at workers and their organisations, at
government, at those half-concealed groups whose subversive activities, although often grotesquely exaggerated, were real enough to do
damage—but ultimate responsibility goes with ownership and a record

of ineffectuality is a condemnation of that responsibility. Employers could not confidently command the loyalty and hard work needed to produce the goods.

Some people work hard because they like to, some because they have got used to it and cannot fill a day without it, but most people work to avoid want: they have to. This compulsion had been removed to the extent that the welfare state had eliminated want.

A *sine qua non* of the capitalist industrial system was that large numbers of people had to work for it, but when these people no longer had to work—or no longer had to work so hard or so regularly—the system stood in need of some other way of getting them to work. It did not do this. Two possibilities exist. The first is to revert to the compulsive fear of real or relative penury, a remedy so indecent that it is referred to only indirectly. Yet sections of the right viewed increased industrial unemployment with covert satisfaction, were quick to suggest that social security benefits were unhealthily high, and magnified the proportion of scroungers among the unemployed. The alternative method of getting people to work is more attractive but not easier. It is to give them satisfaction in their work, to get them to like it more. Central to this endeavour is making people feel that they are working for themselves or for some estimable purpose, not just for somebody else and particularly not for a boss class. The greatest obstacle to what would be a new industrial revolution was not the laziness or cussedness of the working population (i.e. the British people, by and large), or even the conservatism and narrow-mindedness of proprietors; it lay in the very patterns of industry which had developed over generations as adversary patterns. The element of conflict in industry had moreover been sharpened, in key industries and thence in the industrial atmosphere generally, to the point where the private capitalist might no longer be able to control or reduce it. Nor were capitalists or unions sure that they wanted to change the patterns. The unions, with their history of fighting within the system, are warriors rather than reformers and they continued to find justification for battle in, for example, the contrast between the low wages of their members and the careers of recent property, banking and other millionaires. Capitalists remained much less than half convinced that the system might be on its way out, or that its ailments might be their fault. They confused communication with participation: telling workers some things about the business is not a first step towards engaging them as partners, if only because it still keeps them on the other side of the table. Few private capitalists were serious about workers' participation, using the undoubted difficulties as an excuse for not asking themselves how industrial production was to be revived without it. The most urgent of the problems of an industrial nation was, in our period, not faced. The will was lacking.

Work is something a man does; labour is something he sells. There is a great gap between these concepts. Modern industrialism has made work dreary. Modern capitalism has not found—has hardly looked for—a way to give those who do this dreary work a stimulating share of the proceeds. The worker's response has been to seek more pay, to sell his labour dearer. A less obvious but equally desirable corrective is to give him more satisfaction through more responsibility and involvement, an expedient which has however been more typical of the earlier than the later stages of capitalism (e.g. Robert Owen's New Lanark or Tito's Yugoslavia). Workers satisfied in neither of these ways do less work and the system in which they work, so far from growing, decays.

PART III
People

1 Poverty and inequality

There are two ways of thinking about a country. The easier is to think of it territorially, as a state bounded by such-and-such borders, possessing a national identity distinguishing it from other states and a central authority regulating its internal affairs and directing its external activities. In this sense a country is a collectivity which is made intelligible and active in relation to other countries and in terms of government. We habitually speak of countries in this generalised way. But, secondly, a country may be considered not as a collectivity and in terms of similar collectivities but as the aggregate of a large number of people with a bewildering variety of spiritual and material needs. These needs, some of which people ought to supply for themselves, others of which have to be supplied by somebody else, include a home, a square meal, schools, graveyards, parks, medicines, public transport, police protection, concerts, playing fields and so on. The country and the people in it are very different things: for example, there are poor people in rich countries. Looked at in human terms, the first questions to ask about a country and its people are how many people are there and what are their conditions.

The English have become thick on the ground. They compete with each other not only for the good things of life but also for the necessities, however this word may be interpreted. They have moreover been increasing faster and faster until very recently, so that the population of England reached the point at which it was doubling in less than a century. Before 1801, when the first census was taken, this increase had been proceeding very roughly at an average rate of one million per century spread over the seven and a half centuries since 1066. The population of England in 1801 was just under 9 million. The nineteenth century saw a great acceleration. In 1901 it was 32·9 million. By mid-century it was 43·8 million and at the end of our period 49·2 million. By this time the increase had slowed down and seemed about to go into reverse but England had become more densely populated than anywhere else in the world except a few small islands.*

* At these same points—1801, 1901, 1951 and 1975—the population of Wales, in millions, was 0·5, 2, 2·6 and 2·8; of Scotland 1·6, 4·5, 5 and 5·2.

In the present century the death rate declined markedly at the beginning and then became steady. The birth rate declined sharply with a brief exception during the second world war. The old were increasing in numbers faster than the young but both these groups were growing and by 1975 half the population was either under 18 or over 65. Given the determination to make special provision for those not of working age, this shift in the balance of the population from producers to non-producers had great significance. In our period the shift was proceeding at the rate of 2% per decade.

The decennial census of 1971 showed that 3·3 million inhabitants of the United Kingdom had been born outside it. These included children born to servants of the empire, civilian and military, and to merchants and others plying their trades abroad. The largest single element was the Irish who accounted for nearly a quarter of the total but were still barely more than 1% of the population. England was a country of net emigration in most years but subject to waves of immigration, all the more noticeable when coloured. Much of this immigration was a reversal of emigration between the wars or a consequence of the end of empire. Refugees from Europe before the war and from colonies after it were small fractions. Numerically these waves were insignificant, but socially and politically they were not.

The basic requirement of all these millions of people was a standard of living, absolute in relation to the cost of living and also, although secondarily, relative in terms of the standards of other people in the community. Much the most important way of attaining these standards was the personal earnings of work: the British were a people at work. Earnings were supplemented by social security payments and by income from investments, but over 80% of all personal incomes came from work. Social security provided 9·6% and investment 3·5%. Employment and the level of wages were therefore predominant in determining standards of living.

From the mid-forties to the mid-sixties there was no serious unemployment overall but general unemployment reappeared in the sixties, at first tentatively when it spurred Conservative ministers to spurts of reflation (the Selwyn Lloyd and Maudling years), and then massively from 1967, a consequence above all of the fierce deflation of 1966 by which the Wilson government hoped to maintain the external value of the pound. In 1967 unemployment in the United Kingdom crossed the half million mark for the first time since the war, increasing by 60% the total for the previous year. Thereafter it became a major problem and reached one million before the end of 1975. These figures, which give the totals of registered unemployed, did not include those who did not take the trouble to register (in badly hit areas many did not think it worth while to do so) or the self-employed or the under-employed or school-leavers or those temporarily laid off. In some areas the registered unemployed alone were half the work force.

Some unemployment was a consequence of technological change. A given level of productivity could be achieved with fewer pairs of hands and where that level was accepted as adequate the work force was allowed to decline. In the sixties this displacement of men and women by machines was proceeding at the rate of about 2% a year—not in the sense that 2% of the population was becoming unemployed for this reason, but in the sense that productivity could be maintained while reducing the work force at this rate. The main source of unemployment, however, in the years of full employment as well as later was not technological but regional. The unemployed were in one area and the jobs in another. By 1970 the percentage of unemployed in the worst areas was three times as great as it was in the best. This was a continuation, at first on a relatively small scale, of the depressed areas of the thirties and the areas were the same. The shift of the population to the south-east accentuated the traditional disadvantages of north and west England and much of Scotland and Wales. Governments accepted the responsibility to do something special for such areas, trying to create jobs by financial inducements to industry and preferential licensing dispensations, but these were palliatives of limited effect. Apart from these regional imbalances the brunt of unemployment fell on the unskilled poor, on women and on the youngest and oldest age groups in the working population. Throughout our period the duration of unemployment was getting longer, particularly for older people.

The impact of unemployment on the worker and his family was severe because unemployment and other benefits did not measure up to needs. The basic flat-rate benefit was not by itself enough to ensure a decent standard of living nor could it be drawn for more than a year; at times fewer than half the unemployed were drawing it. Very many unemployed persons drew neither unemployment nor supplementary benefit. The family income supplement, rent and rate rebates and a range of means-tested benefits were available to some of the unemployed but the first and most important of these was drawn by only about half of those entitled to it. In national, as distinct from personal, terms the cost of unemployment was high, including not only the goods not produced by those who might have produced them but also reductions in the yield of income tax and excise duties and in contributions to the National Insurance Fund from both employers and employed.

Policies about people, whether employment policies or social policies, are concerned mainly with the poor. They concern the rich if and so far as poverty cannot be relieved without mulcting the rich. Social policy, however, may also be concerned with inequality, comparative deprivation as distinct from absolute poverty. Complete material equality is neither conceivable (outside the tiniest communities) nor advocated by any sensible body of people, but although unacceptable degrees of inequality cannot be defined, they can be recognised. Blatant extremes are easy to condemn as a social irritant and moral obscenity, even in the absence of poverty and even though the point where extremes cease to be tolerable will vary from time to time, from country to country and from person to person. This is a source of conflict which no modern society can escape.

The problems of poverty and inequality, although distinct, in practice overlap. Britain in these postwar decades had both. The main difference between them was that nobody was surprised by the latter but a great many people were surprised by the existence and extent of the former. They thought that poverty was well on the way out. It was to have been removed by full employment at good wages and also by the levelling of post-tax incomes and the redistribution of wealth which were thought to be proceeding at a decent if decorous pace.

Statistics on these matters are hard to handle and perennially open to reinterpretation, but the hard facts are not disputable. A shocking number of people were poor in the sense of being below the official (and by no means generous) poverty level and in need of financial help even after drawing the benefits to which they were entitled and to which they had contributed under the National Insurance Acts. Thus, in the early seventies, tens of thousands of families were living below the poverty line even though the father had a full-time job; about 100,000 families, comprising 300,000 children, were living in poverty; half of all old age pensioners were living in poverty; of those living in poverty much the largest element, over one third, were children. The principal causes of this lamentable state of affairs were inadequate wages, benefits and family allowances and a massive failure by those in need to claim extra help either because they did not know about it or because they did not like to ask. Inadequate in this context simply means not enough to assure basic needs in food, clothing and rent. All in all there were probably two million persons living below the poverty line in the sixties and early seventies although it is impossible to say how many of them were how far below. The chief remedy adopted to counter this failure was to provide additional discretionary and means-tested allowances or rebates, of which by the end of our period there were about forty available from central government funds and a smaller number in the gift of local government—a plethora dispensing as much confusion as relief.

The discovery in the sixties of continuing poverty led to criticism of government policies as well as of the levels of benefits. The criticism, notably by the Child Poverty Action Group established in 1965, was instrumental in raising family allowances in 1967, 1968 and 1975 and in introducing in 1971 the Family Income Supplement—which in effect defined the minimum needs of families of various sizes, and where there was a gap between needs and resources filled half of it. Critics concentrated on the family, advocating larger and tax-free family allowances and the abolition of the child allowance available only to taxpayers (or alternatively its extension to non-taxpayers). The CPAG exposed what came to be known as the poverty trap—the situation created by the introduction into social security of means-tested benefits which made it impolitic for a man to accept a higher wage since he would then lose these benefits and at the same time become liable to pay more in income tax. The CPAG proposed that more lower-paid people should be removed from the purview of income tax, that a minimum should have the deficit made up to them as a social right.

The persistence of poverty sharpened the attack on inequality, the more so since it was easier to become indignant over inequality than to get a hard-pressed government to raise benefits or decree a minimum wage. Inequality was reduced but remained great. Comparisons with other countries showed Britain to have about the most unequal distribution of incomes and of wealth in the world, but such comparisons are peculiarly ambiguous (what is compared is often strictly not comparable) and in any case remote; the more pertinent measures are domestic.

At the end of our period the range of pre-tax incomes was of the order of 160 to 1. In the United Kingdom 21 million people paid direct taxes:

the majority did not pay direct taxes. Much the largest number, 17·25 million, had pre-tax incomes below £3000 a year. The next 3·5 million had £3–10,000, leaving 135,000 above the £10,000 mark, of whom 21,000 were also above the £20,000. These pre-tax figures are an indication of wealth but not of standards of living since the steeply graded income taxes operated to produce a different picture.

The income tax was remodelled in 1973, since when it has been levied at a standard rate of 30% or 35% on all taxable incomes (subject to allowances) and at a higher rate rising by steps to a total of 83% on incomes above £20,000. In addition investment incomes above £2000 (lowered later to £1000) suffer a further tax at the flat rate of 15%, so that the highest rate of direct tax may reach 98%. In effect therefore there comes a point above which virtually all income is forfeit. (In the USA and West Germany the highest rate in these years was 50%.) In the period 1965–75 the tax rate of an average wage-earner rose from 5% to over 20%.

The effect of these taxes was to narrow the gap between the richer and the poorer taxpayers. Of the 21 million taxpayers 9 million were left with incomes of £595–1500 and 11·5 million with incomes of £1500–5000. The remaining 300,000 kept more than £5000 but only 21,000 of them kept more than £10,000.

Wealth is an even more elusive term than income. In particular one man's income in relation to another's varies if assets producing no income (e.g. works of art) are excluded or included. Nevertheless on any assessment the inequality was prodigious. In spite of some loss, perhaps considerable, at the very top and some improvement at the very bottom (of the wealth-owning segment) one quarter of the country's wealth belonged in 1965–75 to a mere 1% of adults and one half to 5%, leaving the other half to be shared between 95%. The characteristic and most accessible form of wealth in this period—stocks and shares—was specially concentrated. 80% of it was in the hands of 1% of the property-owning class and if the view be restricted to equities 96% belonged to 5% of that class. The beneficiaries of the mulcting of the super-rich were the rich. Wealth was concentrated in something like 17 million persons, most of whom owned very little; the rest owned nothing; the concept of a property-owning democracy was ridiculous. Even among property-owners seven out of ten possessed assets worth less than £5000, nine out of ten assets worth less than £10,000. Fewer than two million persons owned half the wealth in the country. But although two million is a small proportion of the total population, there were a large number of people living a long way above the rest. The rich were not just a handful of millionaires.

Taxes on wealth have two distinct motivations. One is to reduce inequality, the other is to raise revenue. In the first postwar Labour administration Cripps introduced, for one year only, a supplementary direct tax which was described as a wealth tax but was in fact assessed on incomes. It was a super-supertax and its motivation was mixed, partly sop and partly revenue-raiser. The first Wilson administration introduced in 1965 a capital gains tax prompted less by revulsion against inequality than by the outcry against the taxfree bonanzas which were being reaped by property dealers. This tax was first imposed on individuals and corporations but was partially replaced a year later by a separate corporation tax on undistributed profits. Capital gains made by individuals on sales within one year of purchase were aggregated with gross income and taxed accordingly; if made beyond the year's limit, at 30%. Wealth remained untaxed as such except in the special case of transfer on death, but estate duty had become a largely voluntary tax which could be avoided by transferring property a given number of years before death (by the seventies it was contributing no more than 2% of government revenues) and in 1975 the second Wilson administration introduced a capital transfer tax which—subject to certain exceptions of which the most important was transfers between spouses—substituted for a levy on transfers at death a levy on all transfers. This government also set up a committee to discuss ways of taxing capital assets annually but the difficulties of devising a sufficiently acceptable way of doing this prevented legislative action within our period.

In its origins taxation had been a way of raising money for the government to spend. Since governments have abandoned lucrative activities like piracy and no longer make money out of war, taxation has become the only way of raising money apart from borrowing at home or abroad, while at the same time the great expansion in what governments are required to do—quite apart from the rise in the cost of doing it—has vastly increased their need for money. If, besides paying the military and civil servants of the crown, the government has to relieve poverty and provide social services, the entire scope of national finance is transformed. In the nineteenth century moreover taxation ceased to be merely a way of finding money. It was expected also to become an instrument of social change, the clearest example of this new function being the introduction of death duties which were an assertion of the (non-budgetary and non-economic) view that wealth ought not to fall like manna from heaven into the laps of lucky beneficiaries who had not worked for it and that the way to take the edge off this social impropriety was for the state to take a cut for distribution to other people.

By mid-twentieth century the dual purpose of the budget was established. The budget itself had already a dual character of a different kind in that it was clearly, although unequally, divided on the revenue side into its two main sections of direct taxation (or inland revenue) and indirect (or customs and excise). The former, in which the income tax was very much the largest element, was the more productive in terms of revenue and also the more socially progressive for two reasons: less than half the population paid income tax at all and the tax itself was graded. Excise and customs duties on the other hand were paid by everybody who bought the goods taxed and at the same rate; the main items in this category were tobacco, fuels, beer, wines and spirits, and purchase tax (replaced in 1973 by VAT). At the end of our period direct and indirect taxes were contributing to the total tax revenues (£28 billion) in the proportions of 2 to 1.

As an instrument of social amelioration taxation, meaning in effect the graded income tax plus death duties, had made only a modest impact on social patterns and relative ways of living. Some people at the top of the scale were incommoded—some of them severely in terms of what they or their fathers had been used to—and some of the more ostentatious gall had been removed from society, although a part of this change should perhaps be ascribed to the changing *mores* of the rich and not all of it to financial screws. Socially, the general picture in 1975 was not so very different from what it had been half a century earlier: too much poverty and too much inequality as well. Neither rising taxation nor the new substructure of social services and social security payments had done more than modify the picture at its edges. This was largely unexpected as well as very disappointing. Yet it should not have been such a surprise. The standards of living of the majority of the population did not depend on the standards of living of the minority and could not be materially altered simply by pruning these standards: the case for redistribution of wealth and the reduction of inequalities was not economic but ethical. The majority depended for their well-being overwhelmingly on payments made to them directly and much the greatest part of these payments was in wages. The largest element in poverty or inadequate standards or unacceptable ratios was the low wages which a conservative society did not regard as low because they were so much higher than they had been. The suggestion that a miner might be paid £100 a week struck many decent and fair-minded people as outrageous or not seriously meant. Yet the only thing that made such a wage grotesque was habit—the fact that nothing like it had been paid, in these areas, before. In this respect, as in others, the fact that Britain had suffered no revolutionary shock such as defeat in war placed a severe limit on the acceptability of change. Britain, an exceptionally decent society, willed the abolition of poverty and the reduction of inequalities too, but not the means to these ends.

This was a failure, but not primarily an economic one. It arose from the mistaken belief that economic growth would pay for social reform. When growth turned out to be non-existent or inadequate, progress towards social justice and the removal of inequalities was postponed: no growth, no socialism. But growth was not essential to reforms; it was essential only to painless reforms. Thus a gap opened between those for whom equality was a consequence of growth and those for whom it was an end in itself.

There appeared in these years a special kind of inequality or inequity in British society. A few years after the war Britain acquired a colour problem. Racial problems without colour had occurred in Britain before. Antisemitism was ancient and established, though rarely extreme, and the largest minority, the Irish, enjoyed less than universal goodwill. During the war large numbers of Poles and Italians reached Britain, the first as a flotsam of central European politics and the latter as prisoners of war, and many of them—particularly the Poles—remained when the war ended: they were absorbed without difficulty after a brief period of unease. Coloured immigrants, however, were different on two counts—first and foremost because they were coloured and secondly because they were Commonwealth citizens.

These immigrants came overwhelmingly from the West Indies, India and Pakistan. Most of the Indians and Pakistanis came from a few distinct areas in their countries. The West Indians were initially much the largest contingent. Many West Indians came to Britain during the war in the services and went back again, but a few years later unemployment at home constrained them to return in search of a livelihood. This flow, which began in the late forties, was boosted by the McCarran Act which severely cut immigration into the USA from 1952; it flagged from the mid-fifties when jobs in England became harder to come by, but then increased spectacularly in 1960–62, partly because the job market in Britain was once more favourable and partly because of fear that Britain would emulate the McCarran Act and impose controls on immigration. The anticipation of controls particularly accelerated the movement of wives and children who hurried across the Atlantic to beat this ban. West Indian immigration rose to a rate of about 65,000 persons a year. Immigration from India and Pakistan was much smaller (consultation between the governments concerned operated as an unofficial control) but here too there was a rush in 1960–62, abetted by agents who found that there was money to be made by organising and encouraging it. When in 1962 controls were imposed there were 660,000 Commonwealth immigrants in the United Kingdom, half of them black: 172,000 West Indians, 80,000 Indians, 25,000 Pakistanis. These were not large figures, absolutely or comparatively, but the rate of increase in the flow gave rise to alarming, sometimes alarmist, questions about where it would all lead. In 1962 the coloured population was 0·7% of the whole but ten years earlier it had been less than 0·2%. In these ten years the proportion had increased fivefold.

The extraordinary increase in coloured immigration in 1960–62 followed hard on outbreaks of racial violence in 1958 in Nottingham and the Notting Hill district of London. This violence was a shock to the public and to prevailing official complacency about the immigration and the integration of black immigrants into the society. It created the view that something had to be done, but initially it divided the political parties over what that something ought to be. Immigration, more obvious and more amenable to government action than integration, became the focus of attention, and while Conservatives favoured controls Labour at first did not. Control involved denying to immigrants their right to use a Commonwealth passport to come to Britain. Since the British Nationality Act 1948 there had been two kinds of Commonwealth citizen: citizens of particular independent Commonwealth countries such as Canada or Australia, India or Pakistan; and all the rest, who were citizens of the United Kingdom and Colonies. By the Commonwealth Immigration Act 1962 all these people of either kind lost their automatic right of entry into the United Kingdom unless they were dependents (wives and children under 21) or could get employment vouchers. The barely concealed purpose of the Act, albeit that it applied to the whole Commonwealth and made no distinction as to colour, was to check black immigration.

The vouchers were of three kinds: A vouchers given to those who had jobs to come to before they arrived, B vouchers for those with special skills and C vouchers for those with neither fixed jobs nor special skills. C vouchers were given to only a very small proportion of applicants, with priority to any who had had war service in the armed forces, and they were discontinued in 1964 when the Labour Party came to power. Between the introduction of the Act and the end of the decade voucher-holders from the three main areas of immigration arrived at the rate of 40–50,000 a year with India now providing half the total and Pakistan and the West Indies splitting the other half. Dependents arrived in numbers which increased from 15,000 to 40,000 a year over the same period.

The Labour Party was uneasily converted to controls before, and no doubt partly by the prospect of, the general election of 1964. In a White Paper of 1965 (Cmd. 2379) it both endorsed the principle of control, limiting vouchers to 8500 a year to begin with and promising tougher measures against the illegal immigration which the Act inevitably inaugurated, and also stressed the need for action in relation to integration. In the same year it introduced and carried the first Race Relations Act. Although limited in scope this Act was a courageous venture. It proscribed discriminatory acts (not attitudes or opinions) and proposed to deal with them not through the criminal courts but through special regional conciliation committees with ultimate recourse to a civil court. This sidestepping of the criminal law was both judicious and a weakness since the mechanisms designed by the Act—investigation and conciliation case by case—had only tenuous sanctions. Moreover the conciliation committees depended preponderantly, although not wholly, on complaints by individuals, many of whom were ignorant of their rights or scared to exercise them. The Act's area of operation was confined to places of public resort, of which pubs provided the committees with the bulk of their work. To this general scheme there was a single and controversial exception: incitement to discrimination was made a criminal offence cognisable by the criminal courts (which could have dealt with these cases anyway under the Public Order Acts).

Within its limits the Race Relations Act 1965 was effective in regulating conduct and so indirectly in helping to affect attitudes but there was evidence of extensive discrimination against blacks in areas outside the scope of the Act, particularly housing, jobs, insurance and other services. A report by PEP (Political and Economic Planning) in 1967 put these allegations beyond dispute and paved the way for a second Act, but before this Act was introduced public attention was redirected to immigration by the episode of the Kenya Asians. These Asians, most of whom were citizens of the United Kingdom and Colonies and holders of British passports entitling them to enter Britain, were no longer welcome or happy in Kenya where their very success in business had placed them in the hazardous position of an envied alien minority. Dispossessed or in danger of dispossession, they began to trek to Britain, thereby reinforcing prejudices and fears of those who foretold a series of waves of black immigration from countless former colonies with dire social, economic and racial consequences. A new home secretary, James Callaghan, bowed to this storm and introduced a bill to remove from Commonwealth citizens their right of entry into the United Kingdom unless they themselves, their parents or grandparents had been born there—a circumstance which applied almost exclusively to whites. This measure, the Commonwealth Immigration Act 1968, was enacted in the same year as the new Race Relations Act, a second positive step in integration policy to balance the negative policy on immigration. The Race Relations Act 1968 made discrimination in housing, jobs and the supply of goods and services illegal. The procedures of the earlier Act were retained. Opposition to the Act and to black immigration (despite the increasing strictness of controls from the 1962 Act to the suspension of C vouchers and the new Act of 1968) was voiced with an obsessive intemperance and apocalyptic prophecies of bloodbaths which made the work of conciliation and integration very difficult.

Prejudice and discrimination could not be eliminated within a single generation but they seemed on balance to be reduced. The main sources of prejudice were hostility based on colour, an emotion different in kind as well as degree from xenophobia, and intertwined economic fears arising from the numbers or supposed numbers of blacks present in Britain or foreseen. These economic fears were checked with the introduction of controls. They were, however, also nourished by the belief that blacks were more prolific than whites. This belief lost much of its validity after the surge in births occasioned by the arrival of wives who had been separated from their husbands and after the adoption by many immigrant families of the smaller family patterns which had become the rule among whites. By 1975 the numbers of blacks presented less of a problem than their very uneven geographical distribution. They were concentrated in certain areas to which they had been drawn by jobs and by their kith and kin; and as a result of prejudice, particularly in relation to housing, they constituted within these areas—mostly poorer ones—coloured nuclei, not yet ghettos but socially unhealthy segregations. Fundamental gut prejudice was affected in these years by experience but experience worked both ways. Familiarity created tension, particularly by emphasising racial differences (e.g. in everyday living habits). But familiarity worked the other way too. Over much of the country the presence of blacks ceased to excite comment. It became normal and the common humanity of the silent majority, unobsessed by racial prejudice, took this strange new influx in its stride.

2 Homes and land

A home is second only to food among the material needs of a human being. The concern of the state with housing has, however, grown out of standards rather than numbers. It originated in sanitation, as public health used to be called, by way of slum clearance and was then given an impulse by two world wars which created a scarcity of housing and so opportunities for rapacity in such landlords as were that way inclined. Hence the intervention of the state in favour of tenants (of private landlords) in two ways: security of occupation and rent control. The postwar history of housing embraces therefore the building of houses, security of tenure and the control of rents, and slum clearance. It is a continuation of a chapter in social history which began with the Report on the Sanitary Condition of the Labouring Poor in 1842 and the creation six years later of the Board of Health.

The creation of slums by the industrial revolution, combined in some places with surviving mediaeval patterns of landholding,* the degeneration of property, and the fear of political disorder generated by squalor contributed to the first statutory interventions in this area. In 1868 an obligation was laid on landlords to keep their property in repair and authority was given to local authorities to inspect premises and if necessary close them. Local authorities had already been empowered in 1851 to build houses. In 1899 they were further empowered to lend money to owner-occupiers and by the Town and Country Planning Act 1919 they were obliged to plan to provide houses for rent—the effective advent of the council house. This Act also introduced the exchequer subsidy, designed to keep the financial burden of council housing off the rates, but two years later the subsidy was discontinued on the grounds that it incited councils to go on a spending spree at the Exchequer's expense. After another two years it was restored, within limits, because

* E.g. in Nottingham where communal holdings on the city's periphery prevented the city from expanding because of the difficulty of buying and selling the land, and so crammed the town-dwellers into increasingly inadequate space. See W. G. Hoskins, *The Making of the English Landscape*, Chapter 9.

its withdrawal had brought council building to a halt. After 1933 the subsidy was restricted to slum clearance which, since 1923, had been financed in equal shares by local and central government. These patterns reappeared after the second world war.

The twentieth century has taken the view that the state should not only set standards for housing but also ensure that enough habitable houses get built and are available at reasonable rents. In the first world war rents were frozen for the duration in 1915 in order to safeguard families deprived of their wage-earner and keep soldiers at the front from fretting about their homes instead of concentrating on the business of killing the enemy. But rent control was expected to end with the war just as the local authority's function in providing housing was seen as no more than a long-stop to cope with an emergency temporarily beyond the capacity of the private building industry. Rent control was extended at the end of the war but in 1923 a beginning was made in de-control by removing controls from a house when it changed hands: a sitting tenant remained protected but the building did not. The policy of decontrol was inspired by the belief that new building was being held back by low rentability. The next year, however, the first Labour government adopted what has remained the standard alternative policy: if private builders would not build because they could not make enough money out of it, then local councils must build. A dual system emerged with private builders building for purchasers with enough money to buy and local authorities building for renting to poorer people. Midway between the wars one third of new houses were being built by local authorities, and by 1939 one tenth of all families were living in council houses.

Decontrol advanced a further step with the Rent Act 1933 and the Housing Act 1938 which emancipated all but the cheapest houses, leaving only some four million protected tenants, but the expectation during the first world war of total decontrol had still not been met and in 1937 a minority of the Ridley Committee on Housing suggested that some measure of control should be regarded as permanent. Another feature of the interwar period was the enormous growth of building societies, the main source of loans to those who wanted to buy rather than rent. By 1939 these societies had over £700 million out on loan and it was largely through their services that owner-occupiers, a mere 10% in 1914, had increased to the point where nearly 25% of all families lived in houses which they had bought or were in the process of buying.

(The percentage was to exceed 50% before the end of the period covered in this book.) In terms of the number of houses built the interwar record was not a bad one—4·1 million in England and Wales with 340,000 as the highest number in a single year—but the distribution by regions and by classes was uneven. The Ridley Committee estimated that between 1914 and 1937 the stock of superior, middling and cheap housing had risen respectively by 47, 90 and 26 per cent. These proportions concealed the fact that in absolute terms the biggest addition had been in the cheap category; but then that was where the biggest need lay too. Slum clearance, in spite of a helping hand from the second Labour government's Housing Act 1930 which aimed to clear slums in five years, had made only a modest mark on this most ugly and urgent problem.

The second world war brought a return to extensive controls and was immensely more destructive of property than the first. In 1945 millions of people were homeless. It was estimated that there were three-quarters of a million more families than homes. Very many houses, perhaps a fifth, were uninhabitable either from war damage or because they were classed as irredeemable slums. 208,000 houses had been destroyed and a further 250,000 made uninhabitable by enemy action; another 250,000 were severely damaged and some three million had suffered lesser damage. There was a great deal of ignorance about needs. The number of new homes required was variously put at a series of points between one and six million. The building labour force had to be reassembled and there was a shortage of building materials. The new government had to make choices and decided to give priority to new building: slum clearance and housing repair, which had been halted by the war, were in consequence not effectively resumed for ten years after it. The government was also determined to keep rents low, partly out of solicitude for the poor and partly to keep the cost of living index from rising too fast. As a stop-gap 124,000 'pre-fabs' were run up by local councils and abandoned military camps were spontaneously occupied by bands of homeless persons. This self-help spread to cities where empty houses were occupied by squatters. Such invasions of property, even in the prevailing circumstances, struck a raw nerve and the authorities resorted to the law of trespass, the police and the disconnection of gas and electricity in order to get the squatters out. But squatting became a permanent feature of city life, acquiring in time its own organisations and codes of conduct.

Property-owners have seldom been a popular class. They did not add to their popularity when, after the war, they found themselves in possession of a scarce necessity. Blocks of buildings were traded for large profits, often remaining unrepaired and unused in the process, and the repute of landlords as a whole seemed to justify strict measures of rent control in order to protect tenants against unconscionable exactions by landlords who acquired property in order to trade in it rather than care for it and who were unimpededly making large capital gains. In 1949 controls were extended for the first time to furnished rooms and houses and to premises let for the first time since 1945. All rent-controlled premises were brought within the purview of special tribunals empowered to adjudicate on rents and by the same Act local councils were brought into the business of building houses for the middle as well as the poorer classes. The councils were no longer a long-stop or even a junior partner in the housing business, and as they enlarged their scope they were acquiring tenants who, unlike the usual council tenant, did not need help to pay a commercial rent.

The aftermath of the second world war saw big increases in subsidies. Rents were subsidised and so too were building costs, which rose steeply, dragging the subsidies up with them. The general subsidy (as opposed to the subsidy for slum clearance which alone had survived the economic crisis of the early thirties) was reintroduced in 1944 and supplemented a few years later by subsidies for improvements granted by the Housing Act 1949 to encourage landlords to repair rentable property. Half the cost of approved improvements might be reimbursed to the landlord by the council, which in turn recovered three-quarters of its outlay from the Exchequer. Any landlord, however opulent, could get a grant provided he did the work. Landlords welcomed this measure although most of them would have preferred to be allowed to raise their rents.

Over a million houses were built before Labour left office in 1951, a remarkable total in the circumstances but not what had been planned. Labour's first target for England and Wales was 240,000 new houses a year but no more than half that number were built in 1947 and in the succeeding years the annual total rose slowly to just under 200,000. Conservative promises to do better were a major plank in their 1950 and 1951 campaigns. They set themselves an immediate target of 300,000 a year with hopes for 400,000 later on. They reached the first figure in 1956 but the effort so strained resources that the target had to be modified by including Scotland in a figure originally intended to apply only to England and Wales. The main thrust of Conservative policy was removal of controls. Licences for private building were abolished in 1954 so that private builders, who had built only 18% of new houses under Labour, quickly doubled their activity and were responsible for 40% of the aggregate for the twelve full years of Conservative rule (1952–63), their share rising year by year. Resources being still scarce, the performance of the public sector declined sharply. This was in line with Conservative policy which aimed to constrict the role of the local authorities in order to reduce the building and rent subsidies funnelled to them and also to concentrate their activities on slum clearance. The general subsidy was abolished once more in 1956, subsidies being retained only for slum clearance and for the provision of bed-sitters and the overspill housing designed to draw people away from the big cities. In general the Conservatives hoped to cure the housing shortage by encouraging private builders, to solve the rent problem by making housing plentiful instead of scarce, and to save money on building and rents in order to channel public funds into slum clearance (via the local authorities) and housing repair (via private landlords). Their principal instruments, after the abolition of building licences, were the Housing Repair and Rents Act 1954 and the Housing Act 1957.

The 1954 Act permitted, within limits, increases in rents in return for the execution of repairs to habitable houses, encouraged the temporary patching of uninhabitable ones and exempted from rent control new houses built after the passing of the Act. The government also gave grants to owners for the installation of specified amenities such as hot water, baths and lavatories (in 1964 owners wishing to let became obliged to instal these amenities, recovering half the cost and borrowing the other half from local authorities). The 1957 Act went much further. It removed rent controls from more than half the premises subject to them—houses rated above £30 (in London £40), houses occupied by their owners, houses becoming vacant and new unfurnished lettings. For the remainder substantial rent increases were permitted varying with the condition and rateable value of the property. The Act was highly controversial. It was attacked not only by Labour but also by a number of Conservatives who were alarmed by the prospect of controls being removed from as many as 800,000 homes in the short period of six months. The Act's sponsors had intended that decontrol, in order to achieve its aim of increasing available accommodation by restoring a free market in housing, should be massive and swift but they were forced by their critics first to resort to the unpopular guillotine to get the Bill through the House of Commons and then immediately to amend it by adding a right for a tenant to go to a court and ask for his eviction to be delayed.

The promotion of home ownership, which was a prime Conservative concern, required the transfer of the freehold in property from landlords to a much larger number of owner-occupiers, not all of whom could produce the necessary capital sums. To meet this difficulty the Conservatives turned to the financial organisations whose business it was to lend money on mortgage or otherwise to home-seekers. They provided funds for building societies to help people to buy the cheaper, pre-1919 houses, thus making government money available in a different way. They also encouraged and revived housing associations. These associations, which first appeared in the nineteenth century and enjoyed a spurt in activity after the first world war, were charitable non-profit making bodies and had had access to modest public funds since the Town and Country Planning Act 1909. Together with building societies and insurance companies they were a principal source of funds for housing. With the help of these organisations a purchaser could become the owner of his home. He was not a tenant and the area of landlord and tenant contracted, but the outcome was to some extent misleading since the position of the private landlord was taken in financial terms, if not in law, by the mortgagee or other lender and the occupier became financially beholden to the latter instead of the former. The ownership promoted by these measures was qualified and the home-seeker who wanted to take advantage of them needed to possess already at least a modicum of property or prospects in another form. What happened was to a large extent a redistribution of the title to property within the property-owning class. Financiers succeeded landowners.

The Conservatives greatly increased the building rate and went a long way towards the abolition of protected tenancies but they were vulnerable to the taunt that the benefits which they provided went preponderantly to the middle-class purchaser and the owner-occupier and they did not succeed in curbing costs. By the Housing Act 1961 they restored the subsidy to local authorities on new houses (subject to ministerial approval) and when they left office the housing subsidies, which had risen from £45 million to £75 million under Labour, were running at £137 million a year.

In the Labour government which took office in 1964 responsibility for housing (among other things) was given to Richard Crossman. For Labour rents were the central issue. So long as there was a shortage of houses rents in the private sector had to be controlled and rents of council houses subsidised. The new government therefore reasserted rent control but tried to make it more flexible. The Rent Act 1965 introduced the concept of the fair rent. Regulation took the place of control. Rents became variable by adjudication—but not by market forces. A fair rent was to be assessed by reference to the condition, location and rateable value of the premises but without reference to the scarcity value of houses or to the financial circumstances of tenants or landlords. These rents were to be fixed by local rent officers with a right of appeal to rent assessment committees. Since any precise definition of a fair rent was impossible, dissension arose between rent officers and the committees with the former often being accused of partiality towards landlords, but these new procedures produced a fair degree of rough justice. Tenancies which had remained under control in spite of the 1957 Act could be converted into regulated tenancies if they were certified as being in good condition and possessing basic amenities.

On building, as distinct from landlord and tenant relations, Crossman modified without wholly reversing the Conservative policy of drawing a line between private building for sale to owner-occupiers or owner-letters and the local councils' more specialised functions of slum clearance and building cheaper houses for renting. Crossman's aim was parity between the two sectors in a new building programme which would eventually reach 500,000 houses a year. This programme was soon overshadowed by the economic crisis and the need for cuts in government spending, while both sectors were hit by rising interest rates as well as by taxation (particularly the Selective Employment Tax which hit labour-intensive industries like building) and the reduction of exchequer grants. Neither in Crossman's time nor later were his targets achieved. In the best year (1968) 426,000 houses were built in the United Kingdom; the average over the last ten years of our period was 358,000. The housing queues remained depressingly long. In England and Wales the net addition to the housing stock, i.e. after making allowance for houses demolished or closed, fluctuated between 200,000 and 300,000. On the other hand Crossman's aim of parity between the public and private sectors was nearly achieved as the former crept up again.

In these years a third aspect of housing received increasing attention. By 1960 or earlier it had become widely accepted that many houses destined for demolition ought instead to be repaired. During the sixties government grants were made for the repair of about 100,000 houses a year and Labour's Housing Act 1969 tried to boost this activity by getting local authorities to designate General Improvement Areas where it would be worthwhile for landlords to spend money (only some of it their own) in this way. Landlords were to be encouraged to apply for grants where buildings were basically sound, the area was not threatened by developmental upheaval, and the inhabitants might be expected to welcome a general facelift accompanied by some expenditure by the council on amenities. Some owners responded, the more so after a further Act in 1971 increased grants from 50% of the cost to 75%, but the overall response was patchy and disappointing. A number of councils embarked on extensive reconditioning where they were themselves the owners, but private landlords were still unable to foresee a sufficient return on their outlay and displayed little of the zeal to improve which was supposed to be inhibited only by costs. The main beneficiaries of these Acts were owner-occupiers with enough money of their own to be able to take advantage of the 75% subsidy in order to improve their own accommodation. In general the Acts failed to salvage whole areas and in 1974 a new Labour government tried again.

The Housing Act 1974 was both a supplement to the 1969 Act and a deviation from it. The 1974 Act retained the notion of area improvement and introduced Housing Action Areas, but these new areas were to be chosen not because they offered the right ingredients for success (the criteria for General Improvement Areas) but because their need was specially urgent. The new phrase 'housing stress' betokened a social need rather than material inducements. Grants were again 75% of cost but could rise to 90%, but action was once more disappointingly limited. By this date council budgets were being squeezed by the economic crisis; councils did not have the money to acquire, whether by their compulsory powers or by private treaty, the property which they wished to improve; and a number of urban councils became reluctant to buy property for improvements which they might be prevented from carrying out with the result that they would merely have taken derelict houses off the hands of private landlords. Once more the poorer housing was left unimproved and the poorer people indecently housed.

Between these two largely abortive excursions by Labour into improvement policy came the ambitious Conservative Housing Improvement Act 1972. The Conservatives wanted to prod private landlords into spending money on their property. Preferring carrots to sticks they allowed landlords to pass on to tenants any increase in rates and also to raise rents by a proportion of their expenditure on repairs. To counterbalance these increases, and in order to help tenants in difficulties with their rents without putting the screws on landlords, they introduced discretionary rent allowances, i.e. an *ad hoc* and means-tested subsidy in place of the overall subsidies entailed in rent freezes. Rent allowances, like the replacement of rent control by rent regulation, were a further step away from the general towards the particular. (Like all such steps they involved more administrative intervention, called by those who did not like it bureaucratisation.) The Conservatives were also successful once more in reining back the public sector; there was another sharp fall in building by councils. In 1974 Labour, with another Rent Act, extended regulation to furnished premises (but not to houses partly occupied by the owner). Evictions became much fewer; so too did privately owned premises offered for rent, which disappeared from the market. Protected tenants rejoiced; prospective tenants, particularly the single and the young in search of small flats, despaired.

Meanwhile the conditions in which many people lived remained shocking. In one sense they were more shocking than before because of changing ideas of what was adequate or decent. What had once been normal now seemed scandalous. Thus in Sunderland in the sixties nine out of ten families living in privately owned houses had no indoor lavatory (some had no functioning lavatory at all); three-quarters had no bath and half had not even cold water. Those without ocular knowledge of such facts found it difficult to believe them and preferable not to. At the end of our period there were in England and Wales some fifteen million houses, of which six million ante-dated the first world war and at least one million were over a hundred years old. Those without baths, lavatories and running hot water were numbered in millions. One million—certainly an underestimate—were rated as slums. Slum clearance was not only a lamentable failure but had proceeded more slowly than before the war. The target of 75,000 demolitions or closures a year in the fifties was never reached and had to be reduced to 60,000. In 1965–75 the actual number varied between 70,000 and 40,000—compared with 90,000 in the best prewar year (1938). The housing survey of 1968 classified one third of privately rented housing as uninhabitable; the number of uninhabitable houses in England and Wales was put at 1·8 million with a further 4·5 million lacking the basic amenities or in need of substantial repair, and these two categories together accounted for 40% of all housing. At least half a million families were sharing and as many as 30,000 were homeless.

Tenants became fewer in our period, the tenants of private landlords much fewer. By 1970 half the families in England lived in homes which they owned (subject or not to mortgages) and the proportion was continuing to rise. Of the other half two were council tenants for every one renting from a private landlord. Four out of five tenants of private landlords were in unfurnished premises. No tenant might be thrown out of the home which he was legally occupying except by order of a court and such an order was not easily obtained except for non-payment of rent, damage to the property or nuisance to the neighbours. In addition certain private tenants—but not council tenants—were protected by tribunals from arbitrary increases in rent and from abrupt eviction, which the tribunal might delay for six months (sometimes extending the delay by one, two or three further periods of the same length).

The story of housing was typical of much else in Britain in these years. Comparisons with the past showed many, sometimes striking, improvements: in the number of houses available, up by about 50%; in the rate of new building; in the average quality of the homes, whether newly built or old houses improved with the stimulus of government grants (which doubled in number after the Housing Act 1969); in the provision of basic amenities. But comparisons with what should be were much more dispiriting than comparisons with what had been. The slum-dwellers and the unhoused were not interested in what things had been like in their grandparents' day. And the cost of these housing failures was huge. In real terms the cost of subsidies almost doubled in the first half of the seventies. Local government was spending more on housing than anything else except education (over £3·3 billion by the end of our period) and was giving little satisfaction in the process. Rents were bringing in less than half of the councils' costs on housing, in some areas a quarter. The local authorities were crippling themselves in their efforts to cope with problems which were beyond them. Centrally, housing became the prime example of a problem which suffered from the shifts in policy which accompanied changes of government.

The provision of houses and their cost were intimately connected with two other things: the cost of the land on which the houses stood and control over the uses to which a particular area might be put, i.e. planning.

Land, as a commodity of finite extent, is peculiarly vulnerable to price inflation. A rising demand cannot be met by making more of it. Further, any proposal to build on unbuilt land, or rebuild on occupied land, automatically sends the price up so that the builder, unless he happens already to own the land, has to begin by paying a high price for it; and if the land is available for the construction of offices commanding higher rents than homes, a developer who wants that land for housing will—in a free market—have to pay office values for it and then either charge office prices or look to some source other than purchaser or tenant for the difference, i.e. a subsidy. There has therefore long been debate about how to limit the prices which may be demanded by lucky owners of land in the path of development. The simplest scheme is to take all land out of the market and vest it in public ownership. The main objection to this scheme, apart from the objections of owners, is its huge cost if anything like justice is to be done to owners. States in different parts of the world have appropriated and paid for large tracts of land but not in advanced industrial countries where money values are highest. (The last person to do it in England was William the Conqueror who became the owner of the whole place without paying.) Moreover the nationalisation of all land would include the cost of purchasing a lot of land not needed for development. At the other end of the scale are measures of piecemeal local purchase, if necessary under compulsory powers, as and when a piece of land is needed. The objection to these measures is that the land in question will have shot up in value by the time the purchase is made; if the need has to ante-date the purchase, the price will first be hoisted by the need. The principal attempt to meet this problem has been to establish two different values for the land—a use value and a market value—and to empower developers to purchase at the former. Finally, and in between these two varieties of scheme, comes the hybrid notion of extensive purchases by a public body which will pay the owner a fair price and resell to developers at a price which may be either higher or lower. The most notable scheme of this kind was propounded in 1960 by the Civic Trust, a non-political organisation, which proposed the creation of a Land Finance Corporation to buy all land needed for development in the foreseeable future, paying the owners current market values and reselling to governmental or private developers at use values. The Trust estimated that enough of these resales could be made at a profit—e.g. sales of commercially valuable property in city centres—to make the Corporation self-financing. This plan was attractive to socialists and to those owners anxious for a quick sale but it was disliked by Conservatives who were congenitally averse to a single large proprietor of this kind and preferred to leave most purchases for development to be made by private developers paying market values to be recovered from development profits—with local authorities as purchasers of last resort armed with compulsory powers for use when no other developer presented himself.

The Labour Party drew a sharp distinction between the profit motive and the public good. It believed that the private owner rarely, and the private developer never, tempered financial gain with social or environmental values. Socialist planning was therefore a conscious interposition of the state in order to prevent the misuse or non-use of land, and the principal instruments of this planning were local authorities who were in the first place required to draw up plans on which different areas would be designated for different purposes—residence, manufacture, recreation, etc. The Town and Country Planning Act 1947 entrusted this function not to the 1400 odd district councils but to the 145 larger authorities, the counties and county boroughs. It gave these planning authorities powers of compulsory purchase and created a Central Land Board to pay compensation to expropriated owners for loss of development value. The Act, following the report of the Uthwatt Committee established during the war (Cmd. 6386), imposed development charges to be paid to the Board by developers, official or private, and the Board was expected to earn in this way as much as it would need to pay compensation. The Conservative government abolished charges, compensation and Board. It permitted local authorities, but not private developers, to go on buying at use values until, by the Land Compensation Act 1961, this privilege was confined to new town corporations. Since market values included the accretions occasioned by the existence of council plans, councils ceased as far as possible to make plans or buy land.

After 1964 Labour reviewed its planning tactics in the hope of simplifying the cat's-cradle of plans, objections, amendments, inquiries and appeals which cumbered the scene and infuriated citizens, but a new Act in 1968 was not a great improvement on its predecessors. Planning still entailed lengthy procedures and safeguards in order to ensure adequate consultation and discussion, and planning still meant the physical planning of the terrain with social considerations coming a poor second. Planners got a bad name on both counts. At the same time the government tackled the land problem by creating a Land Commission which was a relative of the Central Land Board and went the same way as soon as the Conservatives got back to power. Back in office in 1974, Labour tried again with a White Paper (Cmd. 5730) in 1974 and the Community Land Act 1975. This was a two-tiered scheme. Its object was to shift all land required for development into public ownership in two stages. In the first local authorities were empowered to acquire such land, paying the market value. In the second they were required to buy the land, paying the current use value. Owner-occupiers were exempt from the Act's operation.

A special aspect of planning was the creation of new towns. One ancestor of the new town was the garden city, of which a few examples existed (Letchworth 1903, Welwyn 1920) and which had, as the name suggested, come into being as an exercise in planning for the tastes and amenities of the middle classes. Garden cities had been planned and owned by private companies which were profitable. The postwar new town had also other antecedents. It was designed as a receptacle as well as an enticement and was part of a policy to disperse the populations of big cities. During the war the Abercrombie plan for Greater London advocated the creation of ten new or enlarged towns to syphon away half a million Londoners and in 1946 the Reith Committee on new towns recommended (Cmd. 6759) the creation of new towns with initial populations of 15–20,000, whereafter they would grow by the light of nature: each new town would be developed by its own corporation operating as an instrument of the central government and armed with the compulsory purchase powers of the Town and Country Planning Acts. This report was swiftly followed by the relatively uncontentious New Towns Act 1946 by means of which the government aimed to create in England and Wales twenty new towns with 30–60,000 inhabitants each. This measure was followed by the Towns Development Act 1952 for the enlargement of selected existing towns. The most ambitious venture in this field came in the sixties with the planning of the new city of Milton Keynes in rural Buckinghamshire which was intended to grow to 250,000 inhabitants by the year 2000. By 1975 the development of new towns was suffering not only from the economic axe but also from the growing concern about the dilapidation of old city centres and slums, so that it seemed most unlikely that any more new towns would be founded and possible that some would be halted in their half-built tracks.

The world of housing, land and planning was a complex one where, besides officials and politicians, two other clusters operated—those of the wicked and of the illumined. In this period property-dealers amassed fortunes and some property-owners did so too. Never had they had it so good. Money was poured through the magnifying sieves of speculation, and the property market became so lucrative that banks, insurance companies, pension funds and financiers generally hurried into it, helped to promote it by inflationary funds and credit, and deflected to it vast sums which could have been put to more fruitful uses. Property companies multiplied and quickly departed from their original function of filling a postwar need, becoming instead speculative dealers with decreasing regard for this need. Asset-stripping became the rage and no assets were more eagerly stripped than land sites as new companies and old were tempted into this casino by the lure of the quick big buck. Nothing much was produced except cash gains for the successful operators—gains which became so enticing that even banks overcame their congenital caution and joined in one of the biggest misdirections of resources of modern times. The acme of this manic tarantella was in the early seventies.

But fortunately there is more to this depressing story than the shifts of party policies, the graspingness of speculators and the confusions of bureaucracy. The public voice was increasingly heard, if only as yet from the sidelines. To some extent this was an accepted and even an institutionalised fact. Official procedures provided for notice to the public, protests from the public, public inquiries and the like. Nor were these provisions mere formalities, the ritual small print which accompanied fore-ordained results: there was even a case in which a superior court rejected the argument that a man must be held to have read the small print in a contract, the court observing that it was well known that this was frequently not so. Individuals and groups of individuals, instead of moaning about the bureaucratic juggernaut, inquired into their rights and used them in particular cases or formed societies to promote certain aims or protect certain amenities. Without going so far as to accuse officials of malevolence they maintained that officials could be benevolent but wrong, that they were not necessarily in a position to tell what local opinion was, and that local opinion mattered. They discovered they were good for a news story. They interfered—successfully—with plans to build airports where they were not wanted, to route motorways one way when another would do less damage, to permit levels of noise or dirt which could be avoided by requiring a manufacturer to take a little more care or spend a little more money. One of the main enemies of good living was simply traffic—noisy, smelly and philoprogenitive. Among forms of traffic the motor-car with its motorways was the most ubiquitous, the aircraft the most destructive of peace and land. It was easy to regard both as sad necessities of material progress but this fatalism did not become universal, as was most strikingly demonstrated when governments concluded that London must have a third major, four-runway airport.

It is not clear where this conclusion came from, although it appears to have originated among civil servants who had in their charge a disused airfield at Stansted in Essex and wished, as proper departmental zealots, to prevent the land from being assigned to other purposes and other hands. A departmental committee formally recommended that Stansted be taken out of mothballs and converted into this third London airport, the need for which had never been established. Two ministers of aviation of different parties approved. Local inhabitants did not and succeeded in throwing doubt on the suitability of Stansted for the supposed need. A Royal Commission—the Roskill Commission—was established in 1968 not, however, to examine the need itself but to recommend where the new airport should be. Two years later it recommended by a majority a site in Buckinghamshire round the village of Cublington. Local inhabitants organised such determined opposition that it seemed that old ladies armed with pitchforks would have to be forcibly evicted from their homes and fields if the recommendation were accepted. At this point the government changed hands and the Conservatives dropped Cublington and adopted and amplified the recommendation of a solitary voice on the Roskill Commission to build instead, at Maplin or Foulness on the Essex coast, an airport, a harbour and a new town. This grandiose plan was in turn dropped after the Labour victory of 1974, by which time doubts had grown about the need for a third major London airport as opposed to a big airport much further north or no big airport at all. Assessing these needs was clearly very difficult, since a decision would turn partly on prophecies about a number of things including the volume of international air traffic in years to come and its nature. What was, however, clear was that public opinion had played a part, whether wise or blinkered, over the siting of an airport at Stansted or at Cublington. It was a famous victory.

This is not to say that until this time government and officialdom had been insensitive, and the public impotent, in matters of this kind, but both the area of debate and its effectiveness had been largely confined to the dead past as opposed to the amenities of living. Ancient monuments were first officially protected in 1882 when the Office of Works was authorised to take them into custody and this protection was extended to houses in current use fifty years later.* At the end of the second world war the Ministry of Works (as it had become) was required to list buildings whose owners would then be prohibited from destroying them or making unauthorised changes and twenty years later whole areas, as distinct from particular buildings, were given similar protection under the name of conservation areas.† The safeguards and procedures were tightened and tidied up in a further series of statutes which testify to the concern of governments and the activity of non-official bodies in a field in which Britain was an enlightened and effective pioneer.‡ A conspicuous instance of this effectiveness was the abrogation in 1959 of plans for the development of Piccadilly Circus as a result of popular agitation. Besides buildings and architectural areas, national parks and areas of outstanding natural beauty were also established and protected by legislation. There was in these proceedings some adventitious aid from the increased economic importance of foreign tourists and so from the need to care for what they came to see, but it would be unduly cynical to overplay the impact of these material considerations which were subordinate to the growing concern for other values inherent, first, in the conservation of the visible past and later in the protection of the whole human environment and its gifts. There was furthermore a qualitative change from the archaism of those who wanted to restore relics of the past to their primitive shape, to the conservation or rehabilitation of the national heritage as an integrated part of a living society.

---

* The Ancient Monuments Protection Act 1882 and the Town and Country Planning Act 1932.

† The Town and Country Planning Acts 1944 and 1947, and the Civic Amenities Act 1967.

‡ These further Acts included the Town and Country Planning Acts 1968, 1971 and 1974.

All this was creditable and promising, and yet peripheral to the central issues of housing and land use where, as in the areas of poverty and inequality, the record was a disappointing one—a failure and not just an economic failure. In 1975 the blemishes on the record looked bigger than the bright spots and the mood was reproachful. Yet for all the shortcomings there was one noteworthy change for the better. Architects added a dimension to their complex vocation. In the past the architect had asked his rich client what he wanted, but not his poorer clients. A bizarre mistake altered this. For a period much ingenuity and money were devoted to building huge high towers from which, it was supposed, families would gaze enraptured over landscape or townscape, liberated from the noxious urban airs below. But the families, isolated, insecure, deprived of the conviviality of the street and perplexed about what to do with the children, hated their new homes, and when this miscalculation became evident it dealt a severe blow to the view that a professional minority can without inquiry tell what other people like.

3 Education

If the English pioneered industrial revolution in the eighteenth and nineteenth centuries, and political revolution in the seventeenth, they can claim no such laurels in the field of education. The English universities (plural but only just) held an honoured place in post-Reformation humanist studies and the Victorians gave a spurt to secondary and university education, but by and large the English view of education in these centuries was that it was for the few who could afford it and that it had nothing to do with vocational or even professional training which was provided by varieties of apprenticeship. England followed a western European pattern which was narrowly elitist, clerical, classical and humanist. But somewhere in the background a different tradition persisted, the tradition of charitably endowed education which had prompted rich men and women to found colleges and schools for the instruction of people quite unlike themselves. Over the centuries these colleges and schools strayed from their founders' intentions but new institutions appeared to do the job and keep the tradition alive.

From the heyday of the Utilitarians in the early nineteenth century the English universities and public schools, and the grammar schools too, were under attack, accused of lagging behind the times, of teaching the wrong subjects or at any rate failing to teach the newer ones, of betraying their founders' trusts, of inculcating blind deference to the established church and the ruling class. Would-be reformers created University College in London, which they hoped to develop into a new kind of university, and also a number of schools with what were for those days modern curricula and a liberating freedom from partisan prelatical purpose. They promoted Mechanics Institutes and Dissenting Academies and waged campaigns against taxes on knowledge, but they still barely reached the working classes* who were dependent on such

---

* People fight shy of this term nowadays because it suggests that only a manual worker works. Another objection is that it too frequently denotes those who cannot get work. But it is a useful phrase and means what most people think it means.

ventures as Owenite schools radiating from New Lanark or the Hampden Clubs where working men (not women) met to listen to readings of Cobbett and the like. Education was at the centre of social and political reform movements, including Chartism which produced plans—some of them put into execution—for schools of various kinds and teacher training institutions: the Chartists advocated education at public expense. A hundred years later these seeds sprouted as it became widely accepted that what is taught and who is taught should be broadened and that the state should take a hand in making this possible and making it happen. In the nineteenth century, however, the aspirations of middle-class radicals and working-class self-improvers reaped meagre fruit and the main, if modest, stream of reform flowed rather through established institutions, improving but not much supplementing them.

On this comparatively narrow front the Victorians did good work. Accepting the view that education, though a private matter, was also a subject for public concern, they attacked it with their favourite instrument, the Royal Commission, which they directed at Oxford and Cambridge and the public schools. These universities, which had fallen into the comic sloth portrayed by Gibbon, were probed and reanimated (developing empire gave them a new purpose too) and the public schools, which numbered only nine at the time of the parallel inquiry of 1861, were given such a boost that a hundred years later there were over 200 of them: these schools were adventitiously helped by the building of the railways which strengthened the strong ones by extending their catchment area and enabled parents to send their male offspring even farther away from home. But it took a new European power, Prussia, to make real changes in the content of education and in set notions of whom it was for. In nineteenth-century Germany sciences and engineering were raised to the same status as the classics; modern research methods, institutes, examinations and degrees were invented; many more universities were provided; technical schools (*Realschulen*), equivalent in status to grammar schools, were founded; and the first steps were taken towards an integrated, in modern parlance comprehensive, schools system. These German examples were quickly copied in the USA and contributed not a little to the bounding history of that country in the present century.

The education of children in England, outside the public schools, was until recently regarded neither as a duty nor as a benefit to the nation but as a charity, and it was largely conducted by the churches as the residual legatees of mediaeval clerical literacy. (In English law a trust for educational purposes is *ipso facto* a charitable trust.) The state first intervened in 1833 when it was authorised, but not required, by Act of Parliament to spend small sums to supplement the education provided by churches for the poor and from 1839 the disbursement of this meagre aid was supervised by a committee of the Privy Council which was to grow through various stages into one of the great departments of state and, soon after the mid-twentieth century, the second biggest spender among all government departments. The effective beginning of governmental responsibility comes, however, with the Elementary Education Act 1870 (Forster's Act), whose main aim was to fill through state intervention the gaps in the haphazard pattern of church schools. This Act created local school boards charged with the establishment, where necessary, of new elementary schools for the poor. Although still ancillary to the charitable system these boards, transformed in 1902 into local education authorities, were the precursors of the twentieth-century state system. Most of the teachers in these schools had themselves left school at 12, begun teaching the next year and just kept going. Spending on education was equivalent to 1% of the national income—of the richest country in the world. Many schools were insanitary. There were about 80 children to a class.

The Education Act 1902 (Balfour's Act) followed Forster's Act by empowering, but again not requiring, local authorities to provide post-elementary schooling of their own besides contributing to church schools, but the statutory school-leaving age remained at 12. There was still more teaching by churches and other charities than in state schools but the former gradually ran into financial troubles which obliged them to look increasingly to the state for help. At the end of the first world war fees in elementary schools were abolished, the school-leaving age was raised to 14 and local authorities were empowered to appoint education officers. In 1936 Parliament decreed that the school-leaving age should go up to 15 in September 1939 but on the outbreak of war this provision was cancelled. Between the wars schools became differentiated into elementary and senior elementary, but, apart from the few who won places in grammar schools, there was no secondary education distinct from the mere extension of the time spent by the child in the local school.

When the second world war began most of the schools in England were still private schools and most teachers were in these schools. The state sector was the smaller and there was hardly any secondary education for those below the middle classes. War once more stirred the public conscience and parliament. It gave rise to social questioning in the course of which it became clear to many who had not previously given the matter much thought that class discrimination was keeping education from many children who were both entitled to it and capable of turning it to good account, and that parsimony was keeping standards low. All this was not merely a national disgrace but also a national loss and before the war ended a new report (the Norwood Report, 1943) was presented to parliament which in the following year enacted the Education Act 1944 (Butler's Act).

This Act, in the tradition of all the Education Acts from 1870 onwards, aimed to expand the system which it had inherited. It aimed to get more children into the system rather than to alter either the system itself or the nature of the education it provided. In particular Butler's Act set out to provide free secondary education—something that Matthew Arnold among others had been arguing for in the previous century. It followed the Norwood Report in establishing a tripartite pattern of grammar schools, secondary modern schools and secondary technical schools. The last type, derived from a small number of junior technical schools, never came to much and for the most part the new state secondary schools constituted a dual system which quickly gave rise to controversy in professional and then in political circles. The charity schools became either 'controlled' or 'aided' according to the extent of public finance which they required: in the former a majority of the teachers were to be appointed by the local authority. The public schools were untouched by the Act and remained effectively so in spite of schemes to give a handful of places to boys who would not normally go to them and would be picked and paid for by local authorities (an awkward reversion to the role envisaged by William of Wykeham, Henry VI and such benefactors).

Butler's Act did not directly interfere with the basic principle that public education was primarily a matter for local authorities but it strengthened the central and the professional elements in policy-making. The President of the Board of Education (the Board being in theory a committee of the Privy Council) was transformed into a minister and twenty years later into a secretary of state. In most postwar administrations the minister was in the cabinet. He had a statutory duty to report annually to parliament on the state of the nation's education. The Act gave him authority to intervene through statutory regulations concerning admissions to schools, amenities, repairs and the qualifications (though not the appointment) of teachers. He had the power of the purse. He had too a central advisory council and an inspectorate; the former surveyed and reported on broad educational questions from time to time, while the latter—created in the nineteenth century* and now organised over ten areas and 500 districts in England and Wales— acquired considerable respect and so influence through its visitations and reports on teaching methods and conditions in all schools, state and other. The inspectors were recruited from the teaching profession. Locally the Act established 146 local education authorities (the number later grew), conterminous with counties, county boroughs and the London boroughs; they operated through mixed committees of local councillors and salaried education officers. The appointment of the chief education officer of an LEA required the minister's confirmation.

After the war the school population rose sharply, particularly when the leaving age was raised in 1947 to 15 and when the wartime birth bulge hit the primary schools in the fifties. The raising of the leaving age to 15 added about 390,000 children to the secondary schools in England and Wales. (The age was raised to 16 in 1972 with similar effect.) When the war ended there were about five million children in state schools ranging from nursery schools to secondary schools.† Thirty years later the comparable figures were close on eight million. This multitude had to be accommodated, paid for and taught. The need for teachers and buildings became urgent. The number of teachers rose from under 200,000 in 1945 to over 300,000 in 1975; a fifth of them came into the profession through universities and proceeded mostly to the public schools or grammar schools, the rest went to teacher training colleges and thence mostly to secondary modern schools. These training colleges were specialist institutions with their origins in the nineteenth

---

* Matthew Arnold was an inspector for 35 years. W. E. Forster, whose name is associated with the 1870 Act, was his brother-in-law.

† The introduction of the term 'middle school' confused the nomenclature. Primary school includes infant school (5–7) and junior school (7–11). Middle schools take on children from 8 to 10 and have done with them at 12 to 14, transmitting most of them to comprehensive secondary schools.

century and devoted entirely to the vocational training of teachers. On the eve of war they had provided places for 12,000 students doing two-year courses but immediately after the war the number of places was increased by half and by 1950 it had doubled to meet the wartime bulge in the population and the raising of the school-leaving age to 15. In the fifties the number of places was further increased but not so much in order to take more students as to enable the colleges to give three-year instead of two-year courses. Expansion continued in the sixties in anticipation of the further raising of the school-leaving age and the introduction of four-year courses as well as for the purpose of reducing the size of classes by providing more teachers. By 1972 the number of places in colleges stood at 114,000 but in this year a planned reduction was begun by Margaret Thatcher; it was continued by her successors at the Department of Education. This reduction was dictated by financial considerations and facilitated by forecasts of a declining population but it entailed the freezing of teacher-pupil ratios which preceding governments had laboured to reduce—and had succeeded in reducing over our period by 4–5 children per class (the averages in primary and secondary schools in 1975 were 25 and 17.5). During these years too teacher training ceased to be organised predominantly as a distinct branch of education. Although the proposals of the Robbins Committee (see below) for lodging teacher training in the wider ambit of universities was not accepted, government policy from the mid-sixties was to ally it to the polytechnics, to reduce the number of colleges (now renamed colleges of education) and to leave only a dozen or two as separate institutions specialising exclusively in teacher training.

During 1945–75 new building provided 7.5 million extra places in schools, divided roughly equally between primary and secondary schools. In the last ten years of this period new places were being provided annually at rates between 330,000 and 425,000. This building needed money, as too did new equipment and better teachers' salaries and training. Education overtook defence as second in the list of government spending at the end of the sixties (social security benefits exceeding both).

The problems were not simply logistical. This massive expansion, due mainly to the superimposition of free universal secondary education on free universal primary education, emphasised that the difference between the primary school and the secondary school was much more than the difference between the ages of the children in them. The children in the primary school were all destined for the same goal, the secondary school. Some areas had much better primary schools than others; some children were less bright than others, or subnormal in intelligence or handicapped in other ways. These social and educational problems were tackled alongside a general revolution in methods of teaching young and very young children. They attracted considerable professional attention and interest but not much more. The case of the secondary schools was different.

The raising of the leaving age to 15 and then 16 coincided with an observable change in the answer to the question: when is a child not a child? Children were maturing earlier, or at any rate were generally believed to be doing so. Adults were obliged to abandon the notion that schooling and puberty did not overlap. Teenagers acquired a culture of their own complete with dress styles, aesthetic tastes, independent ideas and ultimately the vote. Yet half the time they were still in school. Leading a dual life is neither uncommon nor particularly difficult, but it becomes difficult if the goals of the one life or the other are unclear. The secondary school prescribed no single simple goal, as the primary school did. It might be a road to a job or to a university or what was more vaguely described as preparation for life—or even, for some older children, a nuisance—and if it was all these things the curricula had to be more diverse and flexible—as many educators prescribed, including reports presented by the central advisory council in 1959 and 1963 (the Crowther and Newsom Reports). Pupils themselves were asking for this diversity either explicitly or by manifesting their boredom with existing courses which seemed to them irrelevant to whatever goal they might have in mind; and pupils in secondary schools, unlike pupils in primary schools, were acquiring a voice in their own education partly because they were staying at school until they were older and partly because it was no longer the fashion to say that children should be seen but not heard: it was impossible not to hear them—indeed it was often easier to hear than see them, truancy being what it was.

Teachers, far more numerous than before the war and much less inclined to regard the profession as an enclosure from which the world and its problems were excluded, were divided. Many followed a tradition which taught that the teacher's job was first and foremost to impart his own superior knowledge while at the same time expanding the pupil's mind by some judicious flights into ideas but also protecting the precious years of childhood from the premature incursion of the pains and penalties of adulthood. Others rebelled against this recipe, maintaining that children could only be prepared for life by acquaintance with its problems and should in any case be treated as responsible human beings by the time they reached their mid-teens; there was here more concern to prepare for life than to prepare, more precisely, for examinations and consequently a looser style of education which, however well grounded in educational and psychological theory, was more difficult to conduct, did not always work and tended to irritate parents.

There was therefore conflict within the profession and between the profession and others, particularly parents. This conflict was exacerbated and politicised by another about the organisation of secondary education.

In preferring the tripartite pattern to the single comprehensive or, as it was then more frequently called, multilateral school the Butler Act created a need for some method of selection at the end of the primary stage. Since grammar schools were much fewer (there were not many more than a thousand of them) as well as older than the secondary modern schools invented in 1944 the two kinds of school became immediately typed as first- and second-class institutions. The Act did not, however, reject the comprehensive idea. On the contrary it required local authorities to prepare and present comprehensive schemes to the minister and, although this requirement was widely regarded as a long-term injunction to be taken in a leisurely stride, a number of authorities set about making plans, some experimentally and sparsely, others over their whole field. The basic structure of English education encouraged this diversity of approach but alongside the diversity was also controversy of a different kind. If secondary education was to be comprehensive, what was to happen to the grammar schools and their staffs? Were they to be engulfed or left on one side?

The Labour Party's policy was to encourage local authorities to go comprehensive but neither to compel them nor force the pace. The policy was a typically gradualist Fabian one (though the Fabian Society itself took a sharper line) and anything like an immediate imposition of comprehensiveness was advocated only by a minority centrally or locally. But the maintenance of the dual system was not only offensive to those who were repelled by the division of children into sheep and goats; it was also under fire from a more technical standpoint as psychologists insisted with increasing vehemence and unanimity that the testing of a child's intelligence at the age of 11+ was a hopelessly hit-and-miss affair. The voice of the expert was tellingly added to that of the egalitarian. On the other side of what was soon to become a fairly stout fence Conservatives had begun by taking no very precise attitude for or against comprehensives. Many of them had been more concerned to extol and defend the public schools than the grammar schools with which their leaders were not well acquainted, but the left's increasing championship of comprehensiveness and the emergence of a grammar school lobby in search of political support inevitably produced on the Conservative side a body hostile to comprehensives as such. The grammar schools were not without support in the Labour Party at Westminster and in the constituencies and many Conservatives, including ministers, were reluctant to take an extreme stand against comprehensives, but active groups on both sides within the teaching profession hardened the lines and made a battle of it.

This battle became more than a little tinged with ideological prejudice. On the one side the dual system was denounced as a denial of equality of opportunity and a form of discrimination in favour of children who, more through luck and environment than natural endowment, were able to get the earlier and better teaching which helped them to do well in the types of examination which opened the doors of the grammar school and much else beyond. In this camp the grammar school stood for privilege, but on the other side it stood for quality (both of course were right). Here it was argued that cleverer children, who could be identified, needed and deserved separate schooling, that it was in the national interest that they should get it, and that separate schooling meant separate institutions and buildings. But although the temper of the debate and some of the arguments had echoes of class warfare, the critical element was not ideological but professional. Enemies of the dual system pointed to experiments, notably in Sweden, which disproved the need of the brightest pupils to be segregated; attacked the ability tests in current use on the grounds that, since they were unconsciously framed to pick out a certain kind of child, they did no more than endorse existing methods; and extended the debate about the nature of intelligence to show that it was not simply a gift present or not at birth but a potentiality to be developed by circumstances, of which education itself was one, after as well as before 11+. In 1957 the British Psychological Society condemned intelligence tests as a way of sorting out children and in the same year the National Federation for Educational Research reported that 12% of children were being sent to the wrong schools by 11+ selection. The general conclusion was that intelligence was a product of education and not a precondition for it, and that therefore it could not be evaluated at so early a stage in the educational process.

Local authorities went on preparing comprehensive schemes but the party political involvement made the growth of comprehensives sporadic. During the years of Conservative rule (1951–64) the government vetoed as many schemes as possible but was careful not to obstruct local authorities which wanted to go comprehensive. The result was a slow spread of comprehensives which displeased both sides. Conservatives made headway with parents who believed that a comprehensive must automatically be very big and so less attentive to individual children. When Labour came back in 1964 the number of comprehensives had risen from 10 (in 1951) to 175—against 4000 secondary modern schools and 1300 grammar schools. Of the 2.8 million children of secondary age a quarter were in grammar schools and 6% in comprehensives.

In 1965 the Department of Education issued Circular 10/65 which requested authorities to go comprehensive and cited a number of models from which they might choose. The choices may have confused some authorities and retarded progress, and since the Department was still doing no more than urge the impetus it administered was negligible and often neglected. The central government remained reluctant to give instructions in a field in which traditionally local government had the bigger say, and confined itself to negative pressures such as refusing funds for building when projects were not in line with basic Labour policy. Some authorities went ahead with determination, some stalled with equal determination and many dithered. In local elections in 1967 Labour lost control of a number of authorities—including, surprisingly, the Inner London Education Authority which had been created in 1964 to cover the old London County Council when this area had become part of the much larger Greater London Council. Yet by 1970 the number of comprehensives in more or less working order had risen to 1145 and 31% of secondary school children were being taught in them. The return of the Conservatives put a damper on the process: Circular 10/65 was annulled and local authorities were relieved of the modest pressures or encouragement which it had exerted. But nevertheless the trend was not entirely halted. Labour, back in office in 1974, renewed the pressures and the new secretary of state immediately announced that the 11+ examination, the instrument of discrimination, would be discontinued. Meanwhile the battle had changed. It was no longer a fight over comprehensiveness in general but a fight to retard locally or permit local exceptions to what was becoming the general rule.

For most of our period secondary education ended at 15 (1947–72). Higher education began at around 18. This gap was studied by the Crowther Report which appeared in 1959. Besides recommending the raising of the school-leaving age to 16 at some point between 1966 and 1969 (a recommendation sharpened in 1963 by the Newsom Report which recommended that the age be raised with the intake of 1965) the Crowther Report advocated compulsory part-time education in county colleges for all up to the age of 18 and also the expansion of full-time education for school-leavers until it covered 50% instead of 12% of them. Nothing much came of these proposals and the English upper teenage population remained therefore divided between school-leavers and a minority of school-attenders hoping to go on to university or polytechnics.

The English universities were in 1945 few and self-governing. They set their own standards, gave their own degrees and had preponderantly male student bodies. They became within a generation many, more mixed and heavily dependent on public money—for about three-quarters of their budgets. This change was brought about by a study of the needs of the nation as a whole rather than by any change of attitude about the entitlement of the individual to higher education. Since 1944 secondary education had become a right. There was no suggestion that higher education should be a right, only that there ought to be more of it. The tendency in the USA, begun by the Morrill Act of 1862 and the Land Grant Colleges, to open higher education to something like half the population, was neither practical nor much favoured in England a century later.

In 1963 a Committee on Higher Education under the chairmanship of Lord Robbins reported that there was a need, a potentiality and a demand for much more post-school education than existed. At the date of this report there were in Britain 216,000 places for full-time students, rather more than half of them (118,000) in 31 universities and the rest in teacher training colleges, technical colleges and other colleges for further education. The university population, which stood at 20,000 at the beginning of the century, had been increased after 1945 by expanding existing universities—Oxford, for example, where only one new college for male undergraduates was founded between 1714 and 1950 and which had kept its student body around 3500–4500 for half a century, increased it to 7000 after the war (partly in the expectation that this was a temporary expansion to cater for demobilised ex-servicemen and women)—and by founding eight new English universities which, unlike the civic foundations of the previous century, were set down in green fields or agreeable minor cities.* But the universities could still take no more than 3–4% of each age-group, with other full-time institutions of higher education accommodating a further 2%. The Robbins Committee accepted wholeheartedly the arguments for spending public money on university and other further education and recommended that the 216,000 places be increased to 560,000 by 1980. It was convinced that a big pool of untapped talent existed and that those who had it would respond to the opportunity to use it in this way. It rejected the argument that more means worse, that standards of achievement and teaching would fall if the gates were opened wider. The report preferred further university expansion to the creation of different types of institution such as the Liberal Arts Colleges or Junior Colleges of the USA. It recommended therefore the creation of six more new universities and the conversion into universities of the Colleges of Advanced Technology (so renamed in 1956, originally Technical Colleges), although it was intended that these should remain preponderantly scientific: the six new universities were not created but the CATs were converted. The report also devised one new institution or, more properly, a new name for an existing type of institution of which it wished to see more. These were the SISTERs, Special Institutions for Scientific and Technological Education and Research, two to be created from scratch and three to join the group by including in it Imperial College, the Manchester College of Science and Technology and Royal College, Glasgow. This proposal fell on stony ground. The report wanted teacher training colleges to be renamed colleges of education and absorbed into universities: they were renamed but not absorbed and they tended in consequence to become refuges for those who failed to get into a university, although some of them established a symbiotic relationship with a near-by university. An important and overdue recommendation was

* Keele, Sussex, York, Essex, Anglia, Kent, Lancaster and Warwick. Four new universities were created in Scotland.

that universities should pay more attention to graduate students and have more of them. The English universities had concentrated on undergraduate teaching and the three-year BA or BSc, providing excellent education at this level; but the level remained nevertheless an intermediate rather than a specialist one and graduate students, when they were visible at all, had had to struggle for attention in the narrow ground between undergraduate teaching and the research undertaken by senior members of the university on their own account. The MA degree was little prized (except, before the war, by intending school-masters and clergymen and, after it, by those who found in its pursuit a reason for lingering in the groves of academe), while the more searching PhD tended to be denigrated by a generation of teachers who had got on without it. Graduate studies impinged on undergraduate courses. The increased attention to further degrees, coupled with the growth in the number and variety of first-degree students, raised questions about the nature of the first degree. First-year courses became both more general and more elementary. Many students and teachers wanted the first-degree course to be more variable, a development of certain prewar experiments in mixed courses; greater specialisation was more often postponed to graduate courses.

The Robbins Committee estimated that the implementation of its report would raise public expenditure on higher education from £206 million in 1962 to £742 million in 1980 (at constant prices), increasing it from rather under to rather over 1 % of GNP. It strongly favoured the provision of public money by a block grant to be allocated by the Universities Grants Commission which, though appointed by and answerable to a minister, should continue to consist of university and other educational experts. Government intervention, inherent in the provision of public funds, should be exercised indirectly and, even by the UGC itself, *ex post facto*: the UGC would not normally prescribe projects or earmark funds, although it would monitor the use of funds and turn a deafer or benigner ear to future requests in the light of past performance. The Robbins Report proposed that university fees be raised to cover at least 20 per cent of current expenditure; some members of the committee wished to make this proportion higher.

The Robbins recommendations were largely ignored. The six new universities were not created, nor were the new SISTERs. The colleges of education were not annexed to universities. The principal change promoted by Robbins was the transformation of ten CATs into universities, but all ten were already in existence. Nevertheless a considerable expansion in numbers took place and with nearly 500,000 places available for full-time higher education in 1975 the Robbins target of 560,000 by 1980 would not have been altogether out of sight but for the halt imposed by the economic crisis of these years. Of the places available in 1975 258,000 were in universities, 117,000 in colleges of education and 121,000 elsewhere. (These figures were for the whole of the United Kingdom.)

In addition to higher education there was the confusingly entitled 'further education', the distinction lying in the nature of the qualifications aimed at. Further education had its roots in the technical colleges. These institutions, which existed under a variety of names, had been very popular in the latter part of the nineteenth century, had then suffered lean times in the first half of the present century but had made a robust comeback after 1945. Together with a smaller quota of specifically art or agricultural colleges they numbered about 600, providing mostly part-time courses, teaching largely in the evening, closely linked with industry and commerce in their areas, preparing for a wide variety of vocational or professional diplomas or none. Together with 5–6000 evening institutes they constituted a second arm of post-school education catering by 1975 for nearly 300,000 full-time students as well as over three million others from school-leaving age upwards. This duality, with its inherent dangers of a division into superior and inferior, was deplored by some but could hardly be avoided unless the universities were to be vastly expanded and radically transformed. The binary system received official government blessing in 1965 and a year later a White Paper proposed the creation of up to thirty polytechnics consisting of a single college or grouping of colleges where the full-time students would be concentrated and the teaching would approximate in scope to university work. The full complement of polytechnics was reached in 1971.

The most remarkable educational innovation in the period covered by this book occurred in adult education. The possibilities in this area were diverse and unco-ordinated. They included the Workers' Educational Association, extra-mural departments of universities, certain radio and television programmes of the BBC, an excellent and free public lending library service, public lectures of every conceivable kind supplied (mostly in towns) by innumerable learned bodies. To these were added the Open University, mooted in 1963 by Harold Wilson under the name of University of the Air and endorsed by the Robbins Report. The Open University was created by Royal Charter in 1969 and set up its headquarters on a few unoccupied acres within the bounds of what was to be the new city of Milton Keynes. It began teaching its first 20,000 students in 1971. By its fifth year (1975) it had 50,000 students. Apart from a handful of post-graduate students working at Milton Keynes all these students stayed at home, receiving weekly packages and tasks. They were advised to attend to radio and television programmes devised by university and BBC staff and put out (each programme twice) by the BBC which provided 30 hours of radio and 30 hours of television a week at a cost of £3.2 million. Students were also helped by part-time tutors living near their homes and available at set times and places for groups of students and also informally on the telephone. One of the university's many successes was its ability to recruit these tutors all over the country, who frequently gave far more time to this work than the university asked of them. All students also attended an annual summer school.

Applicants had to be over 21 (but in 1974 a small breach was made in this rule experimentally) and one of the main hopes of the university's founders was that it would cater for older men and women who had had no chance in their youth to sample the mysteries and excitements of advanced learning. Applicants outnumbered available places by 2 to 1 in every year. In the first two years much the largest number were aged 26–40; in the succeeding years the weight shifted to 21–30. Those over 50 were a very small proportion. Fees were comparatively low: £6 per course initially, raised to £25 in 1973 (and to £40 in 1976). Students had also to buy books costing £10–15 per course, to which local authorities might or might not contribute. Each course occupied most of a calendar year, beginning in January. Six courses successfully completed earned a pass degree, eight an honours degree. A student might take two courses in a year but few did. There was no time-limit within which a degree had to be earned. The courses were graded in four levels and a student might not proceed from one level to the next until he had got a pass at the lower level. About a quarter of the new students dropped out in the first few months of the year for a variety of reasons. Some found that they could not keep up intellectually; others found domestic or other current duties too much; yet others discovered that what they were offered was not what they had expected. Besides BA courses and postgraduate research the university devised post-graduate courses of varying lengths (in months) which were designed to help those—500 by 1975—who wanted studies relevant to their careers. These courses were completed by an examination but carried no degree.

The university was financed by the Department of Education and Science (not by the Treasury through the University Grants Committee) and the cost to public funds rose from £6 million in 1971 to over £16 million in 1975 (equivalent to £9.5 million at 1971 prices and for more than twice as many students). This was a cheap way to produce graduates. It was also a method which attracted foreign attention not merely on economic grounds but because its techniques enabled large numbers of students to be taught without assembling them on residential campuses where they might engage in political protest and riot instead of sticking to their books.

The Open University was one of the great inventions of this period and a testimony to the continuing vitality of Britain. Between the wars the cultural scene had been enriched first by the BBC and then by Penguin Books and it was a heartening symptom to observe that as those institutions lost much of their pre-eminent purpose and flavour something else new emerged from the British genius.

At the close of these thirty years, when much in Britain was being questioned and doubted, the state of public education came in for as much criticism as anything else. At the beginning of this period primary education was universal, comprehensive and free. Thirty years later secondary education had become universal and free and had been extended from 14 to 16; it was becoming comprehensive but was neither fully so nor happily so. Higher education was selective but not selective in the sense that secondary education was still partially selective at 11+. The secondary schools discriminated between children of varying capacity in order to direct them into different kinds of institution. University selection on the other hand determined who should enter and who should be debarred. Places, although much more numerous than before the war, were still relatively few and had to be competed for. A University place was a prize and not a right. Successful candidates were largely paid for out of the public purse. There remained islands of private education in schools for all ages, exciting the censure of social purists, providing education ranging from the very good to the very bad, statistically inconsequential. There was also a single venture into the field of university education wholly unsupported by public funds—the

University College at Buckingham—partly an educational experiment and partly an ideological gesture. Education became in these years the largest single charge on public funds.

The question who should be given education was answered to the effect that everybody should be given it, free, up to the age of 16. Beyond that age further education, whether in universities or (though much less so) in technical colleges, polytechnics etc., required certain tests and qualifications, but the ability to pay was ceasing to be one of them.

The question who should provide the education was decisively answered at one level but not so decisively at another. The state should provide. Church and other private schools were all but completely pushed aside, mainly because they could no longer meet the costs of modern education with its expensive equipment, properly paid teachers and higher standards of building and hygiene. This reversal of the laissez-faire principle that the role of the state was to do no more than plug gaps and cough up essential ancillary finance brought England into line with Scotland and continental Europe. What was less decisively settled was where within the state the focus of authority should lie. In theory the local authority dominated, even after other services such as health had been reorganised in broader regions or centralised. The tradition of local control was particularly strong in education and was reinforced by parental interest which was itself increased by the controversy over comprehensives, but the Act of 1944 had conversely given the Department of Education increased authority over and above, if partly in consequence of, its overwhelming financial power. (The universities, with their bizarrely entrenched independence, were much better able to resist intervention by government which was in any case even less keen to obtrude itself into higher education than into schools.) Politicians, with their roots in their constituencies, were not minded to abet any shift of control from the locality to the centre, but teachers and other educational specialists were divided. Many teachers, particularly those with a more experimental turn of mind, distrusted central authority for its remoteness from the classroom, its natural proclivity to uniformity and its wariness of change. Others, critical of the achievements of the schools in these years, looked to the Department, the inspectorate and if necessary the Secretary of State to exercise more authority over the maintenance of standards and results. This trend cut into party politics, since clamour about falling standards came chiefly from the right, which was however congenitally averse to every strengthening of central government. (The left too was worried but more defensively and less clamorously.)

It became common in the seventies to talk about a crisis in education. Polemics apart, this meant that the schools were not producing good enough results. To some extent this was part of the dislocations of the age referred to in the first chapter of this book. The war had been a spur to change and advance. It had also, for the second time in less than half a century, debilitated the nation's resources at precisely the moment when it wished to use them in generous and imaginative initiatives. High hopes and great plans were nipped by diminished resources. The eager kicked against the pricks, the more so when admonished by sour reactionaries who could not be silenced because some of what they said was valid. The Act of 1944 had set a new scene and teachers had begun to try new ideas upon it.

Moreover, like every extension of school education this Act marked a further stage in a process which had been going on for generations—the usurpation by the school of one of the prime functions and justifications of the family: the imparting of knowledge and of values. This usurpation had been little remarked or challenged so long as the school was doing merely what parents could understand and approve, but parents became uneasy when teachers adopted bright new teaching methods which seemed to some undoubtedly new but not so undoubtedly bright. Did the younger teachers really know what they were up to? Did their enthusiasm for the new lead them to forget fundamentals like discipline and the three Rs? How many of the teachers pouring out of the new colleges of education were more interested in changing society than getting little Johnnie along? Did the new methods really benefit the children?

This last and most serious question was difficult to answer because there was no longer agreement on how to compare one school-leaver with another or tell which had been better educated: there was less agreement than there had been about the purposes of education and the tasks of the teacher. On the one hand was an axiomatically held belief that what the teacher had to do was convey knowledge and ideas. On the other was an equally firm commitment to developing the child's personality and potentiality, and not necessarily by stuffing its mind. The pendulum swung between these poles and in doing so raised not merely problems but conflict. It was not so easy to show that a child's personality had been developed as to demonstrate that it could not spell, count or pass examinations.

In these years English education confronted two things which had been perennially at its centre: authority and elitism. The word 'authoritarian' had become synonymous with the Nazi and Stalinist tyrannies. One of the more sinister legacies of these monstrosities was the perversion of language and ideas. A world racked by authoritarianism forgot that authority is morally neutral and that what makes it good or bad are the uses to which it is put. Authority was itself besmirched. The teacher was no longer looked up to in his little world; even the professor, who had been a very superior personage, became little more than a better paid lecturer—partly because professors became two a penny but more so because top people as such no longer commanded respect.

A second cause of this slump in authority was paradoxically better education. Young people were trained to observe and judge and came sometimes to the conclusion that those in authority over them were fallible, intellectually or indeed morally—thick heads and feet of clay. Another cause was the increasing revulsion against privilege when the path to the top was still in some areas smoother for those with the right connections: the cousinage, thought to have given way to the meritocracy, made a comeback. The effects in schools were peculiarly disruptive. The traditional basis of the teacher's position was that he knew more than his pupils and was there to dispense what they were there to receive—an authoritative relationship now undermined by scorn for authority as such and sometimes too by the teacher who was at pains to insist that he was no better than the pupil.

Even more contemned than authority was elitism. This was a source of damaging confusion. Elitism was equated with privilege and snobbery —with which it frequently overlaps but is not identical. The elite are people with superior talents and aptitudes which should be nourished. The problem is how to select them. In English education the elite have been a class elite. This is now unacceptable. French education has been no less elitist than English—perhaps more so—but the French elite did not emerge from a class; on the contrary the elite constituted the class, that of the successful graduates of the *grandes écoles* who came from no matter where but formed a class to run the country. England, edgily conscious of its social class system, reacted against elitism in general and so evoked a radical transformation of the class-conscious structure of its education, even though the more obnoxious class elements were largely absent from the public sector. One result was denigration of the grammar schools.

Education was in these thirty years a strained equation: many more children at school and many new ideas, but too few teachers and other resources to make the best, in this short space of time, of these two very welcome developments; and dissension, sometimes bitter, between the proponents of new methods and an uneasy majority of opponents ranging from the unconvinced to the hostile.

4 Politics

Politics has become a neglected subject. Whether measured by the volume of public debate or published material economic and social issues have outstripped politics. Yet politics is the ground of all since politics determines who has the authority to regulate economic, social and all other affairs.

In an industrial democracy there is commonly a conflict between economic growth and social justice and when a choice has to be made two opposing propositions will be advanced. The first will aver that if priority is given to justice growth will be inhibited, the second that if priority is given to growth justice will be delayed. This conflict between social and economic ends can be resolved only by political action.

The years 1945–75 saw little change in the bare bones of British politics but some vexed questioning about the distribution of political power and its use. The structure of the kingdom, of the parliament and of local government were all questioned and reviewed but remained either intact for the time being or not fundamentally altered. Adherence to the EEC at the very end of this period had considerable political and constitutional implications but in 1975, the year before the presidency of the European Commission was first occupied by a British politician, their impact had been no more than vaguely traced. At the core of British politics the increased industrial and economic power of the trade unions raised questions about their political role.

The Representation of the People Act 1948 introduced postal voting and abolished plural voting in parliamentary elections. At the ensuing election 250,000 postal ballots were sent out and 93% of them were validly returned. Conservative efficiency in this department was thought to have tipped the balance their way in ten seats. The abolition of university graduates' votes affected no more than 250,000 voters while the abolition of the business premises vote affected even fewer, about 70,000. There was a considerable realigning of constituency boundaries by which Labour was held to have forfeited 30–35 seats in the 1950 election through their strict objectivity. The qualifying age for the vote was reduced in 1970 from 21, where it had been fixed in 1918, to 18. The salaries of MPs, introduced in 1911, stood at £600 a year in 1945 and rose in five stages to £5,750 in 1975.

Reform of the House of Lords remained in the sphere of constitutional debate and party manoeuvre. The question was broached in 1948 by Lord Salisbury during the debate on the Parliament Bill which reduced the delaying power defined in the Parliament Act 1911 (see Part One, Chapter 3). An all-party conference was convoked but broke down over the definition of the delaying power which Labour wished to restrict so far that, in Conservative eyes, the outcome would be a single-chamber legislature. There was a fair degree of agreement that the House should consist of paid members, some hereditary and some appointed, and that non-member hereditary peers should be free to stand for election to the House of Commons. The question was revived twenty years later with the introduction in 1969 of a Parliament Bill which proposed to phase hereditary peers out of the House, reduce its delaying powers to vanishing point and give to party leaders the power to appoint members of the House in proportion to their party strengths in the House of Commons. These proposals were opposed by those of the left who preferred total abolition and by others, chiefly on the right, who looked askance at the increased patronage bestowed on party leaders. After delaying tactics concerted by its disparate opponents the Bill was abandoned. Life peerages for men and women became conferrable under the Life Peerages Act 1958, a kind of peerage restricted until this date to those within the ambit of the Appellate Jurisdiction Act 1876, i.e. judicial members of the House. This new source of patronage added disputes about its exercise by successive prime ministers to older disputes about the heritability of legislative wisdom.

A more determined attempt was made to reform local government which had remained substantially untouched since the previous century. Local government in England and Wales had been developed as part of the political and not the administrative structure of government. Local councils consisted of elected councillors answerable to their local electorate and possessed their own (limited) power to tax by levying rates. Local councils and their officials (who, as local government officers, were distinguished from the civil servants who staffed the departments of the central government) were neither answerable to the central government nor offshoots of the departments of state; but they were dependent, and increasingly dependent, on grants from the exchequer and they

were of course subject to the provisions of Acts of Parliament pre-
scribing the limits of their competence or requiring them to do certain
things.

There has been in the present century a shift away from this pattern
by the creation of public corporations which are creatures of the central
government, e.g. for starting new towns, and by the creation of non-
elected regional authorities, e.g. hospital boards covering wider areas
than local councils. In this respect there has been an approximation to
the dual French system of local administration through appointed
prefects as well as elected mayors (Britain's wartime regional com-
missioners were, in the very special circumstances of those years, a
temporary invasion of local government by the central authority's
nominees), and the extension of the powers and responsibilities of
government has raised questions about the nature as well as the size of
local government units. Paid professionals in health, education, planning
etc. were exercising in fact the kind of authority which the creators of
the nineteenth-century local political system had not envisaged, while
many local councils lacked the financial and other resources required for
the discharge of the burdens laid upon them by twentieth-century
legislation.

The principal units in English local government were the county
councils, including the County of London, invented in 1888; the county
borough councils also initiated in 1888 and subsequently increased in
number from an original six; rural and urban district councils created in
1894; and metropolitan (i.e. London) borough councils created in 1899.
There was a conscious effort to divide urban government from rural.
The main difference between the two kinds of authority created in 1888
was that the county boroughs, unlike the counties, had no second-tier
authorities under them. Differences in size and shifts of population
created anomalies but an attempt at overall reform after the first world
war failed to get off the ground. In 1963 the Local Government Act of
that year established the Greater London Council to rule over a greatly
extended metropolitan area and two years later a Royal Commission on
Local Government was set up (replacing two Local Government
Commissions for England and Wales created by statute in 1958). The
Royal Commission—the Redcliffe-Maud Commission—reported in
1969. It recommended changes which were radical within the tradition:
the extinction of the 124 county and county borough councils and over
1000 district councils and their replacement by eight large economic and

social planning councils in England (and one each in Wales and Scotland) and 58 single-tier authorities.* The underlying principle remained, however, unquestioned—namely that the councillor elected to represent a constituency was superior to the appointed official who was trained for a career in local government. The local government officer, better paid and more heeded than in the past, did not in consequence command a higher status—an epitome of the place of the expert in English life.

The Labour government gave general approval to these proposals but they were scrapped after the Conservatives, who wanted less change, returned to power. The Local Government Act 1972 established therefore six new metropolitan councils on the pattern of the GLC but somewhat smaller than recommended by the Royal Commission (i.e. they drew into metropolitan government less of the surrounding countryside) and 51 counties with 406 subordinate districts. In sum the new metropolitan and county authorities were considerably fewer than their predecessors, the counties and county boroughs; and the new districts were much fewer than the urban and rural districts which they displaced, but the big planning areas recommended by the Commission did not come into existence. Their future, if any, was to await the report of another Royal Commission which was set up in 1969 with Lord Crowther as chairman (succeeded on his death by Lord Kilbrandon) in response to growing separatism in Scotland and Wales. This commission presented majority and minority reports in 1973. The majority recommended the creation of new assemblies in Scotland and Wales to be elected by proportional representation and endowed with legislative authority subject to a veto by the parliament at Westminster; and smaller unelected assemblies without legislative powers for eight English regions. The minority wanted to see seven rather than eight English regions and to equate these with the proposed Scottish and Welsh assemblies by having them all elected by proportional representation and by denying legislative powers to Scotland and Wales.

* A dissentient minority advocated 35 authorities, mostly with subordinate second-tier councils, in an attempt to get the advantages of size without losing the contacts and concern that go with more and geographically smaller bodies. The eight planning councils were an echo of the eight planning regions created in 1965 by the short-lived Department of Economic Affairs.

The general election of 1974, by putting Labour back in power without an overall majority in the House of Commons, increased the leverage of the Scottish Nationalist Party and Plaid Cymru, and although Labour strengthened its position eight months later so too did the SNP and, marginally, Plaid Cymru.* The first of these elections was followed by a White Paper on Democracy and Devolution in Scotland and Wales which approved the creation of elected assemblies in both countries, opposed proportional representation and proposed to devolve legislative authority in Scotland only. It further proposed that the secretaries of state for Scotland and Wales should continue to sit in the British cabinet (the former office had existed since 1885, the latter since 1964) and that the numbers of Scottish and Welsh MPs at Westminster should be unchanged. The Westminster parliament would make block grants to the Scottish and Welsh assemblies which would be free to apportion the money as they pleased within their competence.

The further history of these proposals lies outside the period covered by this book. Few people in England had taken much interest in the Scottish and Welsh nationalist movements which they regarded as eccentricities in every sense of the word. Most were then taken by surprise by the strength and seriousness of the movements and politicians addressed themselves in the first place to their impact on the balance of Conservative and Labour at Westminster where Labour had always relied for its majorities on its comparative strength in what were not very tactfully called the Celtic fringes. Tactically therefore the Labour Party had to give minimum satisfaction to Scottish nationalism or risk the overwhelming of the Labour Party in Scotland by the SNP. (The situation in Wales was from this point of view less fraught.) The Conservatives too were in a tactical dilemma, divided among themselves between strict adherents to the union of 1707 and pragmatic advocates of a measure of autonomy. Both parties were hampered not merely by

* The two elections of 1974 produced these results:

	Lab.	Cons.	Lib.	SNP	Plaid Cymru	Ulster Unionists
February	301	296	14	7	2	11
October	315	276	13	13	3	10

In the first of these elections Conservatives got 37.8% of the votes cast, Labour 37.1%.

their own Scottish and Welsh affiliates but also by not knowing how much autonomy would satisfy how many Scottish or Welsh voters. Within Wales independence seemed as yet to be sought by virtually nobody, within Scotland probably by few. But by the seventies both nationalist movements smelt success and were tempted to raise their bids. In the case of Scotland this fervour was nourished by economic prospects as well as electoral successes. The Scots noted that North Sea oil, which was struck in 1970 after a decade of exploration and began to come ashore in Scotland in 1975, was much nearer to Scotland than to England. The more this oil was hailed as the salvation of the British balance of payments (supplementing the heroic performance of Scotch whisky), the more Scotland claimed a say in how the new wealth should be allocated.

The revival of the Welshness of the Welsh and its emergence as a political force had its roots in the economic revival of Wales in the nineteenth century which fortified an earlier cultural revival. This revival, which was not without its frauds and fakes,* was ignored or derided by those English who heard of it, while its principal outward sign, the speaking of the Welsh language, was regarded as a fad hardly less absurd than speaking Erse or Chaucerian English. So long as this nationalism flourished chiefly in the remoter parts of the principality it remained a thing apart, but pride of race and tongue spread and in doing so became allied with a current not essentially Welsh but tinged, in Wales, with a Welsh tone—the feeling of those far from the capital that they were not being properly looked after or listened to. The creation of a Welsh office in 1952 and of a secretary of state for Wales in 1964 were sops which did not suffice. The example of the Scots was a spur.

Rather more than Wales, which had been conquered and constitutionally absorbed in the middle ages, Scotland retained a strong identity despite the union of the crowns in 1603 and the union of the kingdoms in 1707†. The vigour of Scottish culture in the eighteenth century

---

* Edward Williams, *alias* Iolo Morganwg, the Welsh counterpart— and contemporary—of the James Macpherson who invented *Ossian*, fabricated documents to substantiate his fantasies about the Welsh bards as the spiritual descendants of ancient and romantically garbed Druids waving naked swords inside circles of stones.

† Scotland was briefly annexed to England in 1651–60.

affirmed a separateness which was acknowledged by Scotland's distinct legal and educational systems and by the mixture of Calvinism and Roman Catholicism with which Scotland outfaced the flaccid protestantism south of the border.* In bad times Scots migrated southward, in better times there was less to worry about; but by the mid-twentieth century these attitudes ceased to pass. National consciousness and national dignity—reinforced by the feeling that Scotland's special problems, such as white fish or the development of the Highlands or unemployment on the Clyde, received inadequate attention in London —created a protest movement which carried its members into the parliament at Westminster and, on the English side, stirred memories of the troubles caused there by Irish nationalists a century earlier. The English had to take notice that a secretary of state for Scotland seated in London and a Scottish Office dispersed between London and Edinburgh epitomised without assuaging a new political conflict. Nobody in England wanted a debate about the structure of the United Kingdom, least of all in the seventies when economic problems were clamant, but the timing was not under English control. The appointment of the Crowther-Kilbrandon Commission won some time but after the Commission had reported something had to be done (preferably before the next general election) and that something could hardly be less than some degree of autonomy for both Scotland and Wales. The principle was clear but its elaboration unclear. The principle was that if a sufficient number of people in Scotland or Wales wanted constitutional change, they could hardly be denied it. What was unclear was how many people wanted what degree of change, and introducing legislation before seeking answers to this question did not clarify it.

The coincidence of devolution as a problem of government and devolution as a means of satisfying nationalism was unfortunate. The Redcliffe-Maud Commission was set up to make recommendations about the size of local governments. It was partly implemented and partly pigeonholed on the plea that the terms of reference of the Crowther-Kilbrandon Commission overlapped. This, however, was true only if English regions were to be equated with Scotland or Wales, which was hardly sensible—the ancient kingdoms of Bernicia and Deira

---

* The differences between the laws of Scotland and England were becoming something of a romantic fancy as statute law, largely identical in both countries, bulked ever larger than earlier law.

between Tweed and Humber were still happily dead. The Crowther-Kilbrandon Commission was not concerned with the mechanics and efficiency of government but with giving political satisfaction to Scottish and Welsh nationalism, if necessary at the cost of efficiency. There was no reason to suppose that the requirements of good government and the satisfaction of national aspirations were the same thing. As a result of this confusion devolution in England was postponed while the Crowther-Kilbrandon Commission produced a discordant report which not only recommended one solution for Scotland and another for Wales but contained different and conflicting recommendations for each of these countries. It laid bare differences between Scotland and Wales, pointing to differing constitutional arrangements and leaving the position of England anomalous and unclear in an island which could contain a British parliament, a Scottish sub-parliament, a Welsh assembly but no specifically English legislature nor, probably, any English regional authorities (other than the regional Economic Planning Boards and their attendant advisory councils set up by the DEA): the English regions did not even have at Westminster the equivalents of the Scottish and Welsh Grand Committees in which MPs from these areas discussed the problems peculiar to them.

The fourth segment of the United Kingdom, Northern Ireland, was raising questions which went further than autonomy. The problem here was very different, notably because people were being killed in Northern Ireland and because the English—unlike their parents or grandparents —had given up thinking of Northern Ireland as part of the United Kingdom and come round to thinking of it as part of Ireland, a separate country. The English would have liked to be rid of Northern Ireland but hesitated to disbelieve those who prophesied *a priori* that a British withdrawal would precipitate a bloodbath. The unhappy history of Northern Ireland is related in a note at the end of this chapter (p. 192).

Also postponed to a later place (p. 217) is the account of how Britain came to join the EEC. This move, which had profound constitutional as well as political and economic implications, seemed paradoxical alongside the simultaneous Scottish and Welsh campaigns to loosen or even possibly dissolve the structure of the United Kingdom. Devolution within the kingdom was going hand in hand with a quasi-federative European venture akin to the union of 1707 which the Scots were successfully calling in question. This seemed illogical, as indeed it was, but the relevance of logic to situations of this kind is slight.

We have been concerned so far in this chapter with the externalities of British politics but these are far from being the whole. The politics of a living society are constantly in a state of flux as new forces and old jostle for power and prevalence and strain the political matrix. Auguste Comte said that the tradition of French politics was monarchical, of English politics aristocratic. This is a useful aphorism. Comte was not thinking of the aristocracy in the sense of the hereditary nobility. He meant, like Aristotle, the best people whoever they might be, and the value of this tradition is that the concept of best people is flexible. In this sense there are always aristocrats, a group of people fit to do the job whatever it may be, and chosen for it on that assumption. Aristocracy of this kind is not the same as an hereditary nobility.* Britain is a mixed aristocracy and democracy. It deserves the name of democracy because of the dissemination of political power. It is also a pragmatic society which is more interested in results than theories, and this predilection makes for the preservation of the aristocratic tradition. Pragmatists look for the best people and set them to work but hesitate to let too many people in on the act (as the Athenian democracy did) because, on the principle of too many cooks, that is the surest way to get the wrong results or none. Britain prefers the few to the many—though not of course too few—and so the basic question in British politics is how and where to find this elite and how broad to make it. The British are exceedingly proud of their system but in the vaguest way. They would reject the epithet 'aristocratic' and the best that they can find to say about democracy is that it is the least bad of political patterns. They are subconsciously aware that the British pattern is a hybrid.

There is a second point of equal importance to be made about British politics. The one thing that Britain emphatically is not is an oligarchy. Oligarchy is by definition the rule of the few and in practice the same few. An aristocracy is select but, by definition, selected on merit and therefore not closed. Oligarchies are more or less closed and must either fossilise or mutate. An example of the former is Venice which decreed in 1297 that nobody without an ancestor who had sat in the Council of Five Hundred might himself do so. The Senate of Rome on the other hand, by opening its doors to plebeian as well as patrician families,

---

* China provides a parallel. From the time of the Han empire (206 BC–AD 221) noble birth, while it retained social distinction and respect, ceased to be coterminous with the ruling class.

transformed itself from an oligarchy into an aristocracy. As the Roman example shows, an aristocracy finds room for a number of very odd people.

The English tradition of flexible aristocracy has not had a steady or undeviating history. William the Conqueror, who knew all about over-mighty subjects since that is what he himself was in France, took steps to make the crown all-powerful in England. Not even the greatest barons were allowed to possess large contiguous dominions. But the Normans and their Angevin successors did not rule absolutely. They ruled through committees or councils where the great barons and churchmen had their place and (within limits) their say: they were part of a ruling class. An exceptionally powerful king could ride roughshod over some of them some of the time, but no English king in the middle ages—not even Henry II—could afford to affront the whole baronage or the church. There was no monopoly of power in the crown, or in the church or magnates, and so the political system had to comprehend all these powers if it was to work. And even in the middle ages, by no means so static a period as its remoteness may make it appear, power shifted and new powers arose and had to be accommodated. As early as the four-teenth and fifteenth centuries England was practising its genius for adaptability. The warrior society of the first Angevins—a society dominated by roistering illiterates filling draughty halls with din, smoke and beasts—became softened by merchants and their values (not to mention women and theirs). Before the end of the middle ages the ruling class embraced ennobled merchants as well as descendants of the Conqueror's companions. The Tudors, of mixed Welsh and French origins, were less tolerant than the Anglo-Normans, eliminated most of what was left of the magnates after the Wars of the Roses, subjected the church and annexed its wealth, centralised government and made England's most successful bid for absolute monarchy. But the last and greatest of the Tudors, Elizabeth, combined an absolutist temper with a taste for political finesse and religious compromise and so steered England away from a course which her successors, less well endowed with spirit and with money, could not in any case have sustained. The first two Stuarts, absolutists who failed, proved the point.

The rebellion that followed is the first in the series of major modern European revolutions. In this the English were precocious, and their political precocity in the seventeenth century is no less important for subsequent history than their pioneering of the industrial revolution a century and more later. The English revolution of the seventeenth century came so early that it was nullified with comparative ease; and there has been much unfinished business ever since. The eighteenth century had many of the characteristics of an age of recoil. England achieved unprecedented stability. It became also conservative; and the stability and conservatism seemed to be two sides of the same coin. This conservatism was reinforced by the revolution in France at the end of the century which enormously scared a lot of English people, not only the ruling class, as tales of horror and war rubbed in the message that it was impossible to turn the world upside down without a great deal of unpleasantness. (The revolution in America, although it was a revolution against the English crown, caused much less commotion in England. The leaders of the American rebels were country aristocrats with standard eighteenth-century ideas about liberty and no wish to turn anything upside down.)

The eighteenth century also saw the definition of the ruling class which was to dominate England for over 200 years. This class was distinct but neither monolithic nor closed. Within it Whigs and Tories contended, albeit on issues which seem to a later age artificial or superficial. Both factions were conservative and aristocratic without being exclusively so. The Whigs, more open to change than the Tories, produced also in Edmund Burke one of the founding fathers of modern conservatism. In both groups the leaders had wealth, influence and land —which is three ways of defining the same thing. Three other things made these groups more open than they might otherwise have been: empire, trade and speculation, i.e. alternative sources of wealth and influence which could buy a passage into the ruling class. The nabobs who made their pile in India, the City men, the first big brewers—these and other thrusters provided a trickle of new men who could get a foot into the door of politics and bring new ideas with them when they went through it. Even top posts began to come their way as the Pitts and Peels and Gladstones put success in trade to the same uses as the de la Poles and Russells at the end of the middle ages—or for that matter their much more distant precursors in the last two centuries of the Roman republic. Socially the new men might not count as aristocrats but that did not prevent them from acquiring a share in political power and even in time one of the humbler varieties of peerage. (A graded peerage is itself a social solvent.)

In the nineteenth century the pace of absorptions into the ruling class, like the pace of much else, increased and many people began to think that Britain had become a democracy. Yet the widening circle had hardly widened enough to merit that name, and the more it widened the less those on the inside liked the expanding prospect. Whigs and Tories gave way to Liberals and Conservatives. More and more people got the vote. Social problems were aired with high seriousness. The population increased as never before, as did literacy; communications improved out of all recognition; the political scene experienced its swiftest ever transformation. Political parties were invented. Where there had been factions consisting of members of the two Houses of Parliament and their patrons, there were now parties with members all over the country who met at conferences to listen to and even influence their leaders, to draw up programmes and set goals. There was political debate far away from the Houses of Parliament, and the members of the Houses were no longer the only people 'in politics'.

It is not easy to see what politics are about when one is in the middle of them. It is, however, comparatively easy to see what politics were about in time past and since nineteenth-century politics determined the content of twentieth-century politics it pays to contemplate the former in order to understand the latter. The politics of nineteenth-century Britain were about democracy and industrialisation. These were the two most potent processes at work in the realm of public affairs. At that period democracy meant first and foremost the extension of the franchise and by the end of the century universal adult franchise was well on the way, although it was not extended to women until 1918: males became adult at 21 in 1918, females at 30 in 1918 and at 21 in 1929 (but 19-year-olds who had fought in the first world war were allowed to vote in the first election after it).* Reform in the nineteenth century began with parliamentary reform and in spite of enormous changes wrought by industrialism and other forces it is probably true to say that the transformation of the lower house of the legislature changed Britain more than anything else between the Napoleonic wars and the first world war.

Industrialisation was no less obviously a major political catalyst. Its consequences were both economic (largely happy) and social (frightful), but also political because it changed the political players. It ended the

* At work women had to wait until 1970 before attaining equality with men. The Equal Pay Act 1970 came into force in 1975.

rule of the landed aristocracy which had been inaugurated in the seventeenth century when the Stuart monarchy failed to maintain the position
inherited from the Tudors, and it gave to manufacture the priority over
agriculture: the eighteenth century had seen great advances in both and
had bequeathed a choice to the succeeding age which that age semi-
consciously exercised in favour of urban as opposed to open-air industry.
Increasingly the men who grew things were displaced by the men who
made things and traded in them—manufacturers and merchants. Later
still the men who made things were outpaced by the men who simply
made money, the financiers who, with the growth of empire, made
London the financial capital of the world and dominated the politico-
financial complex so long as Britain was a world power—and thereafter.
These new classes were readily fitted into the ruling class.

Industrialisation also brought on to the political stage another group
which was not absorbed into the ruling class—labour which, when it had
been organised, created a new political party and also learned to use its
political muscle through trade unions which were not themselves part
of the formal structure of politics. As a result of these changes politics
ceased to be a contest within a ruling class (Tories versus Whigs,
Conservatives versus Liberals) and became a contest between the ruling
class and those outside it. This was a momentous, if blurred, change.

If politics in the last century was predominantly about democracy and
industrialisation, it would be legitimate to expect that the politics of the
present century would be about the continuing impact of industrialisation on democracy and the introduction of democracy into industry.

Industry in a free-enterprise capitalist system has its own politics
which are adversary politics. The one party, that of the proprietors, had
little difficulty in entering the national political arena and did so both
directly as MPs on (increasingly) the Conservative side and indirectly
through their membership of the ruling class. They had power because
of their success and they were in consequence a political force, however
little many individuals among them cared about politics or politicians;
they were accommodated in a political system which was flexible enough
to adjust to their existence and their power. This accommodation was,
however, half-hearted: they joined the ruling class but were not much
interested in or convinced by its developing democratic institutions
and processes. The other party, that of labour, did not in the nineteenth century have power, largely because it did not have money,
but it learned to make up for this lack by organising and by using a

negative power—the strike. Gradually it became not only organised but richer and so more able to strike without risking destitution; but the power of industrial labour remained, even in the twentieth century, essentially negative and oppositional.

Also it remained to a considerable extent outside the democratic political system. The extension of the franchise to some working men in 1867 and 1884 opened the way to a parliament with a large contingent, even eventually a majority, of working men but they never entered parliament in numbers commensurate with their voting power. The reasons have frequently been given: lack of confidence in themselves, a long tradition of deference, lack of financial elbow-room, the opportunity for the ambitious or the dedicated to make a career in the alternative arena of union politics. The House of Commons remained very much a middle-class and professional body, less representative in fact and in appearance of the enlarged electorate than the unreformed House had been of its electorate. (A middle-class parliament may be efficient at its job but it cannot claim to be representative. It may be democratic in terms of electoral machinery and yet fail in its composition to reflect the electorate.) It in its turn kept away from the politics of industry—a large part of the politics of the nation—except for occasional interventions to prescribe safety regulations or stop the more appalling forms of child labour or, conversely, to hamper by law the growth and freedom of trade unions. The main business of industrial politics, including wage bargaining, was left to employers and unions to fight out among themselves (non-unionised labour was hardly able to fight at all) with the result that a dual political system began to emerge. Parliament, whose historic role was to make laws, vote taxes and redress grievances, allowed the redress of industrial grievances to be mooted and contested elsewhere. Disraeli's diagnosis of two nations, the rich and the poor, was superficial;* there was a newer divide between government and industry, between the parliament and administration on the one hand and the developing forces of capitalists and unions on the other.

Union leaders did not object. They were more at home in industrial politics, which were in any case their main affair, than in the more generalised political field where they would have to give time to subjects

---

* And not new. Five hundred years earlier, at the start of the centuries-long English revolution, John Ball said the same thing when complaining that England was divided between gentlemen and villeins.

they knew little about and where they were regarded as socially inferior. One consequence of this absence of labour leaders and labour members from parliament was that the parliamentary Labour Party developed, particularly from 1919 onwards, a different social complexion from organised labour in the factories and, especially in years when Labour had a poor showing in the House of Commons, the union leaders outside parliament might be politically weightier than the parliamentary leaders inside. The political power of labour, far more than the power of industrialists and financiers, throve outside parliament and to a significant extent independently of its parliamentary links. This growth of a distinct political power centre produced some very muddled thinking. It was commonly said in our period that the unions ought not to have this power. This was nonsensical since there is no ought about power. People and organisations either have power or not. The question is factual and not ethical: the uses of power may be good or evil but its existence is morally neutral. The political position of the unions by mid-twentieth century was similar to that of the church in the middle ages. The church had power. There was no sense in debating whether it should have power or not. The fact was that it had and so long as this was so governments which acted as though the church did not have power frequently came to grief. Good government required therefore that the church be part of the political system and not outside it and in opposition. So with the unions: given their power, good government required that they be part of government, good democratic government that they play a democratic part in the established democratic institutions. In default of this adjustment the system was endangered since the unions' negative power was great enough to maim the system if a government tried to govern against them. The problem therefore was not to curb the power of the unions but to fit it in.

The concentration of union power outside parliament presented a danger to parliament in as much as the evolution of parliament had not kept up with the evolution of politics. In the dual system which had emerged it was possible for the power of the unions to be brought to bear on parliament instead of within it. The unions had become an over-mighty lobby: a lobby is compatible with democratic government only when it is not so mighty that it begins to look less like a lobby than a government, at which point the lobby is on the wrong side of the fence. What happened in practice was that important economic and social issues came to be increasingly discussed and even concluded between the executive branch of government and senior representatives of the two industrial fiefdoms of employers and unions, with parliament playing a relative inconsequential role. The parliamentary constitution was being elbowed out of the way by the corporate state (which had been thought to be a specifically fascist invention but was not).

This trend towards extra-parliamentary deliberation and decision was accentuated by inflation and the instability of prices. Wage bargaining in a period of stable prices was a tussle for money between those who had it and those who wanted it, but in years of rising prices it was no good winning a higher wage if the purchasing power of the new wage was no better than that of the old. Union leaders saw that in order to perform their prime function they must not only get more money out of paymasters but also influence policy-makers—the government—whose actions would determine the value of the money they had won. But their attempts to influence government policy from the sidelines were regarded as outrageous because they were not part of government. Their claim was rational but their stance vulnerable.

Since the business of unions had traditionally been the improvement of the material lot of their working-class members, other classes regarded the unions as their enemies (although in these years they began too to form or join unions themselves). They denounced union power as unconstitutional as well as partisan, in the first case improper and dangerously great, in the second proper if lamentably great. There was, however, a significant difference between the power of unions against employers and the same power against government. Union power had increased steadily in relation to the power of employers who disliked it for sufficiently obvious reasons and disliked too the increasingly successful attempts of unions to make it impossible to fire moderately inefficient employees (very inefficient ones could be fired relatively easily provided . the employer went about it in the right way) and to interfere through the closed shop with the employer's freedom to hire whom he wanted. But in relation to the state the power of unions was different. They were nowhere as near to being on level terms with government as they were with employers. Only on one occasion did they seriously challenge the government and the law—when the inept Industrial Relations Act 1971 (see Part Two, Chapter 1) operated to mulct them of hundreds of thousands of pounds in consequence of the actions of a handful of individuals; and even then they did not so much make the law unenforceable as demonstrate that it was. Nor did the unions repeal the offending statute. That was done by the electorate, which removed the party which had enacted it and transferred power to the party pledged to repeal it. Moreover the unions had no very successful record in getting what they wanted out of governments. Neither the relatively right-wing leadership of the first half of our period nor its more clamorous successors could get governments to maintain food and housing subsidies—high on the list of TUC desiderata.

There was, however, a third area of union activity which contributed to the view that the unions were challenging the right of the government to govern. As a result of the nationalisation Acts of the forties a number of unions, including some powerful ones, found themselves facing the government as employer as well as the government *qua* government. In these areas the functions of unions as bargainers became enmeshed with their functions as a policy pressure group with the result that industrial action against the employer was all but synonymous with action against the state because the employer happened to be the state. (For these purposes the fact that the Coal Board, for example, was not the state was a distinction which the general public ignored, with justice.) The political strike had changed its meaning. From being a strike against private employers for political purposes it had become additionally a strike in an industry which had happened to be nationalised.

Uneasiness about union power was the more intense because of the sheer numbers of the army behind union leaders. The obverse of the question: how many divisions has the Pope? is: how many legions has the general secretary of the TUC? The answer, however, is unclear. In one sense the army is huge. By 1975 the membership of trade unions was close to twelve million in 488 unions: the first figure was rising and the second falling. Ten of the twelve million were in the forty largest union (50,000 members each or more); seven million of these were in the eleven largest unions (250,000 members each or more). In other words a few unions were numerically very much more powerful than all the rest put together.

The power of the unions derived from the fact that, in an industrial society, the men and women who work or make or mind machines are essential, but some are more essential than others and union power was fragmented and also limited in more ways than one. In the first place it rested on a refusal to do something; it entirely lacked the positive or physical authority enjoyed by organs of the state. Secondly, for most unions their negative power rested on solidarity with other unions. The tradition of solidarity, derived from early struggles for recognition and the emotional appeal of the brotherhood of working men, was strong, but solidarity was at its strongest when the unions were weakest and it was institutionalised in only the vaguest way. The TUC was an instrument of the unions and its secretary general as confined in his office as the UN secretary general was hemmed in by the jealous sovereignties of UN members. The TUC therefore was a thinking place, still more a talking place, a co-ordinator so long as members agreed on what to co-ordinate and how, but in no sense a power-house. Effective power lay neither with the TUC nor with the aggregate of unions but with a few unions which were both large and entrenched in industries whose stoppage could make governments shudder. Each of these was more powerful than the trade-union movement as a whole, although each was also in the uncomfortable position of having to go to extreme, unpopular and destructive lengths to win a victory upon which it was determined. It could threaten and it could use the more refined and teasing forms of industrial action which were developed in these years (partial or short or selective stoppages), but the strike was still a union's one effective weapon if and when the talking stopped. The strike and the threat of a strike were powerful weapons in the hands of coal-miners, electricity workers, railway staff, dock workers, motor-car manufacturers and a few more groups, but the record shows how little it was used across the industrial board. In the years 1971–73, a peculiarly troubled three years, 98% of all manufacturing plants were free of strikes in each year and 95% had no strike throughout the whole period. Finally, unions were decidedly unpopular outside their own ranks. They were seldom in the public eye except in relation to strikes or threatened stoppages of one kind or another.

The converse of the place of organised labour in a democratic system is the place of democracy in the industrial system. The phrase 'industrial democracy' had been coined by the Webbs at the end of the nineteenth century and both world wars witnessed ventures into consultation with workers. For the most part these ventures faded away when peace returned. After the second world war there was some marginal interest, chiefly academic, in French writings on the subject, West German legislation (which had its roots in nineteenth-century patterns of industrial organisation in Germany) and Yugoslav experiment, but Britain, said a captain of industry in the seventies, was not ready for industrial democracy. He meant to convey that Britain did not want it but his remark could have been interpreted to mean that Britain had not much thought about it. Those who had were of three kinds: pragmatists worried about poor management and bad industrial relations because of their effect on output and profits, democrats who wanted to extend workers' power in industry as the next step in the evolution of democracy, and enemies of the capitalist system who espied a useful tool for its disruption. The positive achievements were negligible, although at the very end of our period a Royal Commission was appointed to survey the question. Union pressures altered the climate in industry to the extent that proprietors found it expedient to mitigate their accustomed secrecy and give their employees more information about their company's affairs and even on occasion to justify their stewardship, but directors remained the servants of proprietors and hostile to the idea of workers sitting on boards where they would have a voice in decisions and a sight of information and plans customarily reserved to few. Although dialogue between management and employees became more normal and fuller, it remained an across-the-table affair and any meaningful concept of partnership round the table was for the proprietors a strange, unreal and frightening portent. The adversary pattern was but little dented although its conceptual base was badly damaged since the class of proprietors—the shareholders—had become an army of passive rentiers and a shrinking one (2.25 million individuals owned shares and their ownership conferred neither power nor responsibility). The much smaller group of effective proprietors struck a note of unreality, even hypocrisy, when they regulated their conduct and justified their attitudes by referring to the interests of this army at their backs. Their true interests seemed narrower and more selfish.

There was a further obstacle to industrial harmony. The two sides were moving at a different pace and rarely found themselves at the same stage at the same time. As managers became accustomed to consultation, consultation ceased to satisfy employees. They began to reach for participation and more. Participation was a vague term. In what and how? Worker directors on boards might satisfy the theoretical democrats' demands, but would these directors become divorced from their fellow workers and be used by the proprietors as lightning-conductors, and how would they reconcile their obligation to fight for better wages and conditions with their corporate duty to keep costs down? Behind such arguments was the unspoken belief of the managerial class that workers' representatives would not be up to the job and could not be trusted to keep secrets from those they represented, and this in turn raised the question whether much that was habitually treated as confidential needed to be. In their extremest form demands for industrial democracy went beyond participation to control or the self-management introduced in Yugoslavia but, in whatever form, all these demands implied a downgrading of the proprietorial or money interest and almost certainly a relaxation, perhaps massive, of the secrecy in which companies wrapped themselves. Nor was it at all clear how many workers wanted participation of any kind. Particularly in hard times many were happy to settle for benefits rather than power, so that the fight for industrial democracy—like the earlier fight for political democracy—was left to an active minority whom proprietors of businesses, like the proprietors of rotten boroughs, could stigmatise as unrepresentative champions of representation. It is a paradox of political history that democracy, whether political or industrial, has been won for but not by the majority. It is none the worse for that.

If a blinkered majority of entrenched proprietors and managers were an obstacle to industrial democracy, hardly less so were the unions. Since the power of organised labour lay in organised unions, any attempt to introduce industrial democracy which sidestepped the unions flew in the face of facts, but on the other hand many unions were themselves undemocratic to the point of caricature. Not only were elections decided by a pitifully small proportion of those entitled to decide them; more seriously, the basic apparatus of democracy, for which their forebears had fought in the parliamentary field (e.g. the secret ballot), was not present in the internal affairs of many unions. Consequently, in so far as worker power was taken to mean union power, an oligarchy of moneyed proprietors was not being democratised but was being faced by a rival oligarchy, so that industry would become a forum for contending oligarchs with no necessary or likely gain either in efficiency or democracy. If, however, the alternative was to leave things as they were, this was unacceptable to many and of proven inadequacy—if only because too many workers had shown that they were no longer prepared to work loyally and hard in such a system. Furthermore, this alienation of the largely unionised work force was accompanied in these years by an equal alienation of the middle ranks from proprietors and senior management. As it became increasingly apparent that effective power was polarised between proprietors and senior directors on the one side and the shop floor on the other the men in between, with superior education and training but not in many cases superior pay or power, turned their resentment against the men at the top who, by accepting the realities and dealing directly with shop floor and unions, were flouting the established hierarchy. The boss who had in the past used his middle ranks to deal with the workers as an officer uses NCOs was now dealing directly with the workers because power had shifted to them, with the result that the men who had been the bosses' intermediaries found themselves in limbo. But the boss, who had in the past combined the authority of proprietorship with the authority of expertise, had lost the latter half of his authority as industries grew in size and ownership passed to untutored financiers closeted with accountants and lawyers a hundred miles away from the experts in the factories. The industrial yeoman class was squeezed out: its knowledge and its standards were assimilated neither by proprietors nor by unions, both of whom had other things on their minds. Surviving industrial proprietors developed similar resentments beyond the invisible pale which, fifty miles north of London, still constituted a social boundary.

The democracy to which Britain was attached related for certain only to the making of laws and the raising of money by taxation. It was not evident that the British positively believed in a democratic organisation of industry, although they might welcome the introduction of such democratic practises as might improve industrial relations and tempers and so output. It was on the other hand evident that transferring authority in industry from private proprietors to unions was in itself no great democratic advance. And it was also evident that discussion about the politics of industry, although focussing on organisation and management and board-room power, in fact raised the explosive question of ownership and so impugned the capitalist system and the mixed economy. Such discussion called in question the co-existence of a political system which was democratic and an industrial system which was not.

Capitalism had developed alongside democracy but was neither indebted to it nor inspired by it. Rather, early capitalism was allied with nationalism and, with the waning of the European nation state, capitalism became increasingly supra-national or multinational or non-national. Less tenacious of nationalism than the state, capitalism was more successful in creating trans-state organisations. Capitalism is not antithetical to democracy or to socialism because these latter are political doctrines and sets of ideas whereas capitalism is a form of economic organisation. But private capitalism has tended to be scornful of democracy and hostile to socialism.

European capitalism has supplied capital from private pockets in the expectation of profit and, like the church in bygone times, in return for ecumenical powers *in orbe suo*, i.e. in industry, commerce and finance. The alternative to the supply of capital in this way is its supply from government (by taxation) but the disadvantages of this alternative, which is state capitalism, have greatly outweighed the advantages in British eyes: state capitalism is associated in the public mind with Stalinism, with Mussolini's parastatal corporatism and with unwieldy nationalised industries, bureaucratic and insatiable for cash. Moreover governments would have to take risks which traditionally they have taken in diplomacy but not otherwise. Private capitalism has taken the risks. It has also—and this is the main argument in its favour—increased wealth. On how the wealth should then be distributed capitalists profess to have nothing to say. They are not opposed in principle to more equal distribution of wealth—provided they keep enough of it in order to keep on prospering.

Capitalism has been attacked for being short on ethics but the attack rebounds since capitalism has made no claim to an ethical purpose: it claims to do good in a purely materialist sense. Recently and more seriously the case for private capitalism has been weakened in many countries because it is short not on ethics but of capital. In Britain and elsewhere businesses have ceased to produce their own capital and go instead to banks and other financiers and to government. In this situation the case against private capitalism is not that it is evil but that it no longer works. The private capitalist system which worked dominated both the capital market and the labour market. Industry throve largely on its own profits. Neither its bankers nor its labour force called the tune. This situation faded with the increase in the power of the unions and, no less substantively if less obviously, with the encroachment of bankers, insurance companies and other financiers into industrial proprietorship. These new proprietors became in many cases operationally involved (for better or worse) but continued nevertheless to think like creditors rather than owners, like investors rather than operators, and so were ready to discard a dubious investment rather than stick with what they had made theirs—a new version of power without responsibility, the 'privilege of the harlot throughout the ages', which Stanley Baldwin stigmatised as the outstanding characteristic of the barons of

Fleet Street. Harried by unions and liable to be manipulated or abandoned by his new overlords the industrialist was ceasing to be able to boast that the system of which he was part fulfilled its prime purpose of increasing wealth; and if the private capitalist system was either dying of inanition, having had its day, or turning patchily into a state capitalist system, the consequences were not merely economic but certainly also political. The class which had won political power through the industrial revolution would in the end lose it.

Ultimately disputes about forms of economic organisation of this order are political matters, although they may begin as debates about efficiency and become diverted into ideology. We noted at the end of our last Part that the economic failures of our period were essentially industrial and that however the blame might be apportioned among different groups or classes, the main share rested on those with prime responsibility—the owners and their nominees or agents. In Britain the business world, unlike the political, was an oligarchy, but an oligarchy in which the oligarchs had forfeited their claim to efficiency: they had become a mediocre oligarchy. It was not so rigidly closed as the Venetian oligarchy had been but it was more of an oligarchy than anything else, resistant to changes in the structure of the business world and still tainted with nepotism. It courted therefore the fate of most oligarchies which is, sooner or later, to be overthrown. It was perhaps peculiarly British that this process seemed to be taking place in slow motion. But the outcome would contribute nothing to efficiency if it merely substituted a new oligarchy for the old. It would moreover, in the particular circumstances of twentieth-century Britain, do a great deal of political harm since a clash between rival oligarchies was not at all to the taste of the great majority of men and women who would be left outside it and were unenchanted by any kind of closed system, whether capitalist or other. The need, social as much as industrial, was for more democracy, more chairmen's batons in workers' knapsacks. The failures of our period militated, however, against expansiveness. They encouraged timidity and, in a vicious circle, promoted an oligarchic clash in a situation brought about by the hardening of oligarchic arteries. Whether this circle could be broken lay, in 1975, in the realms of prophecy and faith, two uncomfortable fields for the pragmatist and rationalist but not inaccessible to the optimist.

The English in Ireland

The English never conquered Ireland as they did Wales nor mated with it as they did with Scotland. English politics became bedevilled in the nineteenth century by what was called the Irish question, the name for the increasingly successful Irish resistance to English rule. In the aftermath of the first world war English rule was all but thrown off, but a localised piece of it remained, largely owing to bitter English opposition to letting Irish nationalism have its way. This was regarded in England as an affront and a humiliation and since there were those in north-eastern Ireland who, partly on grounds of religion and partly on grounds of race, disliked Dubliners more than Londoners, the break was not a clean one. The United Kingdom of Great Britain and Ireland, created in 1800, was not dissolved but was refashioned with the word 'Northern' inserted before Ireland. Fifty years later war was being fought to complete the dissolution of this United Kingdom and annex Northern Ireland to Ireland. In the course of these years the English had lost much of their interest in Ireland and their pride in maintaining the links, but within this anomalous province of the United Kingdom new conflicts had been added to the nationalist and religious ones.

The complete constitutional sundering of the new Irish state from the United Kingdom did not take place until 1937 because in 1922 the Irish parliament, by a narrow majority, agreed that Ireland should remain in the British empire as a Free State owing allegiance to the British crown which would continue to be represented in Dublin by a governor-general. This decision was followed by civil war which the republican separatists lost. In the north-east, where a border was fixed in 1925, emerged the province of Northern Ireland which inherited from the Act of Union of 1800 the right to send MPs to Westminster and from the Government of Ireland Act 1920 a bicameral legislature of its own with a considerable degree of autonomy (extended in 1948). In practice the province was governed by a landowning Protestant oligarchy, somewhat expanded in its later phase to include middle-class Protestants from the business and professional classes—the last prime minister, Brian Faulkner, being the first to rise from these classes to the top position.

The power of this oligarchy and its representational title rested on an electorate in which Protestants outnumbered Roman Catholics by two to one. This, the most striking and emotive division within the province, gave its politics the air of an antiquated survival from seventeenth-century Europe. It was not the only division. There remained also the conflict between those who wanted Ireland unified and those who did not, and a conflict between rich and poor. This concatenation of religious, national and social passions was made the more lethal because they overlapped. The ruling class was Protestant but not all Protestants belonged to the ruling class, nor were all Protestants richer than Roman Catholics. The partisans of a united Ireland were all Roman Catholics but not all Roman Catholics wanted it.

In 1969 the IRA—descendants of the Irish Republican Army formed to get the English out of Ireland—split into two sections with differing priorities and tactics. The one part, adopting a marxist interpretation of the situation, decided to enlarge its natural base among the underprivileged Roman Catholics by appealing also to the poorer Protestants, while the other part, named the Provisional IRA, continued to lay the emphasis on the essentially nationalist policy of driving the English out by force; the first group was becoming as much socialist as nationalist, while the second remained unmutedly nationalist and military. The English were caught in a position of limited responsibility, limited power and limited concern. They felt an obligation to stand by the established order in Northern Ireland but were uneasy about defending an oligarchy which seemed foolishly and insensitively blind to the need for civil and political reform. Both Labour and Conservative governments committed themselves therefore to upholding an order of which they did not greatly approve. At the same time they deluded themselves into believing that if they could prod Belfast into civil and political reforms no more would be needed and all would be well for a foreseeable time. This was a superficial view.

There had been a foretaste of killing in the mid-sixties. Historic dates had long been occasions for sectarian demonstrations and in 1966 the newly formed (Protestant) Ulster Volunteer Force had aggravated the situation by resorting to killing. The authorities retained control but in the succeeding years the number of killings, although still small, induced the government in London to send troops to Ireland. Anxious to get out again as soon as possible, the British government put pressure on Belfast to introduce reforms to satisfy the Roman Catholic civil rights movement, which successive prime ministers in Belfast were willing to do provided they could satisfy their Protestant supporters that concessions on civil and political rights were not a first step to the unification of Ireland. But it was difficult to separate these two issues and extremists on both sides quickly made it impossible. Protestant intransigence was forcefully expressed by new leaders such as Ian Paisley, an eloquent anti-Catholic of a kind no longer found outside Ireland; and the Provisionals successfully focused attention on grievances which no reforms could satisfy. Reforms were enacted but they divided the Protestants without satisfying the Roman Catholics. Killing on a significantly bigger scale began in 1971. The government was impotent. It had had three prime ministers in three years—Terence O'Neill, James Chichester-Clark and Brian Faulkner—and the last of these resorted in August 1971 with British consent to detention and internment without trial, one of those ostensibly strong measures usually taken from weakness and vitiated in this case first by the incompetence of rounding up a number of wrong persons (and not one of them a Protestant) and subsequently by the ill treatment and torture of detainees which was formally investigated and stopped by the British government itself and then brought before the European Human Rights Commission and Court. These actions added fuel to the flames.

They also failed to break the IRA. Roman Catholic opinion had at first welcomed British troops as protection against Protestant militants but after 1971, when the official IRA joined the Provisionals in denouncing British excesses, Roman

Catholics swung away from the British army towards the IRA. On the other side the Protestants also became more militant. The British had insisted on the removal of their traditional defences by disarming the Royal Ulster Constabulary and disbanding the B-Special Constabulary. Both these bodies were exclusively Protestant instruments of the Protestant ascendancy and were rightly judged by the British to be a provocation to the Roman Catholics. But they were also a reassurance for the Protestants and when they were replaced by the British army Protestants began to form a new self-help body, the Ulster Defence Association, as the counterpart of the Provisionals. The provincial government was abolished in March 1972 and the British government assumed direct control.

Direct rule from London meant direct confrontation with the opposition and as a result of the events of the preceding year the opposition was no longer a civil rights movement but the militant and nationalist Provisionals. Britain had been man-oeuvred into the role of the opponent of the Roman Catholics. It was also distrusted by the Protestants who resented the destruction of their own government and feared a deal behind their backs between London and Dublin. The British army was giving a highly efficient performance in a role which had how-ever no foreseeable end and was not obviously contributing to a political solution or stopping the Irish from killing one another. The Heath government persisted in treating this conflict as a constitutional problem. It adopted two policies which were incompatible. The one was power-sharing, i.e. insistence on Roman Catholic participation in government at all levels, and the other was democratic endorsement by the electorate. But the democratic Protestant majority was in no mood for power-sharing. Protestants were outraged by the murders committed by the Provisionals. Thus British policy, enshrined in a White Paper in March 1973 and apparently triumphant at a confer-ence at Sunningdale in December, was foredoomed and the addition at Sunningdale of a gesture towards the unification of Ireland by the creation of a Council of Ireland only made its rejection by the electorate doubly certain. Two months later this electorate was given the chance to express itself in the general election which Heath chose to call in February 1974 and it decisively rejected the Sunningdale scheme. Although a Sunningdale-type executive had been set up, it was brought down in May by Protestant demonstrations and a general strike. London's only answer was to fly in more troops and resume direct control. The killing multiplied. The British, convinced that their presence was at least preventing the killing from getting even worse, clung on, but the long and mostly unhappy story of the English in Ireland was clearly nearing its end.

PART IV

The World

1 The fateful legacy

2 Which world?

A The American alliance
and nuclear weapons

B East of Suez

C Europe

1 The fateful legacy

There is no need to decry past achievements but there is every reason not to regard them as part of the present.

England had been a very great power and a world power. In 1945 it was so no longer but what people chose to believe was less apocalyptic. They concluded that England, having been a world power grade one, had become a world power grade two. But there is no such thing as a world power grade two. This error, venial but costly, delayed for a generation the British withdrawal from distant theatres, the abnegation of the role of international financier and adjustment to the realities of what was, within limits, still a powerful position.

If Britain was wrongly assumed still to be able to sustain a major part of the amplitude of past performance, part of the reason lay in the fact that British power was still considerable. In Europe Britain was and for some time remained the only considerable power apart from the USSR. It possessed, all but uniquely in the world, the knowledge how to make nuclear weapons and the skill and the resources, and it did in fact make them. It still had bases all over the world and its presence was more widely spread than that of any other state. Its spirit was that of victor, not vanquished. Yet there was a fateful miscalculation: the failure to see that power derives not from stocks of arms but from the economic and industrial capacity to make them, which was ebbing.

British power in its heyday rested ultimately not on the Royal Navy but on the industry which fashioned the ships and guns and paid for them; and the prosperity of this industry was itself derived from a worldwide primacy in invention and a worldwide market for its products.

Britain had been an industrial-naval power. It was not much of a military power, preferring to save the money that continental powers spent on armies. India as a *place d'armes* and the Indian army and the British army in India were important manifestations of British power but without industrial and naval power they were not conceivable. For two or three generations after Trafalgar Britain was not so much dominant on the high seas as unique. There was no fresh challenge from

France and no discernible challenge from anywhere else. Towards the end of the nineteenth century France, recovering with gusto from the Franco-Prussian war, began to rebuild its sea power; and the Franco-Russian *entente*, which might close the Mediterranean to the British at both ends, caused some alarm in London until the Russian fleet was conveniently sunk by the Japanese, whose own growing naval strength was turned from a possible menace into an adjunct by the Anglo-Japanese treaty of 1902. But Germany, which came into being as a European land power, had developed from the last years of the previous century a naval programme which torpedoed the possibility of Anglo-German accord, provoked bitter professional rivalry and popular hostility and became a major cause of the first world war. The essence of this German threat was precisely the same as the basis of British power: the combination of industrial and naval power, the use of the former to create the latter. Consequently the British reaction to the German challenge was not simply a matter of jealousy or pride but a sound instinct which perceived that this threat, unlike Napoleon's or Louis XIV's or Hitler's, matched like with like: there could be no compromise, only victory or surrender.

Germany lost the first world war and its fleets were surrendered and sunk. All existing fleets—the French and Japanese and the new American fleet—belonged to Britain's allies but, more significantly, the Royal Navy was one of several great fleets, no longer unique as it had been a hundred years earlier or even *primus inter pares* as it had been a generation earlier. The American fleet was moving to the top and the Americans did not like the Anglo-Japanese alliance and succeeded in forcing Britain to discard it with the result that Britain was for the first time compelled to envisage a naval strategy which it could hardly afford—a two-hemisphere strategy involving supremacy in the Pacific as well as the Atlantic and Mediterranean which, in economic and industrial terms, was one theatre too many. The equation of naval with industrial power was broken.

Great powers like to ignore the economics of strategic policies. By calling these policies defence policies politicians and chiefs of staff are able to imply that the exigencies and impositions of defence, however construed, are always more necessary to salvation than damaging to the public weal and its economic and industrial base. The economic strains of naval policy had in fact become a worry before the first world war and the question: Can we afford it? forced policy-makers to seek in alliances a way to share burdens which were becoming too heavy. In 1900 Britain could just about afford a two-power standard, i.e. a Royal Navy strong enough to defeat the next two biggest navies combined. But Britain could not afford a three-power standard and when German naval power was added to French and Russian, Britain was driven out of splendid isolation and into alliance politics. By choosing the path of *détente* with France and Russia, leading to *entente*, Britain escaped increasingly intolerable naval and so economic burdens. Alliance with France against Germany enabled British naval power to be concentrated against the German High Seas Fleet in the North Sea without a crippling increase in the overall strength of the Royal Navy. The need to confront Germany at sea was met partly by weakening the Mediterranean fleet and accepting that the Mediterranean must be not a British but a Franco-British lake.

But France was more concerned about the coming war on land and so Britain had to accept, as part of the alliance with France, a continental commitment which it had eschewed since Marlborough's days two hundred years earlier. This commitment, a necessary part of a strategic deal, was however a new economic and industrial burden assumed when the deal itself had been prompted by the need to reduce this burden.

When the first world war ended defence expenditure was severely cut. The army was virtually disbanded. The admiralty was instructed to work to the ten-year rule which said that there would be no war for a decade and which renewed itself automatically every year until in 1932 it became a prophecy of dangerous unreality. (The rule was reintroduced in 1945. At the end of a war everybody feels that the next war must be some way off.) The hope in the twenties was that Germany could be kept permanently enfeebled and that better machinery for handling international disputes would prevent wars. Both these hopes were disappointed. The problems of paying for safety and for a place at the top persisted. A second world war arrived in which Britain had to gird itself to huge and costly exertions with the economic penalties already described. Peace returned and with it generous schemes for social amelioration. These amounted to a social modernisation of Britain to be undertaken alongside industrial modernisation. They too had to be paid for. If the economy were to grow fast enough all would be well. If not, then in a postwar era perhaps defence costs could be cut and all would still be well. The immensity of peacetime defence expenditure in the paradise of modern technology was not guessed.

The industrial base was still the key. The industrialisation of England was a fact which could not be gainsaid or reversed without destroying an economy which had been ordered to produce wealth from industry rather than agriculture. England had moved from agriculture to industry early and profitably but, in the twentieth century, could no longer move back and yet was manufacturing the wrong things and specialising in outdated skills. Fundamentally this was a story not of intellectual or moral decline but of a material and psychological imprisonment in a too successful past: old plant and old attitudes inhibiting the direction of brains and resources into new initiatives.

England had not become an industrial economy by necessity—except in so far as opportunity works imperatively. England had pioneered in agriculture as successfully as in manufactures and might have developed a more evenly mixed agricultural and industrial economy had not the spurs of invention offered even more to manufacturers than to farmers. Agriculture in the eighteenth century and later offered big prizes to the audacious who extended their estates by purchase or seizure, experimented and innovated. But the very opening up of markets overseas, which made the fortunes of manufacturers, had the opposite effect on agriculture. Free trade and a revolution in transport brought in food from new sources; the interests of consumers and manufacturers overrode the interests of farmers. It is not easy to feel certain that the decline of agriculture in the nineteenth century was due solely to these causes. Landowners were to some extent deflected by their very successes. Secure in their fortunes many became absentees. Instead of applying new skills and money to creating an agricultural counterpart to the industrial sector of the economy, they transferred their fortunes into non-agricultural ventures or into landed estates overseas.* During the nineteenth century land in England was sold on a massive scale to smaller owners who were caught by the century of decline which set in around 1850 and was interrupted only by the two world wars which, by making England an island once more, choked off free trade, made

---

* The absentee landlord of the nineteenth century who got his class a bad name has a counterpart in the twentieth century in the financier who has increasingly taken control of industrial and commercial enterprises while remaining both remote from them and ignorant of their processes. The financier rather than the industrialist or merchant has, like the absentee landowner, given a whole class—that of the capitalists—a bad name.

investment funds available and doubled production. In the same 100 years the percentage of agricultural workers in the working population sank from 25 to 5. Even the long and serious depression of 1873–96, which was particularly acute in England, did not lead to a return of protection and farmers, in pessimistic mood, chose to keep to the less competitive fields (e.g. less cereals, except in wartime) rather than modernise and compete. By 1950 England was an industrial economy and had to live as such, and as an industrial economy it had to make its way as part of the world economy. There was no such thing as a viable domestic industrial economy. In this respect, England was inescapably still part of the world as a whole. Having developed a worldwide economy in the context of world power it had to maintain the former without the latter. World power, based on industrial power, had sustained industrial power. Each was the auxiliary of the other.

While industrial pre-eminence was being achieved partly at the cost of agricultural decline, other forces were setting in train an industrial decline. These forces were educational and structural.

As the first in time among successful industrial nations (unless that primacy belongs to China) England owed its success to the first stage of the industrial revolution which was based on coal and textiles. At one point, at least a third of the world's manufactured goods came from England. The succeeding age of iron and steel found England still to the fore but not uniquely so. With the electrical and chemical industries Germany moved to the front and so did the USA. At the next stage— plastics, new alloys, electronics—England ceded ground to Japan and France as well as Germany and the USA, and English industry was absolutely as well as relatively in decline. Having won the laurels of pioneers England failed when the going got competitive.

Something has already been said in an earlier chapter about English education. What needs to be said here is that the nature and thrust of education are an important element in the vigour of a state. In one respect the English universities responded to the expansion of England but in another they did not. They lifted their eyes beyond the borders of the state and trained young men to assume the responsibilities of administration and justice in lands overseas. Nor were the universities alone in this, as witness the example of the East India Company which founded Haileybury school and appointed to it a series of eminent educators beginning with Malthus. But the universities did not respond to industrialism as they did to the imperial adventure. They remained a small elite priding themselves on their elitism and frowning on anything approaching the vocational or impure, and they thereby directed an unnaturally high proportion of the better brains into traditional classical and humanist studies with no immediate bearing on the inventions and techniques of the new industrial civilisation. In this they were followed by the schools whose duty it was to prepare boys for the universities and in which the teaching was done by graduates of those universities. The resulting self-perpetuating system was in its own terms successful but exceedingly slow to do anything beyond carrying on its own norms. Modern scientific education, invented in Germany during the industrial revolution, was disdained and English universities refused—Americans did not—to adopt the fruitful German pattern of the post-BA degree (pursued in England only by clergymen and teachers who got it in the older universities for cash down), the research institute and the new PhD with its emphasis on originality. By 1914 Germany had six times as many university students as Britain, the best of them could spend six years there instead of three, and far more were studying subjects such as engineering. At the same time Germany's standing in classical studies was no lower than England's. The midnight oil was not banished by engine oil.*

The second major clog on England's industrial progress was the conservation of small or medium family businesses and their apotheosis. This was no more surprising, though no less harmful, than the excessive conservatism of the universities. Many of these businesses were the heroes of the industrial revolution. Their very success was a powerful argument against change, and this argument was all the more compelling in the second and third generations (the Forsyte squadrons) where an hereditary plutocracy failed to produce, because it no longer needed, the verve and dedication and austerity which had made the fortunes of the first. The comfortable grandsons of Victorian entrepreneurs lacked the incentive to take the risk of adopting new processes. Whereas the nine-

* This must not be read as a manifesto against classical education. Latin became the language of education in western Europe because it was the only written language. Its standing was enhanced when, in the fourteenth century, the schoolman grounded in grammar and logic were succeeded by the humanists who gave pride of place to literature and language. Its contribution to our culture is immense. The false step was the indifference of the humanists and their Renaissance followers to the scientific and technical studies which had flourished in the thirteenth century.

teenth-century capitalist class had more than a sprinkling of progressive ideas (and even radical thinkers and voters), its twentieth-century successors were almost solidly conservative in thought and in action. Modernisation was evaded so long as old ways remained reasonably profitable, and when they did not the reasons were not clearly grasped.

Education and training on the one hand and business attitudes on the other were the basic determinants of English economic activity and of its product. And the two were at arm's length. Educators were not thinking very much about the business world when they were educating; they were thinking of making more educators, of staffing the civil and colonial services and, at the very top, of throwing up a prime minister or two. Businessmen often preferred not to send their sons—and certainly not their daughters—to a university where they would learn nothing useful, get into bad (i.e. unthrifty) habits and waste a few years better devoted to learning a trade. Although all this has vastly changed, it requires an effort to remember how recently. Yet by going back still further to the eighteenth century, one finds another pattern. In that age English ministers at foreign courts were often glorified agents of English commerce and some ambassadors were actually paid by the merchant community: diplomats were business envoys.* In the nineteen-sixties two reports (Plowden 1962, Duncan 1969) stressed the economic aspects of foreign policy. In urging that diplomats should not only play host to visiting businessmen but also take part in the hard sell these reports were harking back to well established, if largely forgotten, ways of making and marking England's position in the world.

* French agents overseas, diplomatic as well as consular, were also at one time paid by the chamber of commerce of Marseilles.

2 Which world?

A *The American alliance and nuclear weapons*

Historical perspective and day-to-day problems are not easily combined. When war ended in 1945 Britain had one big problem: what was its postwar position in the world to be? It had also many lesser problems of which the most immediate was demobilisation and bringing men and women home. (By the end of the year demobilisation was running at the rate of 12000 a day and yet in some stations overseas there were mutinies.) Then there were problems in re-establishing order and authority, especially in south-east Asia; the occupation, government and feeding of enemy countries; setting up the United Nations; discussing treaties of peace to be imposed on the defeated in concert with allies; war trials; foreign loans, and much more besides which left little time for the broader questions which historians would ask a generation later. In India there was the question whether to stay, not for the sake of staying (which only an insignificant few desired) but in order to preserve the unity of India and protect its minorities, or alternatively to seize upon the ending of war as a cue for a quick exit: Wavell's policy against Mountbatten's, so far as these things can be personalised. The Labour government resolved to quit, but further west it strove unsuccessfully to stay in Palestine, departing in 1948 not because it regarded Britain's day in the Middle East as done but because the Jews took to terrorism and won.

These two cases are instructive. The Middle East had been an anomaly in the British empire ever since the end of the first world war, dominated by Britain but not colonialised (only Aden was a colony, originally of the Bombay presidency and ultimately a British colony). Paradoxically withdrawal or eviction from the Middle East would be a more complete act than withdrawal from India, since it would entail the complete dissolution of Britain's paramount position. India, however, was a part of the British empire and might, upon gaining its independence, become a member of the British Commonwealth alongside others which, since the Statute of Westminster in 1931, had been both independent sovereign states and yet also part of the fabric of British power in the world: independent but still red on the map. India did in fact take this course, becoming not only independent but also a republic and yet at the same time part of an association of states among which Britain was, for a time at least, *primus inter pares*; and the Indian example was followed by Pakistan and Ceylon (but not Burma) and ultimately by dozens of other newly independent countries including every one of the twelve emancipated African colonies. But this new, expanded, admirable, perhaps even useful Commonwealth did not become an instrument or even an extension of British power and it even dropped the word British from its name. It was an association of states based neither on geography nor purpose but on historical accident – and so unique.

The Labour Party took great pride in the Commonwealth as a counter showpiece to the empire created by imperialists and mourned by Conservatives. Its existence helped the postwar government to believe that a radical diminunition of British power need not be accompanied by so radical a diminution in the British role in the world, and it was not until nearly a quarter of a century later that another Labour government drew the obvious conclusion that Britain had ceased to be an Asian power because it could not afford to be.

It was nevertheless an episode in Asia that most particularly fashioned British foreign policy in the first postwar years. This was the war that broke out in 1950 in Korea, a country almost as far from Britain as it is possible to get in this world.

The politics of the war years had been dominated by the alliance with the United States. Compared with that alliance nothing else mattered, for without it the war could not be won. This attitude was carried over into peace, partly by the camaraderie of war and partly for want of any other. The USSR was remote in spirit and menacing; France seemed destined to permanent minor status. In both parties moreover war leaders—Churchill, Attlee, Bevin—became the peacetime leaders. They had prayed for and lived with the American alliance, wished it to continue and regarded it as natural. None of them had played a major role in prewar foreign affairs and, like the vast majority of their countrymen, they did not recall that the ruling mood in Anglo-American relations between the wars had been dislike and distrust on both sides. (The one eminent surviving practitioner in the foreign field, Eden, was overshadowed by Churchill during the war and his day did not come until nearly a decade after its close.) The Korean war affirmed the alliance.

The North Korean attack on South Korea was seen, almost certainly wrongly, as a Russian initiative and therefore a move of global and not merely local significance. It was seen too as a challenge to the principles and the existence of the UN which, in default of a massive riposte, would go the way of the League of Nations after the Italian attack on Ethiopia in 1935. The gravity of the war was enhanced when China joined in six months after the first shots. The defence of South Korea was undertaken by the UN and delegated to the USA which, besides having considerable forces in and around Japan, was the only power capable of sustaining a conflict of the dimensions envisaged. This commitment by the USA in Asia had immediate repercussions in Europe. Committed to a war in Asia the USA needed a bigger contribution from its allies in Europe to make good any transfers of American forces from Europe to Asia. Furthermore, if the Korean war were part of a global Russian strategy the anti-Russian stance in Europe had to be revised: a strategy based largely on naval and air forces would have to be supplemented by substantially increased ground forces. The British government accepted this view of the situation. National service was lengthened from 18 to 24 months. Defence expenditure was immediately increased by nearly 50% to £3.6 billion over the next three years and then, in January 1951 and under American pressure to raise it to £6 billion, increased again to £4.7 billion over three years—an unrealistic figure which had to be abandoned by the next government, though not before it had overstrained the aircraft industry and shipyards, caused the resignation of Bevan and other Labour ministers and wrecked the balance of payments.

The Korean war also precipitated the rearmament of West Germany which likewise was accepted by the British government, although not without misgiving. France, however, tacitly supported by other continental Europeans, fought against German rearmament and began to be propelled along a more anti-American course than any British government would contemplate. But in the early fifties Britain was still in a class by itself among the USA's European allies, and this continuing alliance was symbolised by the presence on British airfields of US bombers carrying nuclear bombs. The North Atlantic Treaty of 1949 was as much a British as an American creation. In Nato Britain occupied a special position, much inferior to the USA but much superior to each and every other member, even Canada. This special position entitled Attlee to fly to Washington in December 1950 to protest to Truman against the implications of General MacArthur's aggressively anti-

Chinese views and his strategy of bombing Chinese territory before the Chinese came into the war. From the British point of view Nato was more than an alliance for the defence of Europe; it was also a forum for the exercise worldwide of the special Anglo-American relationship.

In one respect Britain was incontrovertibly special. It had nuclear know-how and nuclear weapons. Britain had been the first state ever to resolve to make nuclear weapons. This was in September 1941—a date which makes the decision even more remarkable (assuming that 'decision' is the right word for one of those steps of which it can be said that largely it took itself: the knowledge was still imperfect, the outcome most uncertain but a course was open and men just took it). When the war ended nuclear weapons had been made, in partnership with the USA and Canada and on the basis of a complete and mutual sharing of secrets. The USA had dropped two bombs, on Hiroshima and Nagasaki, and was assumed to possess others although it is not certain whether the USA still had a bomb in its armoury on the day after the destruction of Nagasaki. Certainly no other state had a bomb. For Britain two questions arose. Should it have bombs of its own and, if so, should they be home-made or bought from the USA? The second question involved considerations of dependence and of cost. To buy weapons, or parts of them, might be cheaper or more expensive than making them at home, but buying them would go far towards exchanging national independence for dependence on the USA. There was no question about the development of nuclear power for domestic purposes and the Atomic Energy Act 1946 gave the government authority to do this, but bombs were another matter and it was not until 1947 that the decision to manufacture bombs was taken. This decision was taken by a sub-committee of the cabinet and was kept virtually secret until the Conservatives returned to office in 1951. Research and manufacturing establishments were created for the design and production of bombs to be carried by aircraft. That bombs would soon be succeeded by fantastically sophisticated and expensive missiles was not foreseen by those who decided that Britain must have an independent nuclear armoury.

During the war Churchill and Roosevelt had agreed (at Quebec in 1943 and Hyde Park in 1944) that wartime collaboration in these fields would continue after the war. Britain's contribution to invention and development had been significant but the work had been concentrated in the USA and the agreement was meant to ensure continued British access to work in progress and new technical advances. Roosevelt, however, had neglected to file this agreement in a proper place and by the MacMahon Act of 1946 Congress and Truman, in ignorance of its existence, put a stop to further scientific exchanges. This stop embittered the British who were already riled by the abrupt termination of Lend-Lease and the tough terms attached to the loan of 1945 but it was not the cause of Britain's decision to make its own bombs, a decision prompted rather by reluctance to not do what one knows how to do, by determination to make Britain a power in its own right within the Anglo-American alliance, and by some scepticism over the USA's resolve to remain involved in European affairs.

The first British bomb was exploded in October 1952. It was preceded by the first Russian bomb which was exploded in August 1949. At this stage the USA was still out of Russian range and so an uncertain participant in a European war. In any case Churchill and his cabinet had no doubt that the Labour decision had been right. They intended Britain to have its own nuclear weapons, by which they meant weapons made at home and to be used solely at the discretion of a British government. Doubters of two kinds existed: economists who saw in the rising costs and scale of the nuclear defence programme a threat to civilian industries which would be deprived of raw materials, a diversion of resources from profitable to unprofitable manufactures, and consequent damage to foreign trade and the balance of payments; and, secondly, disarmers who regarded armaments as a cause of war (in the late fifties unilateral disarmers appeared in public opinion polls as 25–30% of those questioned on these topics). The American government on the other hand approved of the British programme and even relaxed the restraints of the MacMahon Act in order to help it, first in 1954 and then more substantially in 1958. The USA wanted its allies, particularly Britain, to take a bigger share in the rearmament necessitated by worldwide communist aggression. Eisenhower, on becoming president in 1952, relished the opportunity to renew his wartime partnership with Churchill and also, after the brief interlude of Eden's premiership in 1955–7, with Macmillan with whom he had worked in North Africa fifteen years earlier. Britain still had expertise to contribute and in this era, before the intercontinental missile, the USA was not self-sufficient against the USSR without the use of British bases: missiles on American territory could not yet reach the USSR.

This interdependence was one element in encouraging Britain to embark on the next stage and make thermonuclear weapons. Again this was a logical move and also part of the British government's concern to keep its end up within the Anglo-American partnership, which it could hardly do with a small store of A-bombs to set against an American pile of H-bombs. There was also an element of prestige, a belief that seats at the top table were reserved for H-bomb holders. The first British thermonuclear bomb was exploded in May 1957, three years after the parallel American explosion at Bikini. 1957 was coincidentally the year in which the V-bombers were to come into service. These four-engined jet aircraft—the Vulcan, the Valiant and the Victor—had been commissioned immediately after the end of the war for the carrying of A-bombs. The Vulcan arrived on the due date, the Valiant a bit early and the Victor a bit late. The gap had been filled by the American B 29 and the British medium-range Canberra. The V-bombers were excellent aircraft but by 1957 the aircraft was being replaced by the missile and the V-bombers' life was likely to be unexpectedly short. Nuclear independence required the development of a British missile to replace the bomb. Blue Streak was commissioned to do this. It was a failure and in fact, though not in political rhetoric, that was the end of British nuclear independence.

At this point the British government had no real alternative to a partnership with the USA involving some degree of dependence. It did not contemplate abandoning nuclear weapons altogether; it was on the contrary intent upon running down conventional weapons and manpower and bringing conscription to an end, which it did in 1960. In theory there was the possibility of partnership with France where de Gaulle, returned to power in 1958, was continuing his predecessors' policies of building an independent nuclear force, but although both de Gaulle and Macmillan toyed with this idea, it was not practical politics. For de Gaulle Britain was not an acceptable ally unless it forswore the American alliance, while in British eyes the USA was not only far stronger than France but also a more dependable and more easily understood partner. Since Franco-American relations were bad, an Anglo-French *entente* of this nature must be regarded in Washington as an unfriendly act and the British government neither dared nor wished to sting the Americans in this way. So in March 1960 Macmillan got from Eisenhower a promise to supply Britain with the American missile Skybolt as soon as it was ready. Skybolt would take the place of Blue Streak. In return Macmillan gave the USA the use of Holy Loch in Scotland as a base for American submarines carrying the nuclear missile

Polaris. But Skybolt was to produce an even greater shock than Blue Streak.

By 1962 the American government had decided that Skybolt was a mistake. It was cancelled, mainly because of rocketing costs. This left Britain in the air and with a very big grievance. Macmillan and his colleagues were all the more dismayed because they had oversold Skybolt to the public. They had also probably realised by now that the whole deal had been ill conceived and that they would have done better in 1960 to take Polaris instead. Kennedy, who had by now succeeded Eisenhower, was embarrassed by the breach of faith involved in the cancellation of Skybolt and felt under an obligation to make reparation, but his European policy was fundamentally different from Eisenhower's. Where Eisenhower retained a wartime predilection for the British and a distrust of France and de Gaulle, Kennedy and his generation preferred to look at western Europe as a whole and with less pro-British bias. Kennedy was a strong supporter of the EEC and was even inclined to a less jaundiced view of de Gaulle than prevailed in Washington. So upon meeting Macmillan at Nassau he was prepared to offer Polaris in place of Skybolt but wanted to offer it to a mixed European force instead of solely to Britain. But this was not at all attractive to the British who wanted to be treated separately from the European ruck and Macmillan, making the most of his moral position over Skybolt, fought it off and was able on his return home to tell his party and the British people that he had got Polaris for Britain. Owing to a slip in the drafting of the Nassau agreement it later transpired that financially the bargain was amazingly good, since Britain was to make no contribution to research and development costs. (The agreement was also ambiguous since, in deference to American wishes, it included a vague statement about assigning various arms, including Britain's Polaris submarines, to a Nato mixed force. This notion was developed by Washington into a mixed-manned naval force—the multi-lateral force or MLF—which London never took seriously and regarded, rightly, as absurd. When Labour won the 1964 election it bowdlerised the MLF and produced instead the equally absurd ANF—Atlantic Naval Force—consisting of the British V-bombers and Polaris submarines plus some French element plus some American Polaris submarines plus an experimental mixed-manned non-nuclear force. By this time it was fruitless to conjecture whose tongue was in whose cheek and after a year the ANF, having torpedoed the MLF, itself sank without trace.)

The Blue Streak—Skybolt—Polaris sequence was the story of how Britain failed to manufacture its own missile, opted in 1960 for the wrong alternative but, upon being let down, got the right one after all and got it cheap. The Nassau agreement ensured that Britain would not drop out of the nuclear ranks for another (nuclear) generation. Neither the failure of Blue Streak nor the cancellation of Skybolt was taken as an occasion to review Britain's nuclear role. The Labour Party, although more sensitive than the Conservatives to disarmers and critics of defence costs, did no more than propose to renegotiate the Nassau agreement. This phrase (which was to become famous a few years later in the context of the treaty of accession to the EEC) meant only that the party had not made up its mind what to do about nuclear weapons, but as soon as it returned to office it showed that no major changes in the defence armoury were in the wind. Britain had gone too far down the nuclear road to turn back. People were growing used to nuclear weapons and if France had become a nuclear power was it right or proper for Britain to cease to be one? Nuclear independence was no longer a reality, since the weapons were American, but this had been seen and discounted by the public even while politicians were repeating the old slogans about independence. With four Polaris submarines Britain was still a nuclear power and no government of either party was going to send the missiles back where they came from. The main concern was to limit the costs of the country's armoury rather than to change its composition, and it was becoming inescapably clear that the only way to do this was to reduce the role that the armoury was required to play.

B *East of Suez*

When the first postwar Labour government took office in 1945 it hoped to bring defence expenditure down to 5% of GNP. This was not achieved: the nearest approach was 5.1% in 1973. In 1946 the figure was still 20%. The war establishment was not yet wound down and the costs of occupation in Germany were high. The defence estimates in 1946 totalled £1.7 billion. They were reduced below £1 billion in the estimates presented in 1947, but some Labour members voted against them on the grounds that they could be cut still further. The economic crisis of that year forced the government to reduce overseas establishments (including Germany) to 300,000 but the Chiefs of Staff and Bevin, as foreign secretary, insisted from different points of view on keeping up

British power in the Middle East—Bevin worried about oil supplies and the chiefs of staff, more vaguely, about a power vacuum which seemed to be a veiled way of warning that the Russians would step in if the British stepped out. Bevin and Montgomery, now Chief of the Imperial General Staff as it was still called, were prepared to leave the Suez Canal Zone on certain conditions; Greece (but not Cyprus) was transferred from the British sphere of influence, to which Stalin had willingly assigned it during the war, to the American, about which he might have been less complaisant; and Turkey was similarly transposed. The Mediterranean was now an American and not a British lake. In September of the same year Britain decided to abjure the Palestinian mandate but, moved increasingly by fear over Russian activities in Iran, to negotiate with its traditional Arab associates new treaties preserving a special British presence in the Middle East. It succeeded with Jordan but failed with Iraq and Egypt. (Not that these differences meant much. British forces left the Canal Zone in Egypt in 1956, Jordan in 1957 and Iraq in 1958.) What the cabinet wanted was a reduced world role, which was a contradiction in terms. The choice lay between a world role and a reduced one. The aftermath of victory in a world war was a bad time to be faced with such a choice.

During his short premiership Eden attacked the rising cost of defence. On the eve of the Suez crisis he declared that the manpower of the armed services would be reduced at once from 800,000 to 700,000 and then to 445,000 by 1960. His successor, Macmillan, instructed his defence minister, Duncan Sandys, to review policies with a view to cutting costs. Both prime ministers were looking for ways to cut costs without cutting commitments and were doing so at a time when aircraft were about to be replaced by far costlier missiles and the atom bomb by the thermonuclear bomb. Sandys was also required to end conscription. He proposed to bring the services' manpower down to 375,000 by 1962, to increase the mobility of the services so that smaller forces would be needed in expensive overseas bases, and to rely increasingly on tactical nuclear weapons in all theatres. This new strategy promised to ease the financial burden but it rested on an arm which was untried—tactical nuclear weapons—and another which did not exist—a large fleet of transport aircraft. It did not ensure the second aim of policy, which was the maintenance of the world role.

In the event this world role was not abandoned until more than twenty years after the end of the second world war. Until 1967 both the main political parties were asserting the need and their determination to maintain considerable British forces east of Suez and the Labour Party's about-turn in that year was abrupt and the consequence, not of a strategic review, but of economic stringency.

The determination to stay east of Suez—i.e. in the Canal Zone, Aden, Jordan, Iraq and the Persian Gulf; in the Indian Ocean, Ceylon, Singapore and Hong Kong—took different forms during these years. Notwithstanding the withdrawal in 1947 from India, which had been the heart of the British empire and the reason for maintaining bases and staging posts to west and east of it, there persisted a belief that British interests continued to demand a British presence. In so far as this view was not a mere anachronism it derived, in the Middle East, from Britain's dependence on Middle Eastern oil and, in the Far East, on its dependence on tin and rubber. The fact that other equally dependent consumers of these raw materials maintained no armed forces in these areas did not seem a convincing argument: it was argued in reply that Britain was doing a job for them as well as for itself. This element of service to others was further expanded. Britain, it was said, had a duty to remain in its old haunts in order to keep the peace—the old imperialist turned policeman, and a policeman of the kind familiar to the English, who spreads not fear but security. Finally, the USA which in the past had distrusted Britain's imperial positions and intentions switched in the sixties to a policy of urging Britain to stay and share the burdens of peace-keeping and anti-communist containment.

Even had there been a clear desire to abandon the world role, there were practical difficulties. There were few years without disturbances or emergencies involving British forces or other kinds of intervention. These included: the emergency in Malaya 1948–60; the Mau Mau emergency in Kenya 1952–60 (although fighting ceased in 1958); the despatch of air forces to Thailand in 1962 when that country seemed threatened by Laotian communists pursuing defeated Laotian government forces over the border; help for India against China in the same year when supplies were flown to India and senior British officers and the Secretary of State for Defence himself went to India to manifest active British support for a fellow member of the Commonwealth; still in the same year armed support for the Sultan of Brunei against a revolt, followed in the next year by the Indonesian–Malaysian confrontation which lasted until 1966; armed intervention in 1964 in Kenya and Tanganyika at the request of the new governments of these states to put down mutinies sparked off by revolution in Zanzibar. The Middle East was even more permanently in turmoil: the assassination in 1951 of the King of Jordan, a series of coups in Syria, the overthrow of the dynasty in Egypt in 1952, the oil crisis in Iran in 1951–3, revolution in Iraq in 1958, intervention by invitation in 1960 in Kuwait against Iraq, revolution and Egyptian intervention in Yemen in 1962, emergency in Aden in 1963, and the series of wars between Israel and its neighbours which included the Anglo-French-Israeli war against Egypt in 1956.

In the fifties commitments beyond Europe had to be combined with commitments in Europe which stemmed from fears of the USSR. (European fear of the Russians was greater after the second world war than after the first, when abhorrence would be an apter word than fear. The fear of the fifties was more like the fear inspired by Tsarist Russia between the end of the Napoleonic Wars and the welcome Russian cropper in the Crimean War.) The destruction in 1948 of Czechoslovakia's coalition government in favour of a communist regime subservient to the USSR was all the more alarming since the communists had in any case dominated the coalition after fairly winning an election. That this was not good enough for the USSR was a bad omen. In Britain the national service of conscripts was increased from 12 months to 18 and the defence estimates of 1950 rose even before the outbreak of war in Korea. But in the sixties a different mood prevailed. Europe now seemed the most stable part of the world, the fears evoked by the USSR subsided and were overtaken by new fears of Chinese communist subversion in Asia and a deflection of Russian activities away from Europe and into the Middle East. For much of the sixties British governments felt that the world role was more urgent than the purely European.

But the struggle to keep defence costs under control was lost in the sixties. In percentage terms the record was creditable but in absolute terms the sums required leapt up. As a percentage of GNP defence costs declined modestly and fairly steadily from 6.6% in 1950 to 6.2% in 1960, 5.5% in 1970 and 5.4% in 1975. As a percentage of central government spending the figures were 23.4 in 1950, 24.2 in 1960, 17.0 in 1970 and 13.6 in 1975. (Since all defence expenditure is borne by the central government defence costs as a percentage of total government expenditure, local as well as central, are lower.) Ignoring the changing value of money these costs passed the £1.5 billion mark in 1955, £2 billion in 1965, £2.5 billion in 1971, £3 billion in 1972, £4 billion in 1974, and £5 billion in 1975. Defence, to cut a complicated exposition short, was hugely expensive. It was also an increasing burden on the balance of payments as more and more weaponry had to be bought in the USA. There was no way of making substantial cuts except by doing substantially less, however unpalatable this might be in terms of prestige and allegedly dangerous in terms of security. The two fundamental aims of policy—security and solvency—were in conflict.

When Labour returned to office in 1964 it showed no signs of winding up the British role in Asia. Its approach to defence was financial: how to keep costs to £2 billion. A number of projects were cancelled including a fifth Polaris submarine. In 1965–6 there were more cancellations, notably the TSR 2 and the new aircraft-carrier which the previous government had decided to build. Instead Britain would buy the American F 111 aircraft to sustain the peace-keeping role. The government was trying to square a circle but the role and its cost refused to match; nor could the government make significant cuts in Europe at a time when it was seeking to join the EEC. In 1967 the government decided to halve its establishments east of Suez in 1970 and eliminate them some time between 1973 and 1977. Early in the following year the timetable was revised and complete withdrawal set for March 1971 (extended to December after the personal intervention of the Prime Minister of Singapore). At the same time the order for the F 111 was cancelled. All that would remain were Hong Kong and the islands of Masirah off the south-east tip of Arabia and Gan in the Maldives in the Indian Ocean. This policy had the approval of the shadow Conservative defence spokesman Enoch Powell but of few other Conservatives. Yet when the Conservatives had the chance after the 1970 election to reverse it they concluded that, even in the Persian Gulf where they had vigorously espoused a continuing presence, they should not do so. Both parties thus accepted the end of empire.

c *Europe*

In the first ten years after the second world war Britain tried to attune the wartime Anglo-American alliance to the conditions of peace. The alliance remained firm and continued to do so throughout our period and in spite of dents and jolts, but it was not the exclusive and special relationship which had prevailed during the war. Britain gradually ceased to be the USA's only worthwhile ally, seemed at times to be not even the favourite ally, and itself felt the need for other alliances or associations. In the Middle East there was suspicion and conflict between the allies over the special British position in the oilfields of Iran and over American oil policies in Saudi Arabia; so long as the USA regarded Britain's Middle Eastern positions as essentially imperialist there was small hope of wholehearted co-operation, while the American emotional commitment to Israel and comparatively small dependence on Arab oil gave it a different order of priorities which was only modified and shifted towards British policies after British withdrawals (Egypt 1956, Cyprus 1960, Aden 1968), renewed bouts of Israeli expansion and evidence from the Arab side of a readiness to turn to the USSR, to combine against and even win battles against Israel and to use the oil weapon against the rest of the world. In the Far East Britain's sub-ordinate role, already in evidence during the war, became even more subordinate, culminating in a refusal to give help or even endorsement for American actions and policies in Vietnam. In both these areas a comprehensive retreat, barely envisaged in 1945, was precipitated by economic overstrain and effected between the startling humiliation at Suez in 1956 and the Labour government's declaration of 1968. In the same period and under Conservative direction Britain negotiated its peaceful withdrawal from all its African colonies and most of its Caribbean ones.

The nature of Britain's relations with European states became paramount. Britain's preference was for good relations and precise obligations bilaterally between sovereign states with, in second place, such further but not perpetual engagements to international groups of states as might seem for the time being pragmatically desirable. That such secondary relationships might be necessary either on military or on economic grounds was uncontested but the desirability of entering into organic and permanent associations to secure these aims was distasteful and was avoided as long as possible.

When the war stopped in 1945 Europe was in ruins. The extent of destruction and dislocation was greater than most people in Britain had imagined in spite of their own experience of aerial bombardment in the earlier part of the war. Trade was reduced to barter between states, public services were primitive, political authority and stability were doubtful, starvation was possible. Continental Europe was a place to be pitied and helped but not to be joined and when Churchill and others urged Europeans to bury their hatchets and unite he was not proposing that Britain should join the union—although other Europeans did not realise this. The Labour Party was no less chary. Its hands were full at home with postwar recovery and the creation of a welfare state, and Labour leaders convinced themselves that western European governments were to the right rather than to the left and too much attracted by the idea of creating between the USA and the USSR a third force which would be hopelessly puny and a discordant competitor with the American alliance which Attlee and Bevin regarded as the cornerstone of British policy. Nor were many British, even of the generation younger than the leaders, prepared at this point to see in European affairs sufficient scope for the British genius.

The cold war—the fear of the USSR generated by the size and success of its armies, by the consolidation of this military power over half Europe through subservient and satellite governments, by fear of communist intrigue in western Europe, by the presence of Russians in Europe's central capital cities of Berlin and Vienna and Prague, by Russian reluctance to withdraw from Iran and reputed Russian involvement in the war in Korea, by Russian intransigence at the conferences of foreign ministers of the major powers and at the UN—created the problem of combining two overlapping associations. The one was the anti-Russian Nato military alliance established primarily by the Americans and the British but with the necessary adherence of most of anti-communist Europe. The other was the nascent west European community designed primarily for economic self-help and excluding the USA by its nature and also Britain by British choice. The point at which these two associations, the one formally established in 1949 but the other still inchoate, clashed was in the field of defence where the USA tried to force on continental Europe something it did not want and Britain in consequence was forced to give to continental Europe undertakings more far-reaching than it had been disposed to give.

The core of the problem was German rearmament which France in particular jibbed at. In response to American pressure to strengthen in this way the anti-Russian forces on the ground in Europe the French Minister of Defence, René Pleven, proposed in 1950 that Germans should be allowed to form small units only and that these should be ensconced in larger multi-national formations: German units but no specifically German army. Pleven assumed that Britain too would contribute units to a force of this kind since without a British contribution France would be left to face a new and still half distrusted Germany with only Belgian, Dutch and Italian buttressing. But to the dismay of the French Britain refused to join this new-fangled Defence Community. German rearmament was held up. Secretary of State Dulles threatened France with a reversal of policies. The French parliament predictably retaliated by throwing out the entire Pleven plan. In order to stem what looked like a disintegration of the western alliance the British Foreign Secretary, Eden, stepped in with a new plan whose essential feature was a British promise to maintain in Europe the forces already stationed there (four divisions and a tactical air force) or their agreed equivalent. Although there was an escape clause to allow for emergencies Britain had given a commitment of indefinite duration and had taken the lead in the creation of a new European organisation, Western European Union, of which it became a member. Whereas in 1945 Britain had confined itself to promoting Franco-German reconciliation by fine speeches, in 1954 Britain was constrained to take a more active and permanent part in creating a wider organisation without which this reconciliation was jeopardised. What made the difference and necessitated British participation was the rearmament of Germany.

By saving western European solidarity at this stage Britain also helped it to prosper and soon therefore faced new problems of Anglo-European co-operation. The kernel of all western European organisations was the Franco-German relationship. The Schuman Plan proposed in 1950, which resulted in the European Coal and Steel Community, was a Franco-German functional association (its other members, particularly Belgium and Luxembourg, carried economic weight in it but were politically peripheral) to which Britain was not attracted partly because it disliked this sort of bureaucratic international cartel, partly because it hoped to compete successfully with the European steel-makers and partly because in the prevailing British view these international ventures were more suited to enthusiasts, even cranks, than to hard-headed politicians and industrialists. The trend exemplified by the Coal and Steel Community could have been reversed by the imbroglio over the Defence Community but was not, and in 1955 a conference at Messina took the next step towards the broader Economic Community which was formally created by the Treaty of Rome in 1957 and came into existence on the first day of 1958. Britain sidestepped this one too through a mixture of dislike and scepticism. Many in Britain believed that the EEC was too ambitious to succeed, even in its preliminary phase of removing tariffs and quotas, let alone in its further plans for economic integration and the transfer of political and legal authority from sovereign states to the Community. Britain would have been happy to join an organisation with restricted aims: free trade in manufactured goods, no common external tariff, no common agricultural policy and no political super-structure; and it in fact promoted such an organisation as a rival club of the excluded—EFTA—which came into being in 1959 and was successful in stimulating trade between its members but unsuccessful as a rival or barrier to the EEC. Moreover de Gaulle, who had returned to power in 1958, belied British expectations by not belittling the EEC.

The return of de Gaulle was a critical event. His first preference was for a new three-power association of the USA, Britain and France and he made proposals for a reorganisation of Nato in this sense. These proposals were ignored by his allies who could not get over their dislike of him and were also afraid of offending West Germany. De Gaulle was therefore snubbed and he moved without delay to his second preference which was a Franco-German *entente* (he struck up a close political friendship with Konrad Adenauer)* and the affirmation of the EEC. He had inherited the nuclear programme initiated by the Fourth Republic and after pulling France out of Algeria he established a favourable balance between French commitments and French resources.

Macmillan was now in a quandary. Although he had repaired the rift with the USA caused by Eden's Suez fling (of which Macmillan had initially been a keen supporter) and although he had got Skybolt from Eisenhower to make good the failure of Blue Streak, the old-style Anglo-American alliance was no longer a sufficient basis for British foreign policy, if only because the Americans were embarrassed by talk of a special relationship and wished to play it down. Washington more-over looked with favour on the EEC and disfavour on the kind of free trade zone that Britain would have liked to create. On the European side de Gaulle and Adenauer were both putting their mutual understanding above an understanding of either with London; an Anglo-German front against de Gaulle had been forestalled. In the commercial field British firms were competing with French as well as American aircraft manu-facturers and losing to both. Dubious of the declining value of the American alliance, unable to fashion a French alliance and foiled in the attempt to create the kind of western European organisation most

* British and Americans are habitually taken by surprise by Franco-German rapprochements. Yet there have been repeated bouts of political and cultural association ever since 1870.

appropriate for British interests, the British government embarked on a course which was a long way from the top of its list of priorities. In 1961 Macmillan applied to join the EEC.

The decision lay with de Gaulle who had many reasons for seeking closer relations with Britain either bilaterally or by admitting it to the EEC—but one powerful reason for doing neither. This was his firm belief that the EEC and each of its members must set a distance between themselves and the USA. Britain on the other hand wanted to combine membership of the EEC with the full preservation of what remained of the special Anglo-American relationship. The two positions were irreconcilable. De Gaulle almost certainly got the impression at a meeting with Macmillan that the latter was willing to shift alliances and enter into some sort of political and defence alliance with France which would include a joint and exclusive Anglo-French nuclear programme and deterrent, but such misunderstandings were not the cause of the failure of the British application for membership. Even less relevant was the protracted haggling in Brussels over tariff details. In 1962 the Nassau agreement on Polaris confirmed de Gaulle in his view that Britain was still a satellite of the USA and could not therefore make a good European partner. In January 1963 he vetoed the application.

In the years that followed France overplayed its hand in the EEC and the Franco-German partnership was shaken, but the EEC survived and attained a number of its initial aims ahead of schedule. It played the part of a major international actor in the swapping of tariff cuts called the Kennedy Round, negotiated during 1966 under the aegis of the General Agreement on Trade and Tariffs (GATT, the major postwar instrument for the liberalising of international trade). In Britain de Gaulle's rebuff, correctly appraised as a French rather than a European act, did not long discourage those who, on economic grounds, were becoming increasingly alarmed about being left in the cold outside this populous and prosperous market to which an increasing proportion of British exports was being directed. Wilson and other Labour leaders became converted to membership of the EEC although other senior members of the party remained hostile; whereas the Conservative Party under Macmillan's leadership had been broadly united on this issue but hardly enthusiastic, the Labour Party under Wilson was sharply divided between enthusiasts for and against. But in 1967 Wilson put in Britain's second bid to join.

The key was still in French hands. In 1966 France had patched up its differences with its five partners, and although in May 1968 de Gaulle's authority was severely shaken at home by student riots and workers' strikes, there was still no prospect of the five, who wanted Britain to join, forcing their views on de Gaulle if he remained hostile. De Gaulle, however, was not hostile to British membership provided Britain were not in his eyes a Trojan horse of American manufacture. Early in 1969 he made overtures to the new British ambassador, Christopher Soames (sent to Paris by George Brown to cajole the French government); he reverted to his previous views on greater power co-operation and re-ferred at the same time to adapting the EEC to include Britain. By a peculiarly inept piece of reasoning the British betrayed this conversation to the Germans, apparently in the hope of exploiting a latent rift between France and its partners by giving the impression that France had offered Britain a place in a new association of western nuclear powers which would downgrade both Nato and the EEC. The ensuing public row destroyed any hope there might have been of getting into the EEC by the back door in Bonn, produced a second French veto and destroyed the improvement in Anglo-French relations, but shortly afterwards de Gaulle resigned. (He had incautiously linked, in a referendum, proposals for the reform of local government with a proposal to abolish the senate which he disliked but most French people liked.) A year later the Labour Party was defeated in a general election and the new prime minister was Edward Heath who had conducted the abortive negotiations with the EEC for Macmillan and was one of the comparatively few Conservative enthusiasts for joining.

Heath lost little time in ensuring that the new French president, Georges Pompidou, would back British entry and negotiations for a treaty of accession were completed in a matter of months after a meeting between the two leaders in Paris in May 1971. The treaty was signed in January 1972. Britain—together with Ireland and Denmark—became members of the EEC from the first day of 1973. Two British com-missioners, Christopher Soames and George Thomson, joined the European Commission in Brussels. The Norwegian government also joined but its decision was repudiated by a referendum. Referendums in Ireland and Denmark, required by the constitutions of these countries, endorsed the decision. In Britain no such popular endorsement was constitutionally required but a referendum was nevertheless held two and a half years after the date fixed for accession and confirmed it.

The reasons for this strange proceeding were the fall of Heath's government and the ambivalence of the Labour Party. Wilson's personal ambivalence was sharpened by fears of splitting the Labour Party and ruining its electoral prospects. He therefore attacked Heath's diplomacy, arguing that the terms of the treaty of accession were unnecessarily onerous and would be renegotiated by a Labour government. This was in effect a threat to denounce a treaty which had been properly made and subsequently, in July 1972, endorsed in the House of Commons by 301 votes to 284. Wilson also promised that new terms, if satisfactory to a Labour cabinet, would be submitted for approval to the electorate, apparently by referendum. These threats and undertakings had to be put into effect when Labour won the election which Heath incautiously called for in February 1974. Wilson opened negotiations with the EEC and succeeded in so modifying the terms accepted by Heath that he was able to claim that he had done better than the Conservatives and, in March 1975, to recommend the endorsement of the new terms by the country as a whole. (The main change was in the method of assessing the national contribution to the community's budget, in which the Foreign Secretary, James Callaghan, won sizeable concessions. A secondary change improved the prospects of New Zealand farmers in European markets.) The electorate, confused by rival and protracted arguments about the economic case for joining or retreating and probably reluctant to undo an international treaty validly concluded, voted in June 1975 in the first nation-wide referendum ever held in Britain to remain a member of the EEC by a majority of two to one. Britain thus confirmed its membership not only of the Economic Community founded at Messina in 1955 and created by the Treaty of Rome of 1957 but also of the Atomic Energy Community inaugurated at the same date and of the Iron and Steel Community spurned in 1950 —both of which had been merged with the Economic Community. Whether this Community was to transform the politics and fortunes of Europe or become a gangling adjunct of its ancient sovereignties nobody in 1975 could safely say. What was clear was that Britain's place in the world was as a European nation, however Europe might be organised. The 200 years of successful world imperialism which began when the English and the French in North America exchanged the first shots in the Seven Years' War had ended.

PART V

Notes Towards a Definition of Britain

A Observations
B Weaknesses
C Strength
D Chance and change

Part V: Notes Towards a Definition of Britain

The four preceding Parts of this book have been descriptive and analytical. They are intended to be a contribution to knowledge about Britain and to thinking about Britain. What follows are reflections which have emerged from these chapters.

At the core of these reflections is a view of the weaknesses and strength of Britain at the beginning of the last quarter of the twentieth century. In this view there are two grave weaknesses in British society: excessive inequality and excessive secretiveness. There is also great strength. The essential ingredient in this strength is the rule of law and the essential condition for the maintenance of this strength is the flexibility and pragmatism, in law and in politics, which have characterised the transformation of Britain over centuries.

Round this core are other things. Human societies are perennially exposed to two forces, the one unpredictable and the other intractable: chance and change. This Part ends therefore with a reminder of their disruptive potency. It begins with a few observations intended to evoke some of those intangible characteristics which are easier to recognise than describe.

A *Observations*

In Britain a man, or a woman, may go to an apparatus in a wall in a street, insert a card, wait for about half a minute, receive £10 in cash from the apparatus and walk away with it. He may do this in broad daylight or in the dark. This is remarkable.

Again, at an appropriate and designated spot a person may step off the pavement into the street and walk across it. The traffic will stop. It is not absolutely certain that the pedestrian will get safely to the other side but it is virtually certain. The pedestrian does not wait for a signal to tell him that it is his turn to proceed. It is always his turn if he will take the first step.

This too is remarkable, both for the virtual certainty that the pedestrian's right will be recognised and for the fact that the pedestrian is required all the same to assert himself and take a tiny risk.

The British are a nation who have sustained a creative culture of the first magnificence continuously for 500 years. No other people except the French and Chinese has done this.

In the period which we have been surveying the British have been markedly unmaterialistic. Their favourite pastimes appear to be pottering about in their gardens and watching football. In a more restricted but by no means narrow segment the hours and money spent on music, theatre, art exhibitions, rescue archaeology and buying and borrowing books betoken an age stamped by love of art and pursuit of knowledge. Britain remains also the country *par excellence* of the voluntary organisation and voluntary service.

B *Weaknesses*

The principal weaknesses of postwar Britain are inequality and secretiveness. About material inequality enough has been said elsewhere in this book. One further word will suffice and it will be William Blake's:

> A dog starved at his master's gate
> Predicts the ruin of the state.

Material inequality is the most corrosive and disgraceful source of social divisions but not the only one. Secretiveness comes a close second. Secretiveness is pernicious not merely because it offends against a general duty or injunction to impart or inform but, more positively, because it divides people into those who know and those who do not, those on the inside and those not admitted, those with and those without rights in a prescribed area. Britain is at one and the same time an exceptionally open society and an exceptionally secretive one. It confuses secrecy with privacy. The walls and hedges which the British instinctively set round their homes attest a love of privacy which is entirely legitimate (even if the opposite inclinations of other people also have their validity and value). But the extension of privacy into non-private matters has become unjustifiably pervasive.

The executive branch of government has carried this secrecy to extremes. The Official Secrets Act, dating from 1911 and enacted primarily to make life difficult for domestic spies, has operated not on the limited front of protecting vital secrets from an enemy's agents but on the much broader front of enabling all official activity to be concealed from public scrutiny by official fiat. Government business and government papers have become *prima facie* secret even when they have nothing to do with national security. The citizen has been cordoned off and the press forced to resort to conspiracy, bribery or theft in the discharge of its proper functions. A government purporting to be democratic has become arcane. Government officials, innocent of any nefarious intent and used to this comfortable seclusion, are hurt when accused of having turned themselves into a mandarinate which fobs off the public and corrupts the press. They put efficiency a long way ahead of communication.

This is not a question of ability. A mandarinate may be very efficient, but it cannot be democratic. It opts for secrecy and against communicating.

Another aspect of this attitude is the refusal to open parliament to the public gaze—except in the sense that the doors are open to those who can afford the time and the fare. Proposals to relay the proceedings of parliament by radio and television were mooted in our period, experimentally tested and then timorously pigeonholed. Citizens who want to see and hear parliament at work still have to go there like tourists and the reluctance of politicians to be seen and heard when about their public business is an inept refusal to use methods which lie to hand. The principal excuse—that politicians would use the new dimension in order to play to the gallery—underestimates the good sense of the electorate and overestimates the histrionic abilities of politicians. The one concession made to the advance of the technology of communication was the introduction in 1947 of party political broadcasts which, however, quickly became a fearful bore and so did politics and politicians more harm than good.

Secrecy is not confined to government. It is no less habitual and excessive in business. When private businesses were small and private this was as legitimate a form of privacy as setting a hedge around a garden, but the modern private company is private only in legal terminology. Yet most boards of directors treat the company like a private club, giving shareholders only anodyne statements once or twice a year (tricked out with pretty pictures and modish graphics) and resisting attempts by employees to learn about current activities or comment upon them. Both groups are regarded as unfortunate nuisances. The developing science of industrial or personnel relations is too easily used as an exercise in discovering how little communicating a board can get away with; and the futility of denying to employees information which many of them have acquired in the course of their duties serves only to increase the disregard and suspicions which a secretive *patronat* thus earns.

Secrecy looks from the outside sinister. It is more often merely patronising or inept. But the damage it does comes from what it looks like and not from what it is.

Secrecy weakens a society, be it a state or a business. In technical jargon, *Gesellschaft* will falter and fail without *Gemeinschaft*, society will fail without community.*

Communicating is one of the things that holds a society together and makes it work. History is almost too full of examples. The later Carolingian empire, to take an early one, fell apart because its physical communications were not good enough. In the modern world communist and fascist bureaucracies have provided outstanding examples of secrecy in the service of tyranny—sometimes politically effective for short or long periods but always divisive, nurturing suspicions and hate.

This is the problem of government and the governed, or management and the managed. Secretiveness denotes distrust, which is no basis for any form of government except tyranny. Britain is the least tyrannical of countries and so has the least justification for secretiveness.

c *Strength*

The weaknesses of Britain are weaknesses in a tough structure. Much of this toughness comes from respect for law. Britain is a singularly law-abiding place. Whoever said in the seventies that Britain was becoming ungovernable made the silliest remark of the century.

* The essential difference between *Gesellschaft* and *Gemeinschaft*, in the view of Ferdinand Tönnies in his book of that name published nearly 100 years ago, is size. *Gemeinschaft* is smaller, more homogeneous, less complex. But there ensue qualitative differences since the mass or crowd has values of its own—a line of thinking developed in our own time by Elias Canetti in his *Masse und Macht* (*Crowds and Power*).

Law is not simply what the police use to nail malefactors. It is the cement of society.

Part of Rome's heritage to Europe was to make law the principal regulator of society. European civilisation has advanced as law has gained ground over force and religion. Yet law has no ultimate sanctions. These belong to force, which is this world's last court of appeal, and to religion, whose *post mortem* sanctions are as effective as cold steel in this world provided you believe in another.

Law needs to establish its authority without appeal to force or religion. When it appeals to force it acknowledges its own subordination, and if it depends on religion it is not law but pseudo-law. (Canon law is an attempt to codify god's will and as such a legal absurdity and a theological impertinence.) Law must win and hold obedience for reasons other than fear—fear of prison or fear of hell. It cannot command obedience, only demand it. The rule of law is consensual and not imperative, for as soon as it ceases to be consensual it becomes the rule of something else.*

At any given time or place law reflects the values of the society in which it functions and also the interests of the dominant classes in that society. The continuing rule of law depends upon how these two ingredients are balanced. If and so far as it becomes, or seems to be, an instrument of the dominant classes it jeopardises its function as the servant and cement of the society as a whole: it is then no longer a normative force but a partisan one, the hired referee of the police. To survive as regulator and adhesive law has to be flexible.

The law of England has been extraordinarily flexible, and this flexibility has greatly contributed over the centuries to the transformation

---

* This is neatly illustrated by the Hindu caste system which puts priests and warriors at the top of the tree. Cf. also in Islam the *ulema* and the feudal aristocracy (in the Ottoman empire the *timariots*). Unlike Hinduism and Islam, Christianity was never more than half of the civilisation to which it contributed so much. In this European civilisation it was wedded perforce to the Greco-Roman culture which was partly atheist and partly of resounding religious inadequacy. The founder of Christianity himself told his followers to render part of their obedience to the Roman Caesar. Hence, in part, the special character of European civilisation, its swifter intellectual emancipation and even, I would hazard, its relative stability and tolerance. No other civilisation save the Chinese has had a matrix so markedly non-religious.

of Britain from a polity based on command to one based on interplay. The continuing flexibility of the law is essential to the preservation of a consensual society in an age which has seen a resurgence of 'command' societies all over Europe.

The creative flexibility of law is commonly underrated by comparison with its resistance to change (a natural consequence of the law's attachment to precedent). Judges tend to be conservative but the law itself opposes no barriers to change. These barriers are erected by society or by a class and in Britain the law has continuously absorbed changes, good and bad. The chief reason for this receptivity to change is the absence of any judicial body or sacred text specifically created to withstand change—more particularly, the absence of constitutional laws which have more force and immovability than other laws, and the absence of a constitutional or supreme court empowered to review and undo new laws. Whether this situation is good or bad depends on each individual's forecast of the nature of changes in the making. Those who seek to import into Britain a constitutional document and court do so because they foresee changes which they do not like: they are at once prophets and pessimists. They cannot be proved wrong because they are talking about the future, about which even the most prescient cannot be certain, but in trying to build a dam against menacing change they run the risk, possibly more damaging than the risk they seek to forestall, of making the law so much more inflexible as to deflect it from the service of society to the service of a class. A constitutional court could tilt the balance between the law's ingredients the wrong way and fatefully distort the conflict in British society between its strengths and weaknesses. A constitution and a supreme court would diminish the sovereignty of parliament and imperil the rule of law. They are the radical recipe of pessimists who have lost faith in democracy.

There is a choice between a sovereign parliament where the citizen is represented but not present in person, and a supreme court where the citizen in person may question the validity of laws made by the parliament. Both systems have disadvantages. The sovereign parliament may become the instrument of a class and make partisan or otherwise bad laws. The supreme court, owing allegiance to the tables of the law, may petrify the law. The British democratic tradition has preferred to vest ultimate authority in a larger, representative (if indirectly popular) body than in a small, unelected and judicial one.

There is an inescapable conflict between preservation and change, between preserving freedoms and yet adapting to change. Britain claims with some justice the title of the world's freest country and is right to be proud of the title, which is one of the enduring gifts of the rebellion against the crown in the seventeenth century in the name of the free-born Englishman. Intricate debates about the meaning and varieties of freedom should not be allowed to obscure the fact that there is such a thing. The co-existence of freedom and law and their mutual support are among the most difficult and the most vital of the problems of politics; particularly at times when freedoms inherited appear to conflict with freedoms claimed. The postwar period was of this kind.

These years witnessed great changes in freedom of personal behaviour which both flouted convention and altered the criminal law. Not all these changes were welcome to everybody; some were certainly shocking and arguably excessive, so much so that another word was commonly used to describe and decry these freedoms without earning the reproach of opposing freedom itself. This word was 'permissiveness' and its use denoted a reaction against the pace of change in patterns of behaviour.

The most obvious of these changes were in sexual behaviour. Whether things were done that had not been done before it is impossible to say, but they were certainly done more openly and probably by more people. The prime agent of change was not moral but technical: contraception became much easier and nicer. Consequently avowed copulation outside marriage became common and marriage ceased to be a precondition for sexual relations, even long-term ones. The opportunities presented by the pill were seized by the young and hearty (better health and nourishment produced earlier maturity) who took to sex so young and so unfurtively that their elders were shocked, envious and disturbed. The exploitation of sexual aims and fantasies by advertisers proved the power of sex-appeal and helped to stimulate it with a lack of reticence which the advertisers themselves preferred, hypocritically, to describe as lack of hypocrisy. At the next remove practices described as natural were supplemented by others which had hitherto been restricted to *cognoscenti*. The market for pornography broadened and pornographers, moving from back streets to prime sites, made a lot of money. While many deplored these developments as inherently nasty and dangerous by their example, others defended them as part of the right to decide for oneself how to behave.

The civil law was concerned with sexual behaviour only so far as adultery was grounds for divorce—for long the only grounds—but the gradual extension of these grounds culminated in 1969 in the introduction of the new concept of breakdown of marriage to take the place of the matrimonial offence. Divorce in a court of civil law had not become available in England until the Matrimonial Causes Act 1857 created a new court to exercise the jurisdiction hitherto vested in the legislature, which granted divorce by Act of Parliament, and the ecclesiastical courts, which granted a limited kind of divorce or judicial separation which did not permit remarriage. The grounds for divorce remained severely restricted, more restricted for women than men until 1923, and divorce could only be granted on petition to a spouse who could prove a partner's matrimonial offence. The offending partner had no right of petition. The grounds for a petition were extended, notably by the Matrimonial Causes Act 1937 associated with the name of A. P. Herbert, but after the war the very concept of a matrimonial offence was contested and the Divorce Reform Act 1969 extinguished it in favour of a single new ground, irretrievable breakdown of marriage. The Act specified the circumstances which a petitioner had to establish. They included the ancient offence of adultery although this ceased by itself to be sufficient grounds since the petitioner had to assert under this heading not only an act of adultery but also that he or she found married life with the respondent intolerable. By this Act, which came into force in 1971, marriage became a terminable legal and social contract and not the basically indissoluble bond or sacrament which it had become under the influence of the Christian churches. In effect divorce became available on request as it had been in pre-Christian Rome.

From 1959 children born in adultery might be legitimised, a step previously available only for children born out of wedlock but not adulterously. This last reform was a small triumph for humanity over dogma. Other humane measures were the abolition of hard labour and penal servitude by the Criminal Justice Act 1947, the raising of the minimum prison age to fifteen and the abolition of the death penalty. The House of Commons voted in 1948 for a five-year experimental suspension of capital punishment. The majority was small (23) and was emphatically reversed in the House of Lords—215 votes to 34. Abolition had to wait until 1969. An attempt to rescind it four years later was defeated in the House of Commons by a majority of 142.

The criminal law was more interested than the civil in sexual activities including rape, prostitution, male homosexuality, the seduction of very young girls, abortion and obscene publications. Rape, essentially a form of assault, remained a serious criminal offence although constructive rape—i.e. the seduction of a girl presumed by the law on account of her age not to have consented—was treated more leniently when the girl was in fact nothing loath and the man had reason to believe that she was above the age of consent. Prostitutes were discouraged from public appearance by the Street Offences Act 1959 which increased the fines for soliciting and introduced prison sentences. This Act, designed to conceal rather than impede this trade, was an amenity measure rather than a moral one. It was welcomed by those who were offended by the sight or solicitations of prostitutes but interfered little with commerce. Males on the prowl remained immune from the law unless they made the mistake of accosting a taintless woman who complained of molestation. Male homosexuality between consenting adults in private, which had been made a crime in 1885, ceased to be one under the Sexual Offences Act 1967, ten years after a departmental committee under Sir John Wolfenden had recommended to this effect. This Act did not apply to the armed forces. The main argument for this relaxation, apart from the general tendency of the age to toleration, was that it would reduce blackmail. This was a weak argument so long as homosexuality remained socially obnoxious, but the removal of criminality contributed to candour and tolerance with liberating consequences. Lesbians, whom the law did not pursue, also benefited from this movement towards behavioural freedom.

The legalisation of abortion by the Abortion Act 1967 was an attempt to divert abortions from incompetent and often insanitary practitioners to authorised and so safer ones. The main opposition to the Act, which persisted after its enactment, came from those who disapproved of abortion on principle—mainly religious arguments about the right of a foetus to live—and so of any measure to facilitate or endorse it. The Act defined the circumstances in which abortion might be legally performed. Some of these were already common practice: where the mother's life was at risk, where the child might be born handicapped, or in an emergency which threatened the mother with death or permanent ill health. The Act added other situations which became the commonest grounds for abortions after the Act: risks to the mother's mental health and risks to existing children. The Act stopped short of giving a woman a right to an abortion simply because she did not want the child and forced her in such a case either to bear it or to plead mental damage to herself or some other damage to the children she already had. Nor might an abortion be performed later than the twenty-eighth week after conception. After the Act legal abortions rose to about 130,000 a year, slightly over half of them for unmarried women; 15% of those seeking abortions were also sterilised at their own request.

Law and behaviour also affected what might be published and what not. Changing tastes and values led the way, the law followed. Two well intentioned lobbies clashed. The worlds of literature, art and (to some extent) learning tilted against restrictive laws which, although designed to suppress pornography, sometimes had the effect of suppressing too works of artistic or other value. Moralists on the other hand pressed for stricter control and execution out of the familiar mixture of altruistic concern and personal outrage. The pursuit of obscenity in the courts troubled a third group, the lawyers. It is not self-evident that the excitation of sexual desires is a proper concern of the law unless it leads to violence (with which the law is equipped to deal without enactments specifically directed to obscenity); it is anomalous to bring juries into court to pronounce in effect moral judgements instead of being confined to their true function of finding facts; and the definition of obscenity has given rise to more than normal difficulties and has led to situations in which an individual may be convicted for the effects of his act independently of any criminal intent such as the criminal law basically requires. Nevertheless, in response to social pressures, the law has long taken cognisance of obscenity, has defined it negatively as something other and worse than indecency (which can be prosecuted under the Vagrancy Acts 1824 and 1838 and the Indecent Advertisement Act 1889), and has provided two weapons: seizure and destruction of offending material, and imprisonment or fining of individuals.

The Obscene Publications Act 1857 empowered magistrates to order the destruction of books and pictures whose publication would be illegal under the common law. The nearest this Act got to defining the words in its title was to predicate an intention to corrupt which, in a leading case ten years later, became the tendency to deprave or corrupt which remained the basic formula for a century. At this stage of comparative psychological innocence the relationship between an obscene publication and the moral standards or subsequent actions of a person reading or looking at it was not debated: it was generally supposed that there was a causal relationship and that the effect could be inferred from the cause by any reasonable and responsible person who might be required to pronounce upon it. Common sense held greater sway in those days than scientific learning, and magistrates were happy in that they were confident of possessing the former and were not expected to acquire the latter. A great many orders for the destruction of indubitably obscene material have been made annually under this statute but so too have orders against publications of an altogether different kind and purpose including, in the present century, *The Rainbow* by D. H. Lawrence and *The Well of Loneliness* by Radclyffe Hall.

The prosecution of individuals for obscenity is based on the criminal law's fundamental function to prevent or punish a breach of the peace. The most famous prosecution of this kind in the nineteenth century was that of Henry Vizetelly in 1888 for publishing English translations of *Madame Bovary, Bel Ami* and other French classics including in particular Zola's *La Terre*.* Seventy years later and more by coincidence than design a series of similar prosecutions was brought against reputable publishers for publications which, whatever their literary quality, were neither issued for pornographic gain nor obscene by current standards. The literary fellowship, indignant and alarmed, decided to promote fresh legislation and after a number of failures a new Obscene Publications Act reached the statute book in 1959. In its final form this Act was a compromise between its promoters and its opponents. It made it an offence to publish an obscene article but it permitted a defence of literary, artistic, scientific or other public benefit. The publisher's intention and the absence of *mens rea* or guilty intent remained irrelevant, so that the test of obscenity was still the tendency of the article to deprave or corrupt, now modified however by the burden on the prosecution to show that the persons liable to be depraved or corrupted were likely to see the article. A supplementary Act in 1964 created the new offence of possessing an obscene article for publication for gain. Under this new legislation Penguin Books were prosecuted in 1960 for publishing D. H. Lawrence's *Lady Chatterley's Lover* without cuts and acquitted, but another publisher was convicted in 1967 for issuing Hubert Selby's *Last Exit to Brooklyn* (the conviction was quashed on appeal on the grounds of misdirection of the jury).

These changes in the law were not very substantial. Obscene material

---

* The English view of the French as an oversexed and unrestrained race stems from the considerable influx of French books and photographs of varying artistic level but consistent emotive purpose into Victorian England.

continued to be seized by the police and consigned by magistrates to the flames or the incinerator. If less was seized than some thought was desirable, this was not from any weakness in the law or the police but because opinion and standards had changed. Works of merit and their creators and publishers continued to run the risk of being brought to court. The defence might adduce evidence of literary or other merit to offset the corrupting tendencies of the work but the ultimate judge of these aesthetic issues was still the jury functioning in the unaccustomed and inappropriate role of *censor morum*. No way had been found of preventing good books from slipping into the net designed to catch the pornographic swarm, nor any way of convincingly using a court of law to distinguish a good book from a bad one. The question how good an obscene book had to be to gain acquittal or how obscene a good book had to be to earn condemnation remained, of necessity, uncertain. Meanwhile pornography flourished because the appetite for it was sharp and the tabus on it were lessened; the spirit of the age found it neither so disgusting nor so harmful as it had been judged to be in times past. The temper of the times had changed much, the law less so but enough to show that it could respond to the times.

The pace of change and its openness were affected by a decline in authority. Freedom is constrained by authority and sees authority as an enemy, but in postwar Britain authority was unusually at a discount.

The causes were partly historical. A new generation refused to give to its elders the respect or obedience which age has been used to claim; the older generation was accused, with some justice if less charity, of having failed to prevent a devastating war or care enough about slums and unemployment. Authority was devalued too by its associations with authoritarianism. The ruling class was distrusted more and revered less. *Quo warranto?* its critics were asking in the language of the twelfth century or—in a more modern idiom—who are you to tell us? The teaching class, another repository of authority, also lost its superiority. Teachers, properly sensible that in many ways they might be no better than their pupils, forgot that as teachers they knew more and were in the business of dispensing man's greatest asset—knowledge. (Man is distinguished from other animals first and foremost by his ability to transmit knowledge, to make knowledge cumulative so that each generation may begin where its predecessor stopped and not back at the beginning.) In universities the search for knowledge became confused with the search for wisdom, and the mediaeval tradition of learning became muddied by socratic disputations about virtue which were necessarily endless, seldom rigorous and hardly required a senior director. Only one class retained its authority virtually unimpaired, the higher judiciary both south and north of the border. Judges were sometimes attacked or made fun of, but there was nothing new about that and the prime requirement of the judiciary, integrity, was inviolate. The continuing respect for the Bench in an iconoclastic age was partly due to the fact that judges, unlike professors, did not go out of their way to pretend that they were just like everybody else.

The authority of the British ruling classes has been challenged by democratic and populist currents. Democracy has in general been accepted, populism rejected.

The distinction is important. Modern democratic theory requires that the people (now identified as non-imbecile adults of both sexes who are not in prison) must decide at fixed and not infrequent intervals who is to have power for the next few years. It also requires, although less insistently and less successfully, that people should be kept informed; in democratic theory this is a duty of those in power, but in practice it has been left to and arrogated by the press.* Democracy, finally, seems to require that the people be not only informed but consulted. It does not require that the people, when consulted, should have their preferences adopted, and this is one of the weaknesses of democracy since it seems illogical and can be hazardous to ask people what they want and then gainsay them. Populism endorses all the requirements of democracy and goes further. It requires more frequent and more formal consultation (the referendum being the principal means) and it at least implies that opinions canvassed should be followed. Consequently populism is clearer than democracy about where authority lies. It lies with the people, even though they cannot in practice be consulted about everything all the time. It therefore gives greater standing to the parliament or

---

* This is the source of the view, held by the press itself but not by the public, that the fortunes of democracy rest with the press. Luckily this is not so.

In a period much concerned about freedom and its limits a good deal was heard about the freedom of the press. This vague phrase usually meant freedom for editors, from proprietors or unionised workers. The equation between this kind of freedom and good newspapers was in practice hard to discern.

assembly than to the cabinet or executive and even more to the town meeting. It also tends to destroy the concept of a ruling class by making all adults members of that class. Ancient Athens practised a form of populism, often with strikingly unsatisfactory results. In modern and much more populous states populism has been so impracticable that it has operated only as a critique of representative democracy. But technological progress, notably in radio and television, have made populism less implausible. These inventions do not affect the desirability or otherwise of populism but they have weakened the argument that it is practically unworkable and have made it more difficult to know where to draw the line. Are President Carter's phone-ins an up-dating of democracy or an aberration into populism? If a man may be questioned on the hustings before he is elected, should he not also—technology permitting—be questioned in his office afterwards? To put it another way: have technical inventions made Athenian democracy, which is in our terms populism, possible once more? And if so, do we want it? Should *vox populi* be direct or representatively mediated?

A system or society needs more than cements and authority. It needs too the pragmatic sanction that it works. Workability is more important than logic. Here is a cautionary tale to conclude our thoughts on the rule of law.

In the Roman republic where, as in Britain, politics was something men did rather than something they theorised about, the constitution was a bizarre balance which worked so long as it was not under too much pressure. Laws were made by the people, but the people might propose no laws. Laws were proposed by the magistrates. The magistrates were elected by the people and changed every year but the people almost always elected nobles (whether of patrician or plebeian stock). The most important institution was the senate which was the only permanent feature in the political landscape and consisted of nobles, but the senate might not meet unless convoked by the senior magistrates, the consuls. The people were represented in this scheme by the tribunes, also elected annually, but the tribunes came from the ruling class and sat in the senate and almost always included at least one tribune who was in the senate's pocket. Such a system sounds lunatic but was for centuries one of the more effective forms of government ever known in Europe—subject to one proviso. If any group within the system stood on its rights, the system broke down. It depended on an ultimate understanding or solidarity between these groups. If that consensus failed too frequently the ruling class and the established order disintegrated, which is precisely what happened when the republic was destroyed by the conflict between the traditionalist and conservative section of the class on the one hand and men like the Gracchi and Julius Caesar on the other who led a party of change or progress and put this cause above class solidarity—as the conservatives too put their cause above class solidarity. The importance of Augustus in history is that, if and so far as he yearned like so many of his contemporaries for the restoration of the good old days and ways, he knew that it could not be done. Something new, better or worse, had to be made. In the new order force played an increasingly evident role.

D *Chance and change*

This book has attempted to sketch a brief period in a small area as a contribution to history. Its range and focus have been narrow and it is therefore fitting to recall in conclusion two mighty forces—chance and change—which shape the present more than we like to think or are perhaps able to grasp. According to Shelley they bow to nothing except eternal love.

Chance is an element in history never absent and never calculable, a perennial potent actor usually out of focus. The narrow margins of fickle fortune were most piercingly bemoaned by that most notable of English political failures, Henry St. John Viscount Bolingbroke who, writing to Swift on 3 August 1714, the morrow of the dashing of all his almost attained ambitions, exclaimed: "The Earl of Oxford was removed on Tuesday; the queen died on Sunday. What a world is this! and how does fortune banter us?"

Change is among the most taxing of the forces with which man has to contend. Rapid or fundamental change is hugely disconcerting. Attend to Matthew Arnold apostrophising the *Scholar Gipsy*:

> For what wears out the life of mortal men?
> 'Tis that from change to change their being rolls
> 'Tis that repeated shocks, again, again,
> Exhaust the energy of strongest souls,
> And numb the elastic powers.

The thirty years which followed the second world war were a segment of a century or more of accelerated and bewildering change which brought a profusion of new knowledge, outlooks and opportunities, accompanied by new puzzles, choices and confusions. Private lives, public life and the universe itself were altered.

The physical world was conquered in the sense that, although much of humankind still lived at the mercy of natural phenomena, the techniques for taming and using nature had been discovered and were available to those with the requisite wit and resources. This was a change so vast that it is almost impossible for a twentieth-century Briton to think himself back into the moods of fear and helplessness which prevailed in even the most educated and emancipated circles up to about 1800. This book is not a history of ideas or of science but it would be incomplete without a reminder of this feature of an extraordinary century: the triumph of Descartes' vision of the mastery of nature through science.

A second and even more disturbing change was the undermining of certitudes. More revolutionary than Copernicus, Kepler or Galileo, scientists and mathematicians such as Planck, Riemann and Einstein said that what everybody regarded as obvious was not so. What they said has still been assimilated only by a few, not merely on account of its complexity but above all because it astounds. Time and space have become not only larger but utterly different. They are not what they seem, and what they are is barely comprehensible. The meaning of small and simple words has come unstuck. Yet our faith is such that we believe what we do not understand—an ancient religious rather than a modern scientific frame of mind.

To everybody's surprise and discomfort the new science reintroduced uncertainty and mystery, and the shock was all the greater because the nineteenth century had been dominated by the confident certainties of positivism. Positivist thinking allied with scientific discovery promised certitudes which not only never arrived but were displaced by uncertainties claiming greater intellectual respectability and greater scientific confirmation. Things turned out to be not fixed and deducible but relative and shifting.

Artists too, as well as scientists, looked afresh at the world and portrayed it utterly differently. From the middle ages the European arts took their departure from conventional notions of space and time. The painter placed objects on a wall or canvas in relation to one another and distinct from one another. Music was an art of intervals, of the relations between distinct notes whether they were sounded in sequence or together. European art was essentially discrete. It dealt with objects or notes and the spaces between them.

The Renaissance consolidated this attitude by providing it with an aesthetic theory and with classical authority. Beauty, the artist's aim, was the product of harmony; harmony was in fact synonymous with beauty; and the ancients, whom the Renaissance revered, notably Pythagoras and Plato, had shown how harmony and so beauty were to be extracted from nature by measurement; art was a province of geometry and arithmetic. This aesthetic theory began to crumble in the eighteenth century when, in England in particular, there appeared the contrary and mildly anarchic view that beauty was not the product of objective and measurable harmonic laws but lay in the eye of the beholder and the ear of the listener. But this change of theory, flattering rather than confusing, did not require painters or composers to stop dealing in objects or notes and the spaces between them.

During the last century, however, the spaces have disappeared, and with them the familiar objects and notes. The spaces have been filled in until the objects or notes are no longer discrete. The impressionists filled up their canvases with light where their predecessors had sorted out objects. Composers filled in the continuum of sounds: the twelve-note or all-note scale, one of a number of new tools evolved to help this process, was the musician's counterpart of the impressionist painter's all-pervading and dissolving light. Holism conquered discreteness and dissolved solidity. (This transformation has fascinating, even disturbing, implications which cannot be pursued here. Discreteness—sorting things out in time and space—involves intellectual exercise, the intelligence acting upon the continuous and non-discrete flow of information to the mind from the senses. Discreteness therefore requires an intellectual effort; but sense perception undifferentiated does not call on the intellectual as opposed to the sensible segments of the mind.)

This infringement of the rules was not the only one. The impressionists were followed by the expressionists. In their work objects retained their familiar shapes, but external forms and superficial decoration concealed something else, for the expressionists set out to portray the inner nature of man or beast as well as his shape. This purpose was not unprecedented—Leonardo expressly sought in his portraits to convey

243

inner meaning as well as plastic appearance*—but it was also in its way unsettling. Those on the receiving end of the arts were, for a time at least, baffled and affronted, feeling mocked or excluded rather than delighted.

Within this muddling context of cosmic change what was the biggest change which came over mid-twentieth-century Britain? It was the fact that Britain ceased to have and to be an empire. This loss of empire was to some extent a loss of purpose too but the effects of it are hard to gauge. One of the unresolved puzzles of nineteenth- and early twentieth-century history is to discover how many people were affected and in what ways and what degree by empire. There was a class which profited from it. There was a different class which found not profit but employment and pride in it. There was a glow, specially from India, but the British cannot have spent much of their time contemplating this glow or warming themselves at it. There is some literature and a little painting—again mostly from or about India. There was a cast of mind, now so irredeemably obsolete that it is difficult to remember that it was not only genuine but generous.

But more obsolete than hankered after. The loss of empire has not, one opines, cut deep; and the reason is that having an empire did not cut deep either. It did not transform the British way of life or even the British ruling class to the same extent as, for example, the Roman empire transformed its possessors.

Cicero believed that the quintessential characteristic of the Roman was his feeling for his family and he meant by this not only people but place, not only living kin and ancestors but also the hearth and the gods which localised and perpetuated the kin. The British, more particularly the English, are like this too and the wealthier English, whose school fare was in their heyday more Roman than Christian, have shown the same territorial clannishness and loyalty, with their worshipful ancestors hanging on the walls. For the Roman this way of life was destroyed by empire which ruined the economy of Italy and disrupted the psychology of the Roman ruling class. For the British there was no such trauma because the empire was enjoyed without having to raise, maintain, bribe and settle great armies and because it was so far away that personal and family lives had to be adjusted only by those who wished to.

* His success is attested by all those who, returning Mona Lisa's gaze, have asked themselves what her smile hides.

Empire was external to the lives of most British people. The British empire was more apparent to foreigners than to the British themselves. Loss of empire was loss of purpose and perspective, temporarily disconcerting, for a few.

So, did Britain need a new purpose and if so what was available? Life without purpose, great or small, good or bad, is almost a nullity. Many individuals find sufficient purpose within themselves or their immediate families but others want to be part of something wider. National or other communal purposes fill this need. One such purpose, which was to the fore in 1945, was the building of a welfare state: to make Britain a place to be proud of.

The social policies of the postwar years were grounded in British democratic socialism, parliamentary, pragmatic and gradualist; a traditional radicalism stretching from the Great Rebellion through eighteenth-century explicators of the Rights of Man to Victorian intellectuals and agitators; an insular and secular pedigree acknowledging no god or guru save vaguely an English dissenting nonconformist ethic which paid scant attention to foreign *savants*. This body of thought was most unusually well placed in 1945. It faced no serious communist challenge. It was embroiled in no *Kulturkampf*. Conservatives and liberals were half way to being democratic socialists themselves. There was nowhere else in the world quite like this. It was the antithesis of empire. It was embraced by a new generation which was delighted not to have to worry any more about the rest of the world.

It was also very demanding. Democracy is about sharing power. Socialism is about sharing goods. Social democracy is about sharing goods and power. Sharing is easier said than done.

Socialism aims to make people care about many other people instead of a few, about far more people than the small family circle in which caring and sacrifice come naturally. For caring implies sacrifice and not merely commiseration. Socialism involves doing something about deprivation and inequality, giving up something of one's own whether money or other material possessions, time or independence. The difficulty for the socialist—like the Christian—is that most people do not want to do this. What they get from socialism, or Christianity, is a bad conscience. Only a small minority acts. But, given deprivation and inequality, a community without socialism is worse off than a community wrestling with it. That is the case for socialism. The case against socialism is that happiness, a supreme human good, is only to be had by the few and in a narrow circle; that it is better for these few to have it than none; and that the wise man therefore will lower his gaze from the *flammantia moenia mundi* of over-sized stoic endeavour and cultivate his own garden in, if possible, peace of mind. The choice is eternal and in practice most people try to get, in varying proportions, a bit of the best of both worlds.

The history of Britain has for centuries been in the direction of caring, sanctified by a willing acceptance of gradual and imposed sacrifice, illumined by the few who voluntarily practise much more and urge it by saintly example or furious indignation.

Empire was a distraction for a particularly vigorous and influential class. The disappearance of empire set this class temporarily adrift. A new commitment—to the welfare state—appeared but, far more than empire in its heyday, this new cause was soon weakened by doubts. A second failure of purpose within a generation of the loss of empire threatened. If consummated, it would leave the British without any obvious purpose, given over to a sterile nostalgia, without much interest or faith in the future, and exposed to the contempt of posterity.

The doubts were various. There was the cost of socialism about which enough has been said in earlier chapters. It was unexpectedly and alarmingly high. It hurt people, who then readily concluded that it was also harming the state and must quite simply be axed. The higher the cost of social services the more did these become the prime target for attacks on government spending—with the incidental result that the quarter from which these attacks came shifted as traditional left-wing criticism of defence expenditure was replaced by right-wing complaints about the size of the social budget. But there were other doubts too, in particular a distrust of bureaucracy and a fear that socialism was incompatible with parliamentary democracy.

Bureaucracy means people in offices but is commonly used to mean people in government offices. If these people in their offices are efficiently performing worthwhile tasks they are not only unobjectionable but actually necessary unless the tasks are to be abandoned. Tasks do not perform themselves. The objection to bureaucracy is that people in offices are either doing nothing or nothing much or nothing useful—which is doubtless true of some of them and also true of people in non-government offices. Bureaucrats are commonly judged guilty of inefficiency or laziness or other crimes until proved innocent: Dickens' characterisation of officialdom as bumbledom in *Oliver Twist* has proved hard to live down. Government bureaucrats earned special unpopularity when they alone seemed to be protected from getting the sack—but that condition is now enjoyed in practice far beyond the ranks of the civil and local government services. They suffer too from the prejudice that paperwork is inherently inferior to handiwork or footwork.

This hostility might be written off as ignorant and unfair if it were not for a further factor. Critics of bureaucracy almost always have in mind big bureaucracies and assume a correlation between size and inefficiency. There is something in this. Large organisations, whether governmental or not, are without much doubt wasteful and frequently over-manned, although there is little reason to suppose that the over-manning in, for example, some departments of local government are grosser than in some industries. Moreover the larger an organisation, the more people does it impinge upon; and what these people experience some of the time is a maddening delay in getting an answer to a question or a permit to do something. The obvious way to reduce the delay—i.e. to have more bureaucrats to deal with questions and permits—is *ex hypothesi* unacceptable and so the irritated citizen wishes to get the questions stopped and the need for permits removed. He may sometimes be right but any substantial trimming of the government bureaucracy requires the abandonment of tasks by government, above all in the social services which is where most government employees are engaged. If people are to be given pensions and dozens of other advantages whose abolition is now hardly conceivable, if the individual is to be restrained from altering an historic building without permission, there has to be a bureaucracy. A bureaucracy which cannot be improved does not exist; nor does a bureaucracy which can be dispensed with.

Sniping against the failings of a bureaucracy—whether it is the state or a public corporation or a privately owned business—is both permissible and desirable but should not be allowed to obscure the fact that more important than its inefficiencies or its size are its purpose and its standards. For a century and more the British government has attracted to its service a large number of exceptionally intelligent, hard-working and honest men and women. The civil service has, however, been confined to certain kinds of task and it has consequently come to be thought unfit for others with the result that government is advised not to extend its tentacles into areas with which civil servants have not been familiar. This is a specious argument, for government's success in the past in attracting the best people for the jobs then on hand augurs well for its ability to attract in future the best people for whatever kind of service it may require. Nor should the break with past practice be exaggerated. Government has long been employing not only clerks, administrators and policy advisers but also a variety of technical and other experts from, for example, the creation early in this century of the Medical Research Council.

For anything larger than a mini-state the alternatives to bureaucratic government are arbitrary government—usually military and incompetent as well as arbitrary—and anarchy. The British are prone to ignore this fact since, unlike other peoples, e.g. the Chinese, they have had from very early times little direct acquaintance with these unwholesome alternatives. (In China the Sung, who were the most successful dynasty in keeping political strife pacific, faced also the stiffest criticism for the growth of bureaucracy.)

Bureaucracy has nevertheless a peculiar capacity for infuriating people by its questionings and delays and some capacity too for dealing unfairly with people, and it is little to the point to argue that other forms of officialdom dispense things more unpleasant than irritation and unfairness. An attempt was made in these years to salve some of the irritations and remedy some of the unfairness by the creation in 1967 of the parliamentary commissioner or, as he was more commonly called after his Swedish prototype, Ombudsman. This innovation was at first opposed by Conservatives who held that an aggrieved citizen's proper recourse was to his MP, and even the more favourably disposed Labour Party restricted the Ombudsman's sphere to instances of injustice caused by maladministration. This sphere was extended by the (Conservative) National Health Act 1973 and a year later four similar commissioners, three in England and one in Wales, were created by the Local Government Act 1974 with parallel functions in regard to maladministration in local government.

The modern state is necessarily bureaucratic. But it is not necessarily or even normally democratic and democracy needs therefore to be defended in theory and justified by its works. Opponents of socialism and the welfare state fear that the advance of these concepts entails a loss of democratic forms and freedoms. They pose therefore a choice between ends and means, alleging that socialist ends cannot be reached without doing violence to democratic ways and that socialists are ready to sacrifice to their ends parliament or democracy or both.

On the socialist side there was by the sixties unease because the socialist purpose seemed to be failing. At a superficial level rediscovered poverty and other social failures might be blamed on right-wing governments which, having captured power in 1951 and held it for thirteen years, did not care enough, but there were also more serious questionings. Some socialists, examining themselves and their handiwork, began to blame the Labour Party and its democratic socialist assumptions for not doing better, for getting its priorities wrong. Politics in the fifties, conditioned by the democratic parliamentary system, had become a fight for the middle ground and the suffrages of the middling classes; it was for a while commonly accepted that there was little to choose between sensible men on either side of the House of Commons, the Butskells as they came to be called by those who gave equal admiration to Butler and Gaitskell. But the results of this parliamentary benignness were meagre outside parliament; and it made the political battle look phoney. The democratic socialist belief in parliamentary debate and legislation as the road to socialism seemed to be belied and the New Left came into existence as a reaction against a parliamentary charade in which parties put sterile consensus before social action and grew in the process too much like one another.*

The New Left seemed ready and willing to use undemocratic short cuts as a road to a socialism which might or might not then turn out to be democratic. It had no indigenous British socialist tradition to oppose to the Attlee–Wilson bourgeois pragmatism, nor did it fashion one. It looked abroad. The various groups comprised within the New Left (a term denoting an omnium gatherum of opponents of the established Labour and Communist parties rather than any coherent new force) wanted more action on social issues, more rigour and more fight. They were internationalists in the sense that they sought support and inspiration from foreign groups and writers—particularly Trotsky, Gramsci and Mao, many of whose works had not before this been translated, or adequately translated, into English. Their base was small and mainly academic rather than industrial. The thinkers among them were engaged in the same task as an older French generation which had acclimatised marxist sociology and its variants in France. Like continental thinkers, they were ideologists in the sense that they sought

* Cf. the old tag: Caesar and Pompey were very much alike, especially Pompey.

a coherent intellectual framework for their activism and in this respect at least they could claim some British ancestry in the late nineteenth-century English idealists who, like Marx, had been disciples of the idealist systematisations of Hegel and Plato. They were contemptuous of British pragmatism which seemed to them sloppy and slow, but in practical politics their impact was minimal. Their tone of voice was too harsh and too careless of liberty and they belonged at the extremity where, by definition, adherents are few. They affronted the settled British method of progress without compulsion and the unstated British motto: Better free than fast. Nevertheless these aberrant groups had significant marginal effects, giving British politics an unaccustomed ideological tinge and British socialism a bad name.

Part of the British right, having in practice subscribed a number of socialist aims, had grown uneasy about using the word 'socialist' as a term of abuse. When therefore towards the end of our period the motley New Left groups came to be compendiously called marxist, this term crept into the political vocabulary not to designate the ideas of Marx or his followers but as a battle-cry to impute a detestation or at least contempt for parliamentary democracy with more than a suggestion that any form of socialism must lead to undemocratic practices—a new instance of the abuse of language to prejudice rather than illumine. Thus the New Left, by saying that democratic socialism meant democracy without socialism, helped the right to assert that socialism threatened democracy. One consequence was a revulsion from socialism which, tarred with marxism so interpreted, was made to appear un-British, uncandid and undemocratic.* But this retreat from socialism left a void since its enemies propounded no positive alternative. Whereas socialists had views, right or wrong, and policies, good or bad, their adversaries had only warnings.

Finally, these doubts about socialism—the financial cost, the bureaucratic apparatus, the anti-democratic charge—were crowned by one

* Anybody wishing to add to the semantic confusion might point out that the one clearly marxist ingredient in the formative process of the Labour Party was called the Social Democratic Federation. At the turn of the century social democracy, presumably not very different from democratic socialism, was equated with marxism. Seventy years later these terms were used to describe warring sections in the Labour Party. Marx himself said of England that its social revolution would be non-violent.

other: doubt about its performance. What was achieved within the span of thirty years was much less than had been hoped. While it might be said that the hopes had been too high or the span too short or the accidents on the way too many, there was also a tendency to brush aside these arguments as mere excuses and allow pessimism or cynicism to rule.

And so behind the economic failures and social disappointments of these thirty years there lurked an uneasy feeling that the country and its leaders did not know how to cope with change or develop a new purpose. This incapacity is epitomised, however unfairly, in the images of Britain's leaders seen in retrospect from 1975. The Attlee team did a great deal of constructive work but some time before it fell it was showing and feeling its age. It built bravely for the future but belonged by 1951 to the past. The succeeding Conservative government was even older. The kindest thing that can be said about Churchill as prime minister after 1951 is that he was not a success. Eden's administration was colourless in its course and catastrophic in its collapse. Macmillan rescued the party but gave the nation euphoria in place of direction. He too belonged to another age; behind a façade he presided over its crumbling. Douglas-Home as prime minister was one of the crumbs. Then at last came new men: Harold Wilson and Edward Heath, two men with considerable attributes. Yet sadly both failed. It is too early to unravel the causes of these failures but one common factor is discernible. Both the one and the other had too many enemies in his own cabinet. Wilson became prime minister a year after a sharply contested election for the leadership of the party. A majority of his cabinet had voted for another leader and most of them continued to believe that they had been right to do so. Heath, having affronted the core of his party by a dogged and heavy-handed insistence on proscribing retail price maintenance, also won a contested election for the leadership and then failed to reconcile his colleagues to his success by importing into his cabinet an unmannerliness which hurt. He was given extraordinarily short shrift after losing a general election by a narrow margin. A prime minister's closest advisers, particularly in hard times, should be among his cabinet colleagues. Of neither Wilson nor Heath was this true. Wilson looked for sustenance to an indecorous entourage, Heath to a highly decorous but equally peripheral group of friends outside the great offices of state. This was not presidential government as practised in France or the United States but neither was it cabinet government.

Of their successors it is fortunately not necessary to say anything within our chosen time-span but the failures of Wilson and Heath and their sequels displayed a disintegration within the parties which suggested some degree of loss of nerve in the ruling class as a whole. They seemed at sea.

But the failures of individuals are as a rule not to be explained solely by their personal inadequacies, however grievous these may be, and in the second half of our period the lot of the British politician was harder than it had been for his predecessors. The emphasis in public affairs shifted from politics to economics. It shifted, therefore, from things which politicians can more or less control to things which they can barely control. This is not because politicians are no good at economics, nor because the business of politicians is politics (however defined). The reason is that politics have remained largely national, whereas economics have become increasingly international and so manageable by national governments only within narrowing limits. Within these limits culpable mistakes could be and were made, but people in general did not understand how narrow the limits had become. Since politicians and others constantly spoke of the national economy, it was pardonable to assume that there existed a nationally manageable economy and to ignore how far all national economies had become mere slices of an international economy which it was within nobody's power to control. One collateral consequence of the pre-eminence of economic problems in a world articulated into nation states was to lower the repute of national politicians who could not cope with them but talked as if they could.

A subliminal awareness of the intractability of economic problems was matched by the conscious realisation of the limitations of government in other spheres. Governments had neither abolished poverty nor materially reduced inequality; by failing to elicit a critically necessary improvement in industrial relations and output, they had not only exposed their uncertainties in this field but had also given new prominence to an underlying constitutional question of the first importance: Where, in an industrial society, does power lie? The gap between rich and poor, the distrust between workers and employers (making for shoddy performance by both) and the fragmentation of authority were different aspects of a divided society which, albeit far less divided than many another, seemed to be becoming divided to the point of danger in the context of the stresses of the times. Optimism gave way to cynicism, and this cynicism about the art of government and its practitioners reinforced the bewilderment occasioned by the pace of change and the vacillation occasioned by the weakening of authority. All these things gave force to the pessimism and fears which characterised the seventies.

Optimism and pessimism—a department of prophecy—are largely matters of individual temperament. Yet there were objective grounds for optimism about the condition of Britain. The tale of hopes deflated by failures which has been told in this book contains encouraging elements.

First, the hopes were proper ones and are so today. Britain has been on a right course. In so far as the hopes have been defeated, this is because they were large and not because they should never have been entertained.

Secondly, the cause of the failures can be analysed and understood. The account of the thirty years presented in this book will not be accepted by everybody in all its details, but broadly speaking this is what happened and broadly speaking this is why, and—most important of all—British people can grasp the essentials and wish to do so. They are serious, intelligent and reasonably well educated people.

Thirdly, the British are also steady people. In the face of disappointments and sometimes cruel failures they have neither panicked into reaction nor bolted after precipitate panaceas.

Fourthly, the chief problems of these years were not created in this period. They were there before, in some cases long before, but were more tellingly revealed by the postwar experience. The shocks—if that is not too strong a word—have been shocks of realisation, of gradual revelation rather than catastrophe out of a blue sky.

And finally, British democratic instincts and institutions remain intact. This does not mean that the democratic processes cannot be improved or that they do not require vigilance. But they have persisted and functioned despite the pressures and perplexities of the most taxing age in British history, and this may well be the single most important feature of the British case. Without them Britain would be unrecognisable, which it is not.